IMAGES
of America

MEXICAN AMERICANS IN TORRANCE

On the Cover: On December 12, 1954, La Rana residents honor the Feast of Our Lady of Guadalupe. This annual celebration took place in the community from 1935 through the 1960s. The all-day celebration for La Rana and neighboring community members included Mexican food, crafts, and music. Children dressed up in traditional attire. The procession would begin on Van Ness Avenue, continue on Del Amo Boulevard, and culminate at St. Joseph's Mission. (Stella Gassett.)

IMAGES
of America

MEXICAN AMERICANS IN TORRANCE

Alice Duarte Solis

ARCADIA
PUBLISHING

ISBN 978-1-4671-2773-8

Published by Arcadia Publishing
Charleston, South Carolina

Printed in the United States of America

Library of Congress Control Number: 2017943695

For all general information, please contact Arcadia Publishing:
Telephone 843-853-2070
Fax 843-853-0044
E-mail sales@arcadiapublishing.com
For customer service and orders:
Toll-Free 1-888-313-2665

Visit us on the Internet at www.arcadiapublishing.com

To all the descendants of La Rana, I cherished all the time I spent with you for all your stories, pictures, and patience; Alex Areyan for your encouragement; my sons Mark and John, granddaughter Nicole, and friend Virginia Valencia; but most of all to God for strength and good health.

Contents

ACKNOWLEDGMENTS

My purpose in writing this book was to provide some insight into the people who lived on Del Amo Boulevard, a street called "La Rana." I want readers of this book to see that many great stories and achievements and strong family values came out of La Rana. These precious memories are shared and recollected when we gather today. In addition, many relationships also continue, and we keep in touch with those who have moved away from the area.

As a Torrance business owner for nearly 46 years, I have shared with my clients all of the many wonderful things that came from that one street nearly two blocks long. We started off as settlers who relocated from Mexico and worked many difficult jobs in manual labor and advanced to become businessmen and women, with many achievements along the way. The progression in society through our children's education allowed us to elevate from the lower class to upper middle class. Our triumph and survival in the United States is a story of hard times that led to a great life.

Alex Areyan, author of several books, suggested I write this book of the stories that I reminiscence about with my childhood friends. Even though I never had any experience writing a book, I was still encouraged by many friends to share the memories of La Rana. I want to thank the following for all of their encouragement and support: Alex Areyan, Virginia Valencia, Marilyn Brashear, Mark and John Solis, Melissa Merritt, Nicole Hutchinson, Olivia Fernandez, and Don Lechman.

Many thanks to those who shared their family pictures and their time and precious stories for the use of this book: Gloria Castaneta, Dora Camou, Conchita Grajeda, Armida Grajeda, Virgina Ybarra, Eleazar Ybarra, Longa Alvarez, Dorothy Mora, Stella Gassett, Irene Ordaz, Judy Ibarra, Artie Martinez, Rachel Acosta, Angel Acosta, Madeline Acosta, Carlos Acosta, Peter Hernandez, Robert Guerra, Connie Molina, Hector Molina, Gilbert Griego, Gerald Laird, Albert Hernandez, David White, Dolores White, Carol Solis, Larry Grajeda, Clara Rios, Maggie Olvera, Beatrice Castillo, Randy Yniguez, Rudy Vega, Teresa Vega, Gloria Salce, Sally Alonza, Sally Bernal, Ernestine Castillo, Linda Chavez, Dora Duran, Linda Ortiz, Laurie Martinez, Jessie Valencia, Manuel Olloque, Raymond Vidal, Henry Escobar, Ramireo Ordaz, Alfonso Ordaz, and Lucy Villegas.

INTRODUCTION

The story of the small community of La Rana begins in 1908. Today, this area is known as Del Amo Boulevard, with Crenshaw Boulevard to the west and Arlington Street to the east. In the early days, it was known as Harriett and 203rd Streets and sloped at the highest point of what is now Crenshaw Boulevard. The area was covered with tall, picturesque eucalyptus trees, and behind these trees was a low, marshy area where water would collect when it rained. Water would stream down both sides of Del Amo Boulevard as it filled with pollywogs, which eventually developed into frogs. This is how the community was named for the Spanish word for frog, *la rana*. My grandfather, Don Lauro Torres, told me this history and other fascinating stories of the colorful people and thriving early times of my cherished neighborhood of La Rana.

The history begins in the early part of the 20th century. Mexico was engaged in a fierce revolution characterized by religious persecution. Many Mexican families fled north to the United States to escape the bloodshed, seeking a more peaceful existence. California soon became known in Mexico as a place for employment opportunities and hope for a better life. Torrance, California, became home to a small settlement of Mexicans because of a steel mill that offered jobs to many of the men who came from towns in Mexico such as Purépero, Michoacán. Many of these men settled in La Rana. They later brought their families from Mexico, and as the years went by, some moved to surrounding areas such as Redondo Beach, Hermosa Beach, Gardena, Harbor City, and Wilmington. Families intermarried and today include second-, third- and fourth-generation Americans. Many people lived and stayed in La Rana and raised their children in their newfound homeland—the United States of America.

La Rana is located in the City of Torrance, which is about 25 miles south of Los Angeles and six miles northwest of the Port of Los Angeles. When the immigrants first came to Torrance, it was a very small community of fewer than 10 families, and many residents lived in tents until housing became available. When houses were first built along Del Amo Boulevard, it was an unpaved road with no electricity, sewage system, or telephone lines. Along the four miles from Crenshaw Boulevard to the ocean, there was nothing but farmland, open fields, and oil derricks. Travel outside the community was via trolleys that went from San Pedro to Los Angeles.

Clothing and just about anything other than groceries had to be purchased outside the community. Torrance had several small clothing and shoe stores, but Los Angeles had a wider variety of shops and retailers, so people often traveled out of town to buy the things they needed.

Torrance had one high school and two grammar schools. Since there were few schools in the area, many students came from nearby cities surrounded by farmland such as Gardena, Harbor City, Carson, and Lomita. Grammar school grades went from kindergarten through sixth grade, while high school was from seventh through twelfth grade. There were no middle schools as there are today. Classrooms were much smaller in terms of student size, and there was only one classroom for each grade. Back then, the bus systems were larger, as they had to transport many students from other cities. The size of each graduating class was approximately 25 to 50 students.

Many of these new citizens came in search of employment and were able to find jobs with U.S. Steel, a steel mill located within three blocks of the La Rana community. More people continued to flock to the La Rana area after the first settlers arrived because the residents spoke the same language—Spanish. During the Great Depression, many jobs were lost as businesses closed, but U.S. Steel remained open and provided at least part-time work for many families.

In addition to the steel mill and oil refinery, there were many farm jobs in the surrounding area, with several dairies and a chicken and pig farm approximately three miles away. Because the residents did not have automobiles, they had to walk nearly three miles each day to and from work. Many children went to work in the fields during the summer to help with costs for school in the fall. The economy in the surrounding area near La Rana was thriving.

At night, while lying in bed, we could hear the horns from the port and smell the fragrance from the flowers in the surrounding fields. The nearby trains coming in from the port to the refinery would blare their horns late at night. The honking from the trains at night can still be heard to this day.

We are proud to say that this little street of two blocks of immigrants gave the country 102 GIs during World War I, World War II, the Korean War, and the Vietnam War. These GIs served in the Army, Marines, Coast Guard, Navy and Air Force. In total, six servicemen did not return—four from the Second World War and two from the Korean War.

This book honors many of the descendants who were the first settlers of La Rana, the little community that was the start of the American dream for so many. It was a place where peace could be found and strong values could be created. Many generations found success and have maintained relationships that started in La Rana from 1908 to the present day.

One

FAMILIES

In the early 1900s, many families in Michoacán, Mexico, were forced out of their homes and fled to the United States to escape the fighting and save their lives during this extremely violent and chaotic time. Civilians were taken to the village plaza and shot or hung to show that the revolutionaries were in control.

Families flocked to the welcoming neighborhood of La Rana as a refuge. This two-block area became well known to immigrants who were far away from their homeland. Once settled, those who secured jobs and escaped poverty often relocated to neighboring cities such as Redondo Beach, Hermosa Beach, Harbor City, Wilmington, and Gardena.

The immigrants who arrived in the early 1920s to the little neighborhood of La Rana had a difficult time communicating. Spanish was the only language spoken by these early immigrants.

La Rana was surrounded by mostly farmland and oil fields, but it provided many jobs for the immigrant families thanks to a thriving steel plant and farming industry. The simple life in La Rana provided great unity in the neighborhood, which made life more bearable. Everyone knew and helped each other, and children were taught to respect adults. In the evenings, locals would sit outside their homes while children played in the street. There were no televisions at this time, and radio was the only electronic form of entertainment. The neighborhood of La Rana provided a safe environment for its residents.

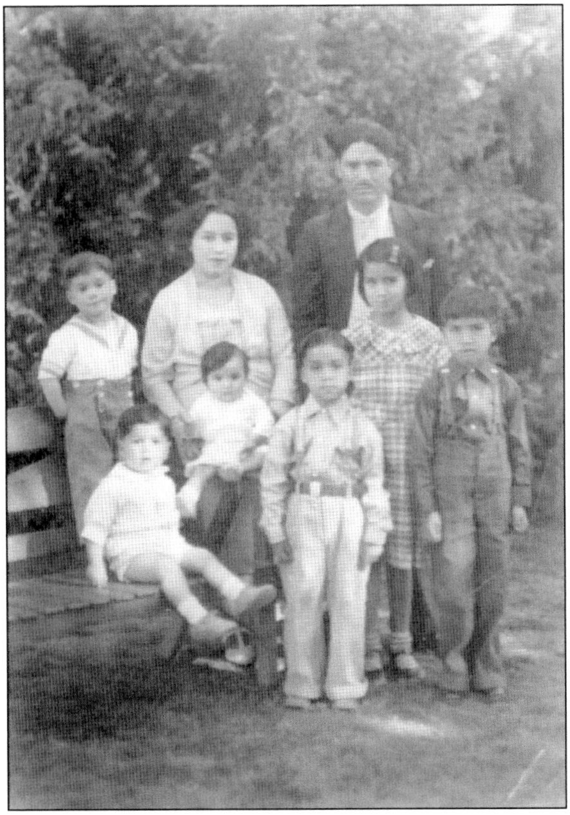

Paulo Acosta (born in 1900) and Eloisa Juarez Acosta (1910) were both born in Penjano, Guanajuato, Mexico. The family had six children born in the United States. The Acosta family moved from Anaheim, California, to La Rana in 1942. Sadly, Louie Acosta was killed in a car accident in 1954. Pictured here in 1936 from left to right are (first row) Aurelio, Margaret, Jose, Virginia, and Louise; (second row) Angel, Eloisa, and Paulo. (Angel Acosta.)

The Acosta family had a reunion every year at the VFW in Gardena, California. Pictured at the family reunion in 2000 are, from left to right, (first row) Margaret, Eloisa, Virginia, and Magdalena; (second row) Peter, Mary, Carlos, Chavie, Angel, and Aurelio. (Angel Acosta.)

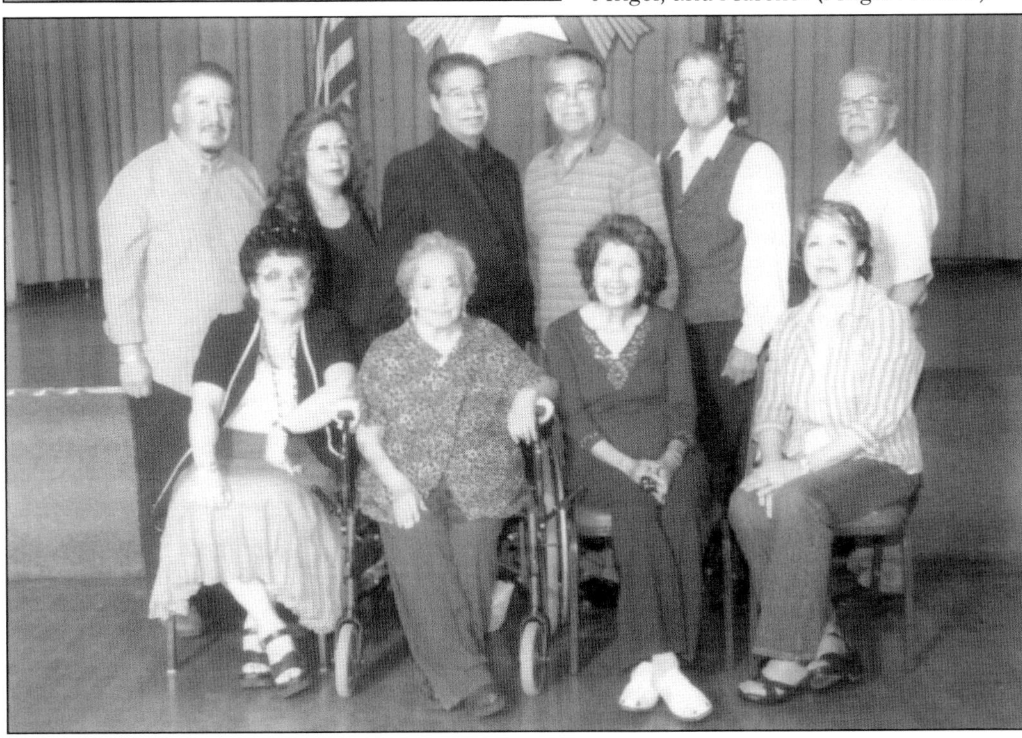

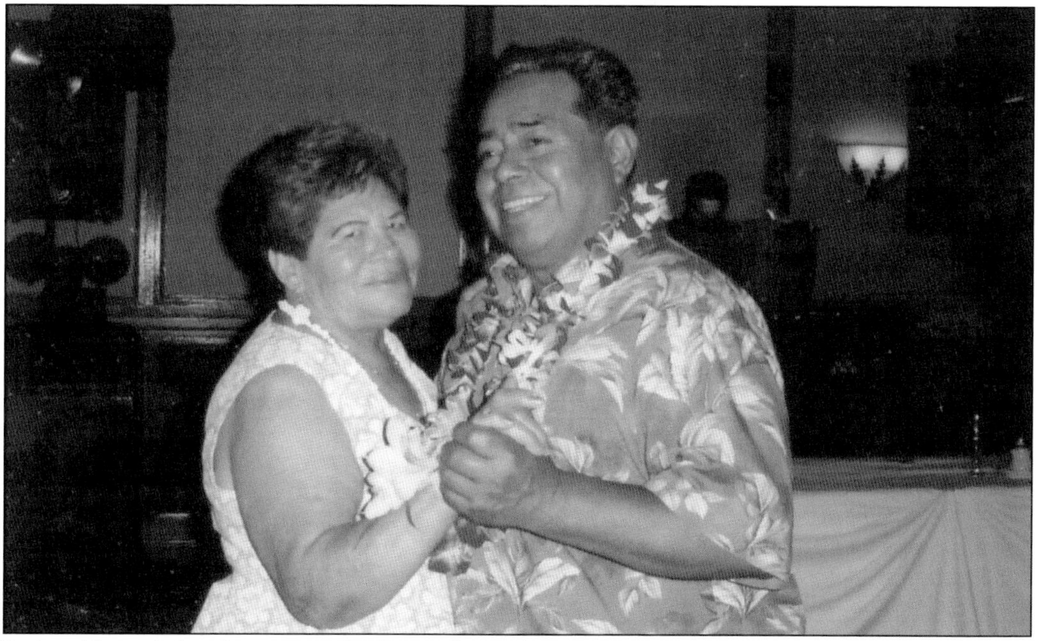

Pedro Alonzo's family came to La Rana from El Paso, Texas, in 1963. Pedro was born in Silo, Guanajuato, Mexico, on April 27, 1937. Esther was born in Fresnillo, Zacatecas, Mexico, on September 14, 1937. Pedro and Esther are pictured enjoying themselves in Hawaii in 1992. Esther passed away in December 2008. (Sally Alonzo.)

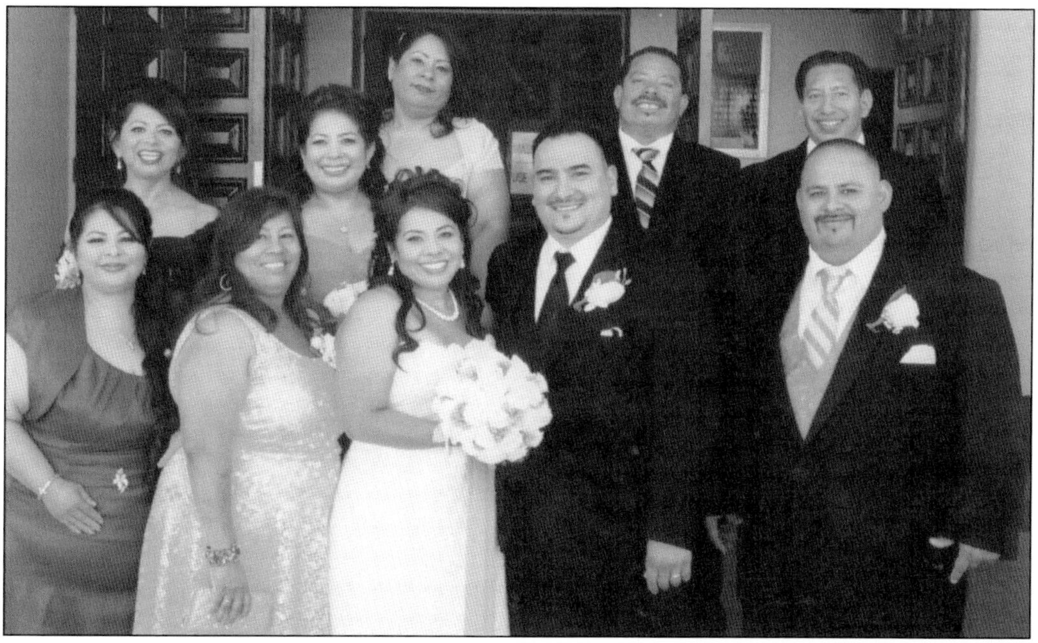

Martha Alicia and Richard Armenta are pictured at their wedding in July 2013. Martha Alicia is an educator with the Los Angeles Unified School District, and Richard is employed by AT&T. From left to right are (first row) Sally Alonzo, Elvira Diaz, Martha Alicia Alonzo, Richard Armenta, and Pete Alonzo; (second row) Theresa Alonzo, Elizabeth Alonzo, Virginia Guzman, Manuel Alonzo, and Jose Alonzo. (Sally Alonzo.)

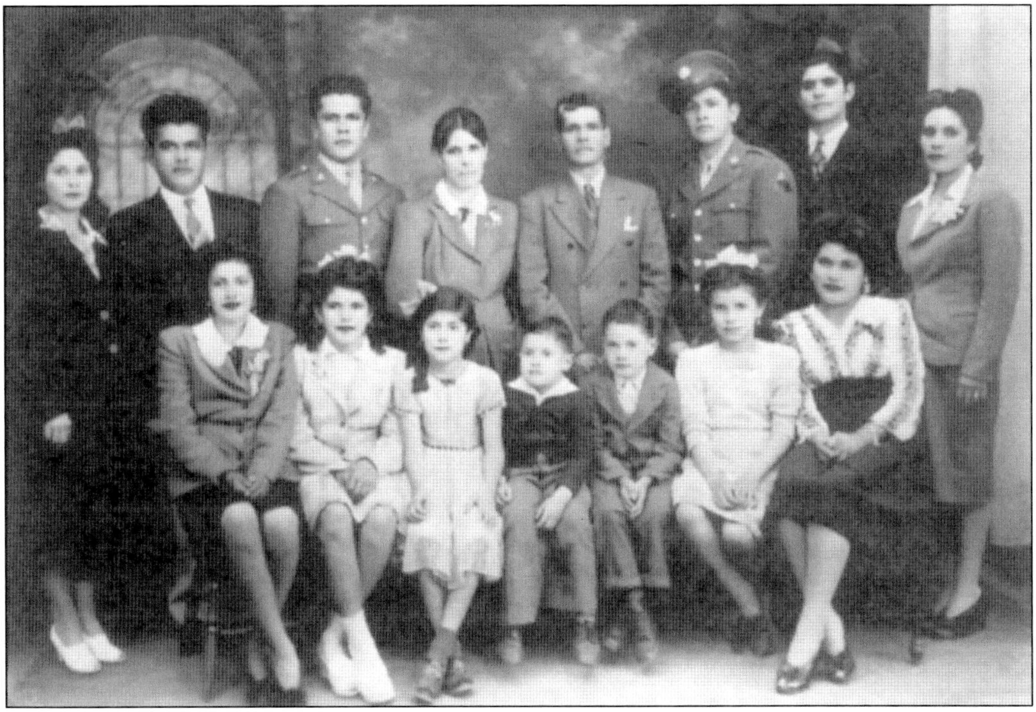

The Andres Alvarez family came to La Rana in 1931. In 1943, Agapita Alvarez was ill, so she called her 13 children together for this picture. From left to right are (first row) Julia, Connie, Phyllis, Raymond, Joe, Hermelinda, and Frances; (second row) Maria, Robert, Andres Jr., Agapita, Andres Sr., Luis, Jesus, and Sabina. (Longa Alvarez.)

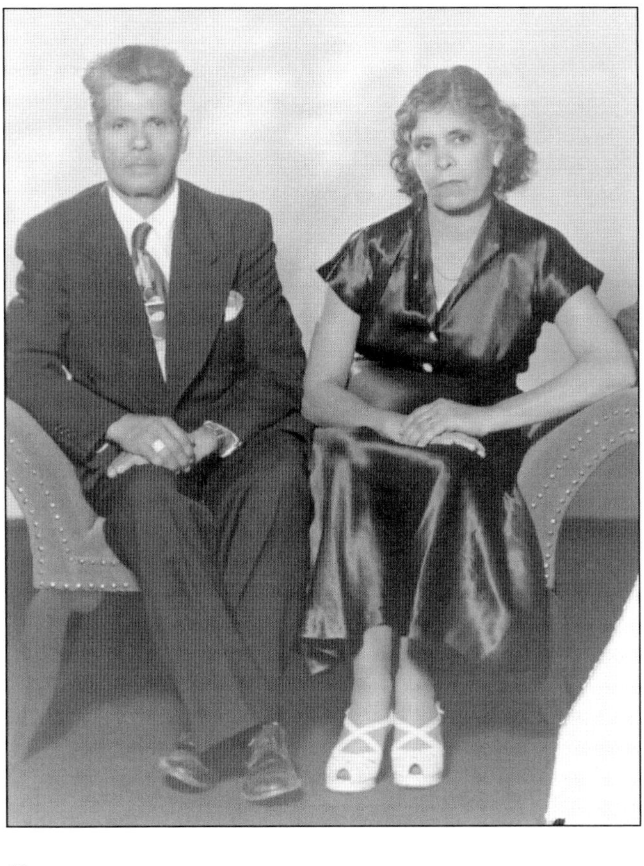

Andres Alvarez (born in 1881) and Agapita Fernandez Alvarez (1894) were both born in Purépero, Michoacán, Mexico. In 1919, they settled in Eagle Pass, Texas. The Alverez family later moved to Kansas and eventually came to live in Huntington Beach in 1920. In 1931, Andres and Agapita moved to La Rana. Andres was employed by U.S. Steel for 33 years. (Longa Alvarez.)

Lupe Flores Alvarez was born in Los Angeles in 1916. She married Manuel Alvarez and was employed by Torrance Laundry and Dry Cleaning. Lupe is pictured on Christmas morning in 1972 (seated at center) with her children (from left to right) Rachel, Manuel Jr., and Tony (standing). (Rachel Acosta.)

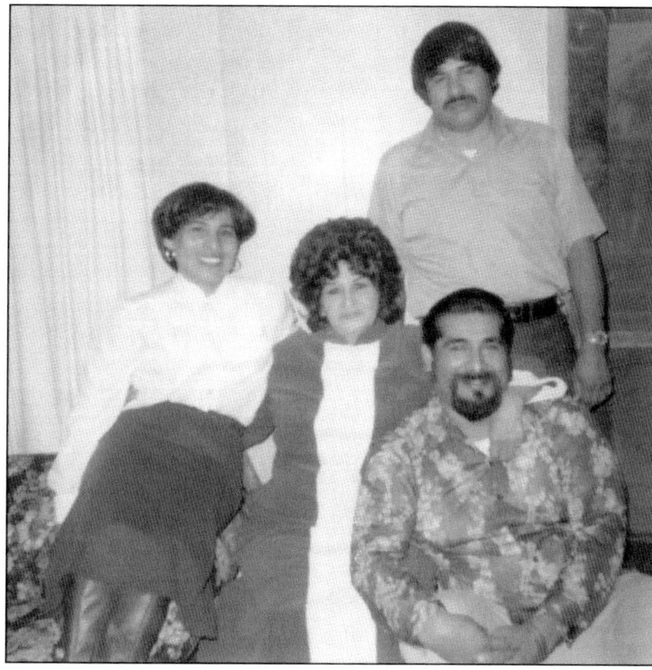

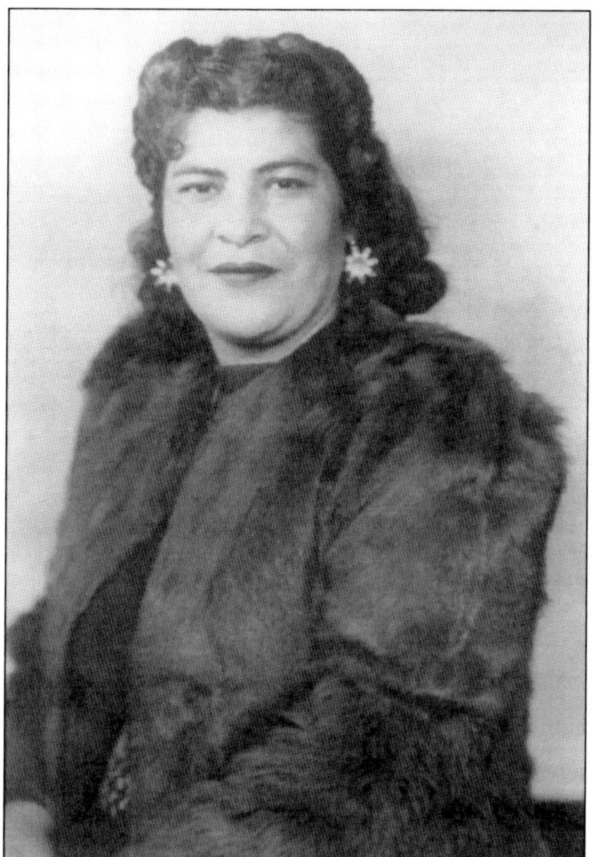

Josephina Arrellano came to La Rana in 1920. She was the daughter of Pedro and Petra Gutierrez and the mother of Dora, Rosie, Trini, Virginia, Daniel, and Angel. She was instrumental in reopening St. Joseph's Mission; it had been closed down for years until Arrellano and others began a fundraising campaign to reopen the church in the late 1930s. (Dora Camou.)

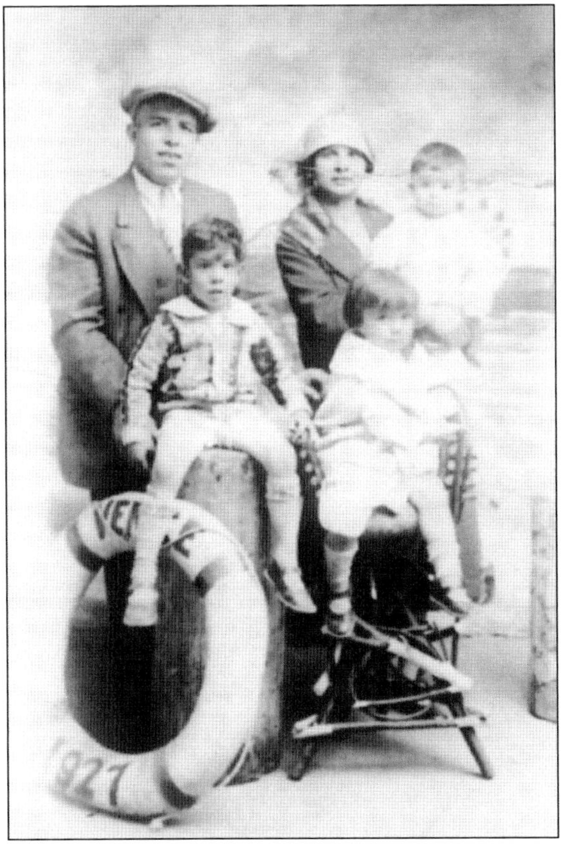

Enrique and Cuca Camou were both born in Sinaloa, Mexico, in 1900. The Camou family came to La Rana in 1937. Enrique worked at Torrance Laundry and Dry Cleaning, and Cuca worked for Star-Kist Tuna in San Pedro. Pictured here in 1927 are Hank Jr. (seated in front of his father, Enrique), Cuca (holding Clemente), and Olga. (Virginia Camou.)

The Camous are shown celebrating the wedding of Joe and Gerry Dominguez in 1960. Geraldine (Gerry) was Charlie's daughter. Sadly, Charlie was shot and killed after attending the Turkey Bowl football game in 1985. (Each year, the Turkey Bowl is still played on Thanksgiving morning.) Pictured are, from left to right, Hank, George, Virginia, Charlie, Olga, Clemente, and Richard. (Virginia Camou.)

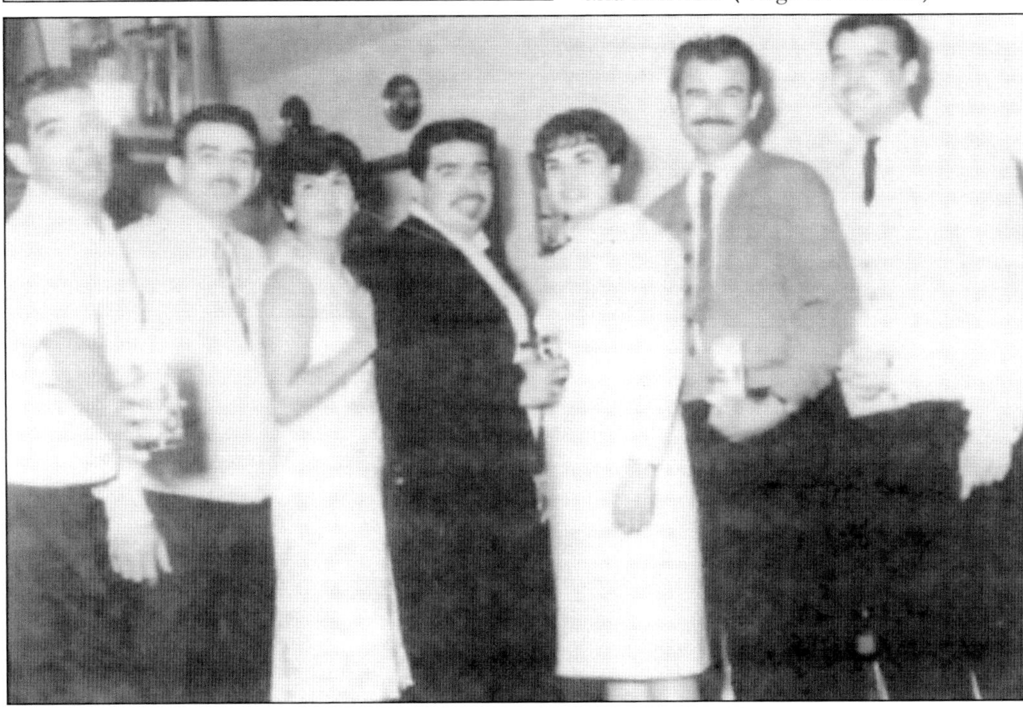

Dora and Clemente ("Clem") Camou are pictured at a formal event in 1960. Dora is the daughter of Josephina Gutierrez, and Clem is the son of Cuca and Henry Camou. Clem worked for Torrance Laundry and Dry Cleaning as a truck driver. Dora also worked for Torrance Laundry and Dry Cleaning and later worked for an aerospace company. (Dora Camou.)

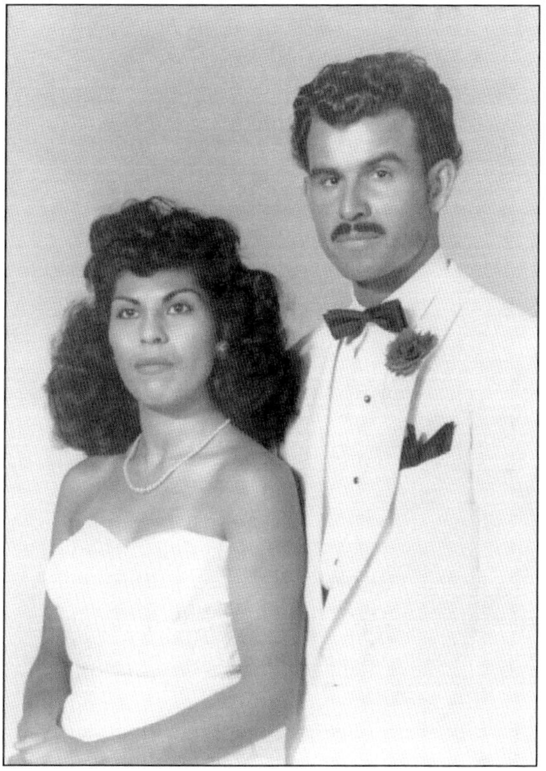

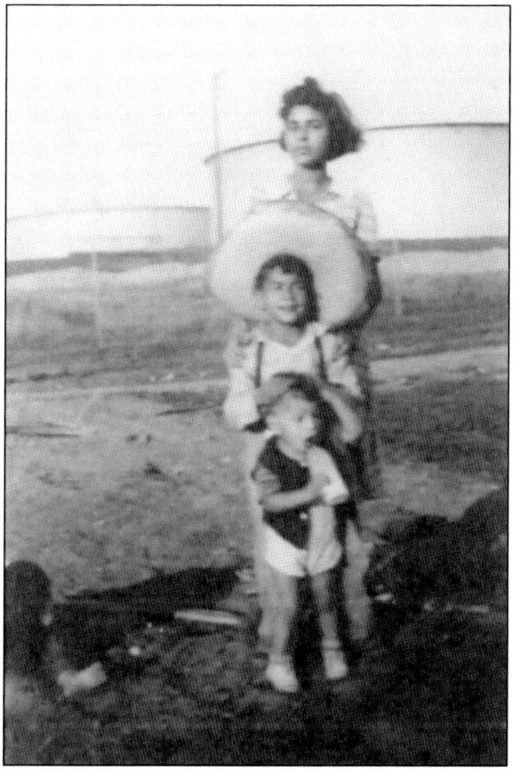

Kate Castillo (top), Louie Flores (middle), and Valente (Chino) Molinar are pictured here around 1937. Kate was the daughter of Eloisa Castillo, Louie was the son of Emilia Flores, and Valente was the son of Angel and Delfina Molinar. This is where the La Rana neighborhood geographically ended and is currently known as Del Amo. The oil tanks still exist. (Linda Ortiz.)

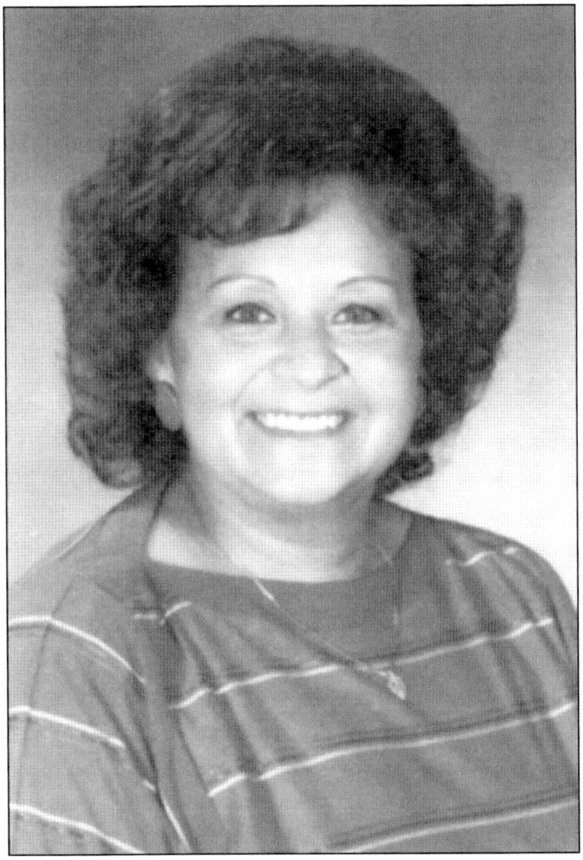

Virginia Sezate came to La Rana from Meza, Arizona, in 1947. She was married to Raul Chavez and worked for Torrance Elementary School for 10 years. Sezate was very active in church functions, and dancing was her favorite pastime. She passed away in 1987. Raul and Virginia had three children: Roberta, Rita, and Jeannie. (Linda Chavez.)

This 1938 photograph shows Artemio (born in 1904) and Dolores Duarte (1910). Both were born in Purépero, Michoacán, Mexico. They entered the United States and made La Rana their home in the 1920s. Artemio's first job was working as a laborer helping to erect the science building at Torrance High School. He worked for several steel companies and eventually became employed by U.S. Steel in 1933. (Alice Duarte Solis.)

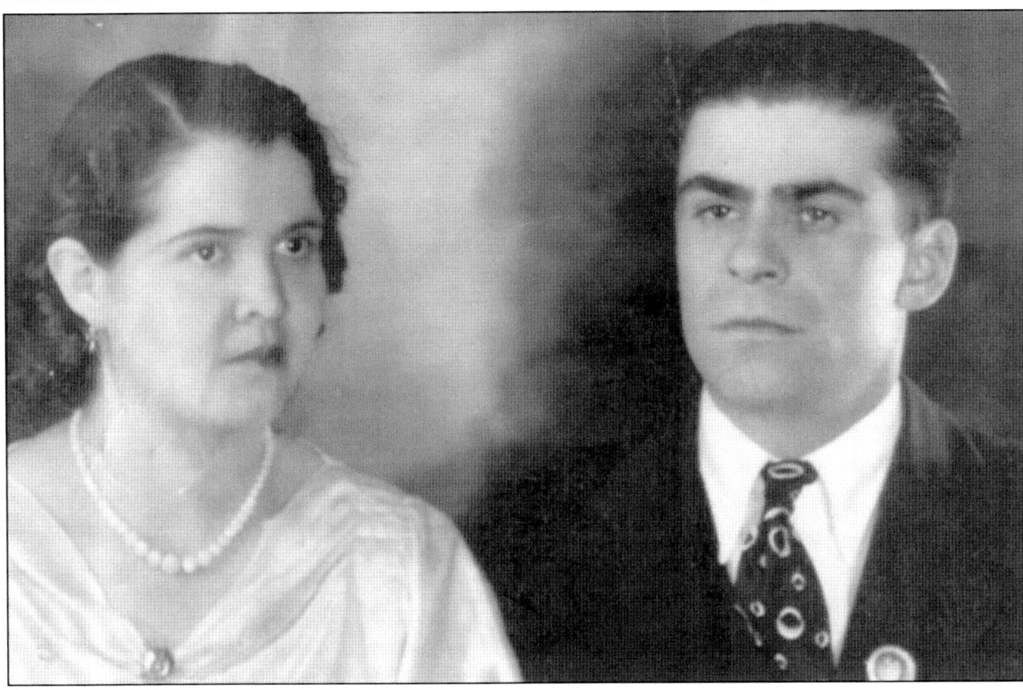

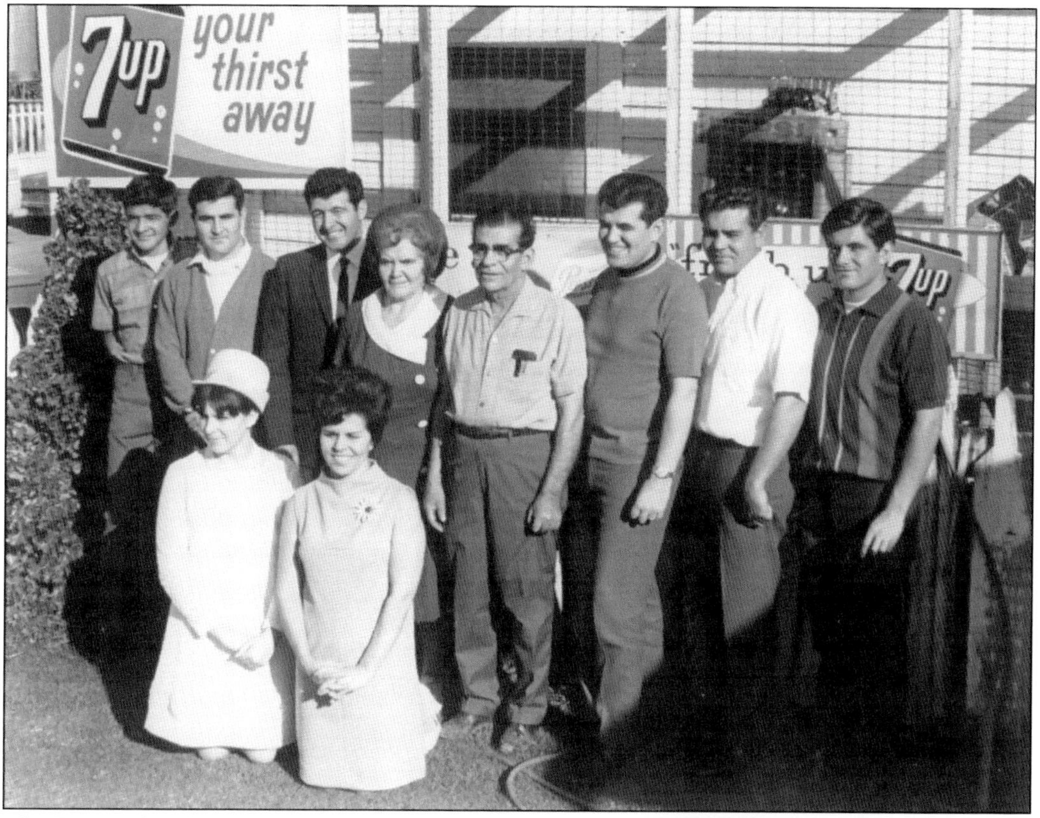

The Duarte family owned and operated a grocery store and tortilla factory in La Rana from 1946 to 1970. Pictured here in 1968 on the side of the grocery store are, from left to right, (kneeling) Marta and Alice; (standing) Michael, Henry, Hector, Lola, Artemio, Artemio Jr., Javier, and Albert. (Alice Duarte Solis.)

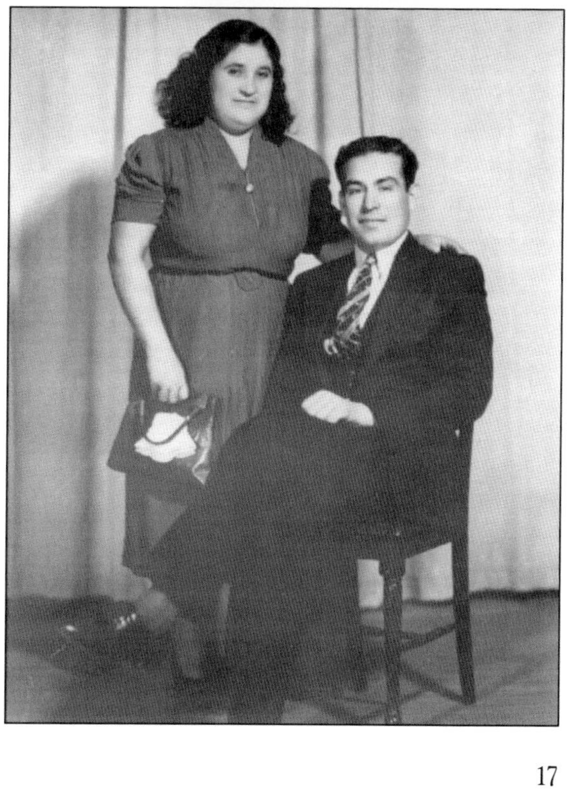

Dario Duran was born in Zacatecas, Mexico, in 1906. Antonia (Guerra) Duran's family was one of the first to come to La Rana in the early 1900s. Dario and Antonia are pictured on their 25th wedding anniversary. Dario was killed in a car accident while coming home from work in 1957. (Dora Villarreal.)

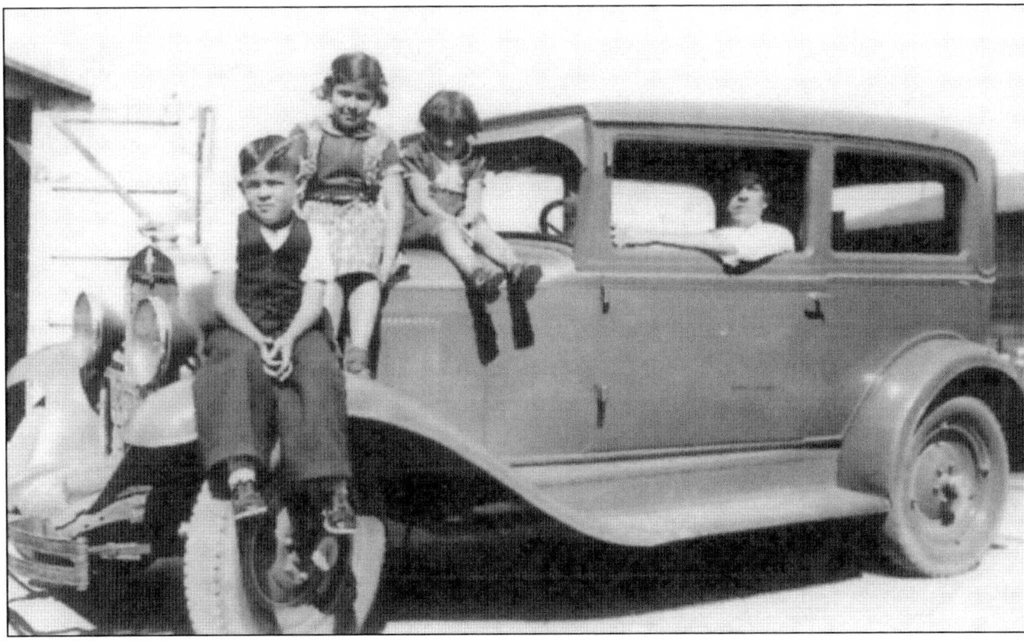

In 1939, the Duran children posed while sitting on top of their father Dario's car. Gilbert is sitting on the fender, Margaret and Dora are on the hood, and Dario is in the driver's seat. Dario was employed by California Salvage on Anaheim Street in Wilmington, California. (Dora Villarreal.)

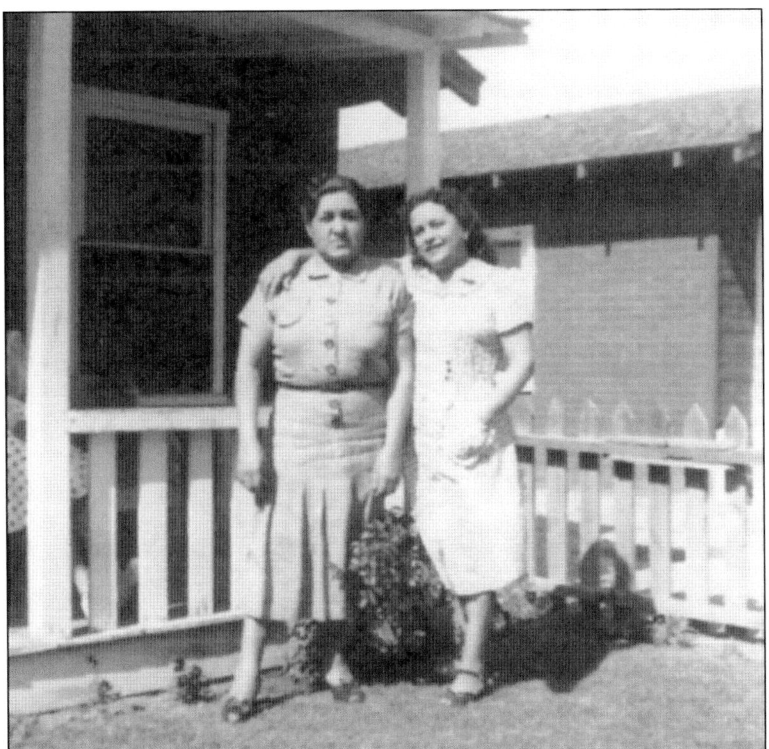

In this 1948 picture, Eloisa Castillo (left) and Emilia Flores are in front of Antonia Guerra Duran's house. Eloisa was mother to Helen, Kate, Henry (Chato) Leo, and Beatrice. Emilia Flores was mother to Louie Flores and Linda Ortiz. (Dora Villarreal.)

Olia Fernandez was born in San Pedro, California, raised in La Rana, and attended Torrance High School. She was active in all the functions at St. Joseph's Mission. Olia, daughter of Jovita Fernandez, became her mother's caretaker until her mother's passing. Jovita was one of the early settlers of La Rana in the 1920s. (Longa Alvarez.)

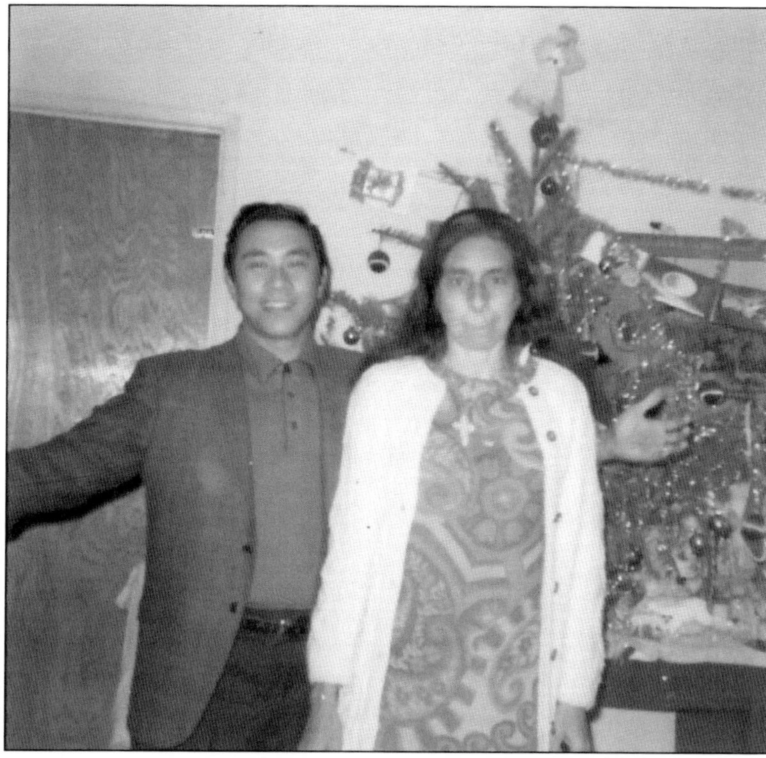

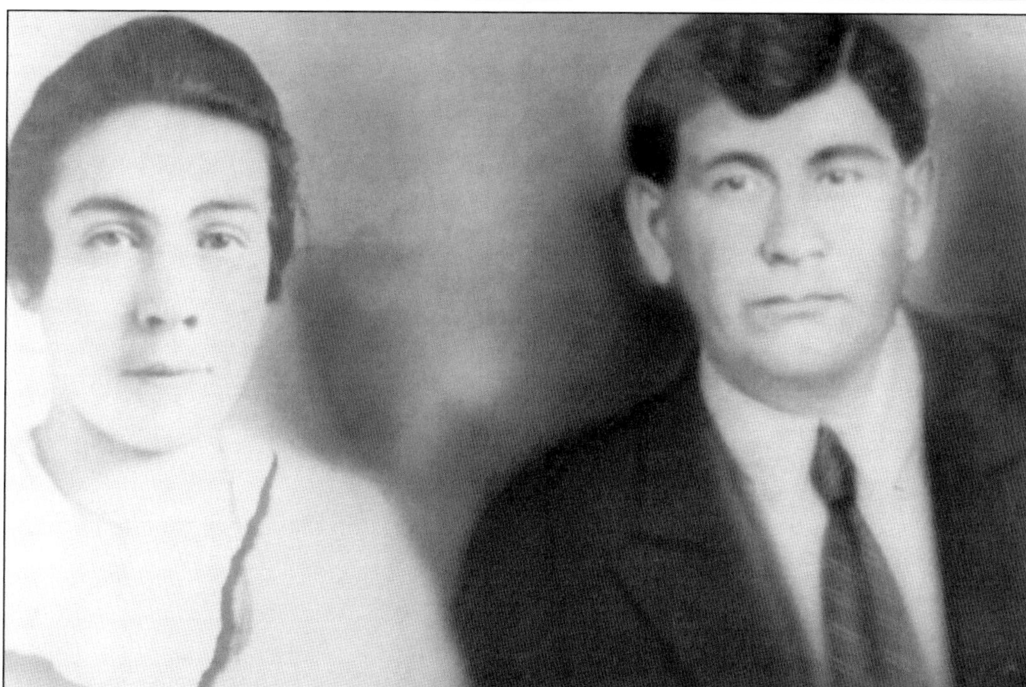

Nestor Flores (right) was a widower with three daughters—Soledad, Lupe and Concepcion—when he came to La Rana from El Paso, Texas, in 1919. In 1921, Nestor married Victoria Quinones (left), who was from La Paz, Baja California, Mexico. They had eight children. (Gloria Castaneda.)

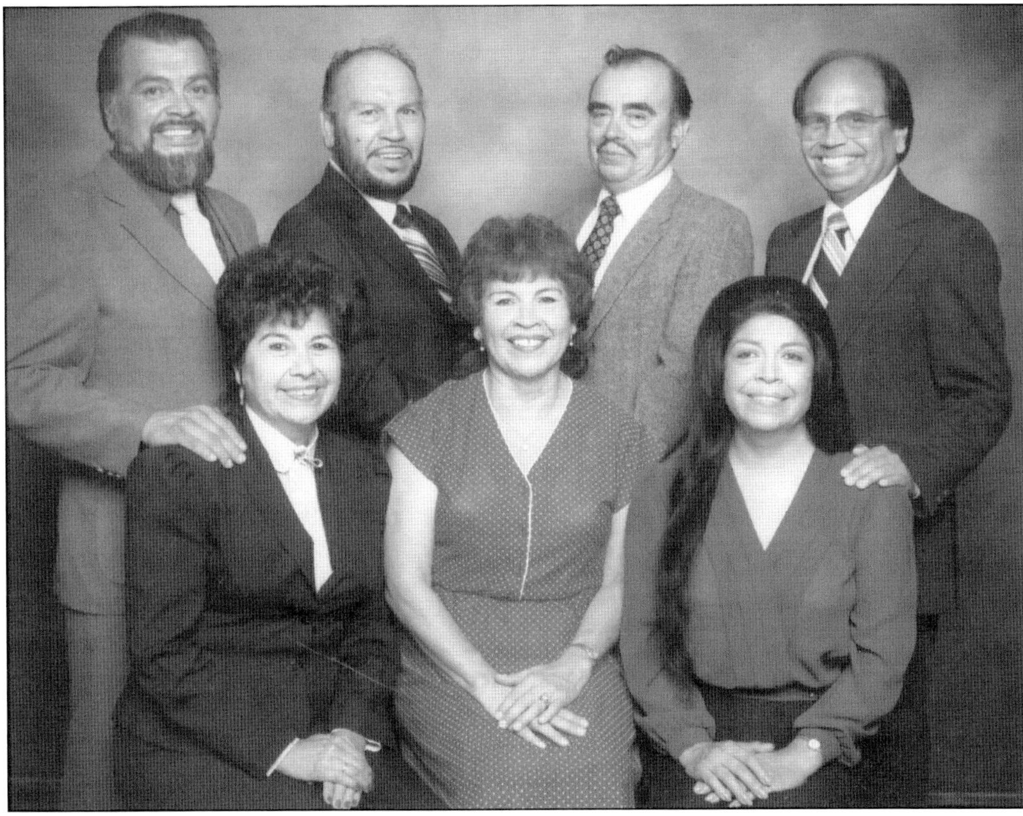

The Flores children pictured here in 1984 are, from left to right, (first row) Gloria, Mary, and Helen; (second row) Benny, Joe, Tony, and Rudy. Five Flores sons served in the military during World War II and the Korean War. (Gloria Castaneda.)

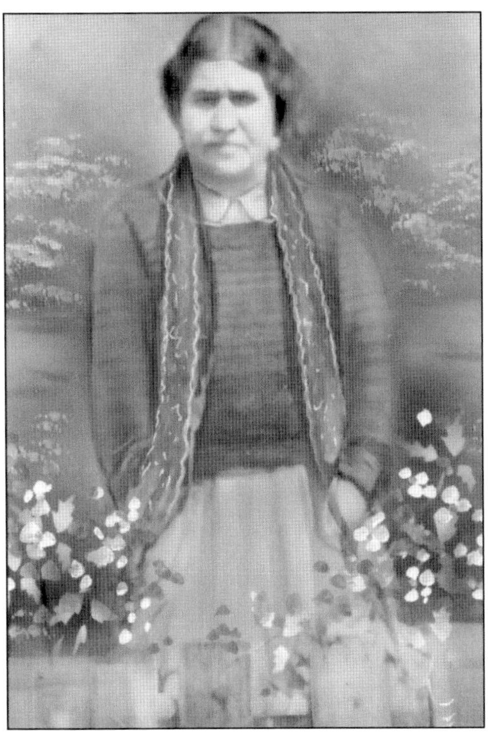

Rosario Garcia Flores came to La Rana from Jerome, Arizona, in approximately 1916. She cooked for the workers who were new arrivals from Mexico during the time of the Mexican Revolution. Rosario was the mother of seven children: Jose, Lupe, Leandro, Eloisa, Antonia, Cruz, and Emilia. The Flores family tradition of excellent cooking still continues today. (Armida Grajeda.)

Lupe Molinar, daughter of Rosario, came to La Rana in 1916. Lupe opened a restaurant called Los Tres Aces on Carson Boulevard in the mid-1940s and later opened another restaurant called Joe's Place in the early 1950s. She is pictured here with her three children (from left to right), David, Rosario, and Angel (background). Lupe is the grandmother of Armida Molinar Grajeda. (Armida Grajeda.)

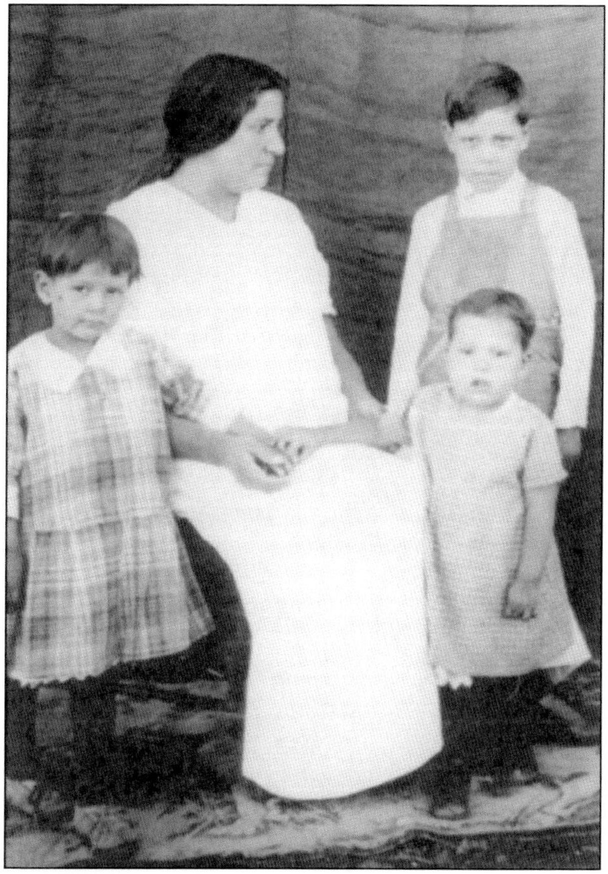

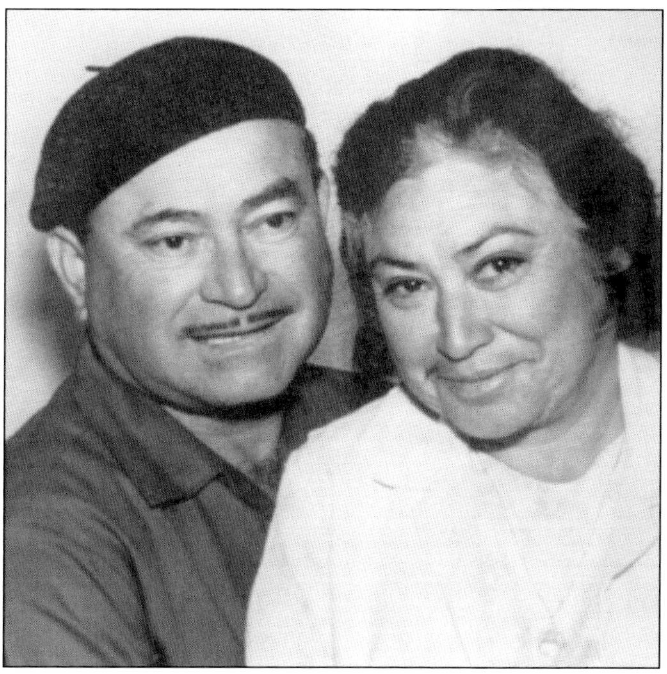

Jesus Camarena Gassett (left) attended a Catholic seminary in Sonora, Mexico, in 1926. Religious persecution broke out during the Mexican Revolution, and instructors ordered him to leave the country for his own safety. His name was changed to Gassett when he came to the United States. He married Inez Annette Ortega (right) in the early 1940s and moved to La Rana in 1944. (Stella Gassett.)

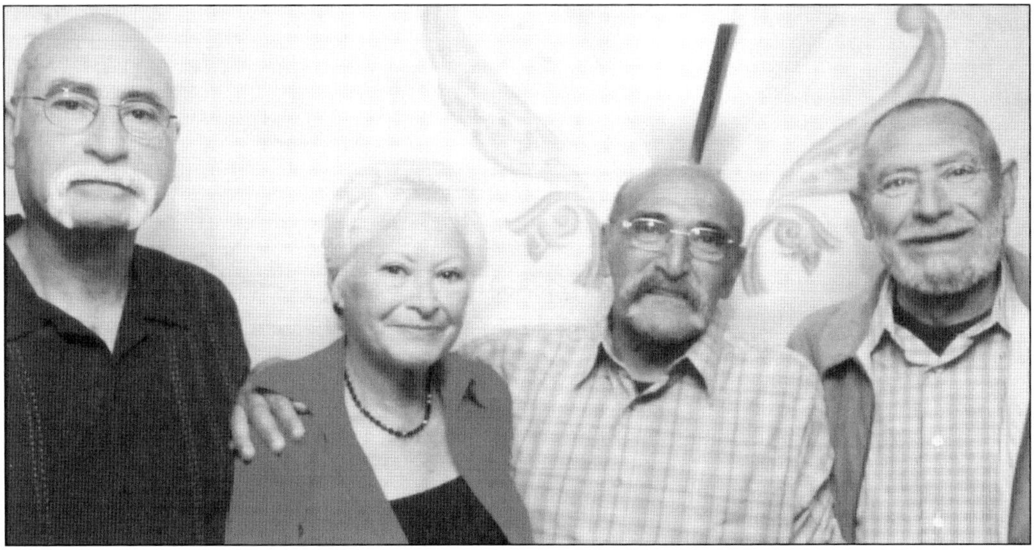

The Gassett children were raised in La Rana and attended Torrance schools. Pictured from left to right are Tony (Zapata), Irene, Terry Boy, and Richard. They were attending the graduation celebration for Tony's granddaughter Danielle Prado when she graduated from California State University, Fullerton. Tony was employed by the Torrance School District, Richard was employed by the City of Torrance, and Irene was a housewife. (Stella Gassett.)

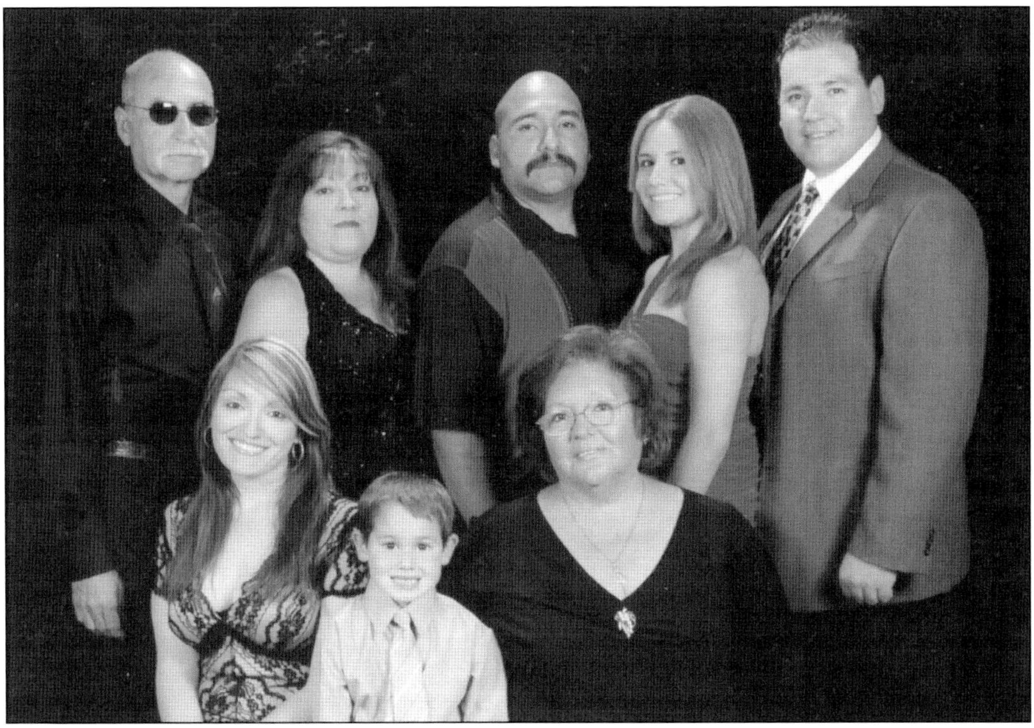

Tony Gassett (standing, left) and Stella (Ordaz) Gassett (seated, right) are pictured with their family in 2005. Tony and Stella were celebrating their 45th wedding anniversary on a cruise to Ensenada, Mexico. Stella is the daughter of Tula and Ruben Ordaz and has lived her whole life in La Rana. (Stella Gassett.)

Jesus Grande and Juanita Solis Grande were both born in Tonalá, Jalisco, Mexico, and settled in Douglas, Arizona. Jesus came to La Rana in 1927, and Juanita came in 1933. Pictured here in 1948 are, from left to right, (first row) Connie Solis and two unidentified; (second row) Jesus, Rosa (Chena) Grande, and Juanita holding Virginia Solis. (Ernestine Castillo.)

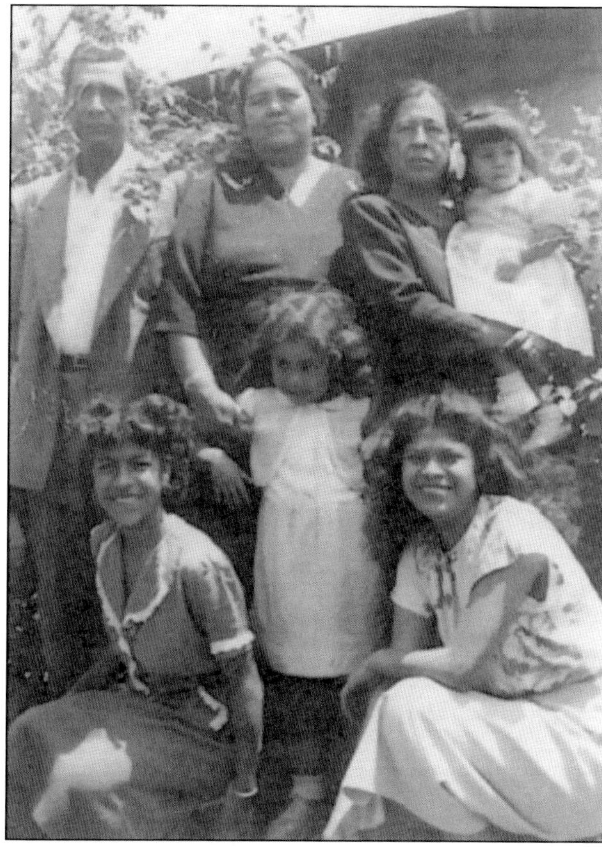

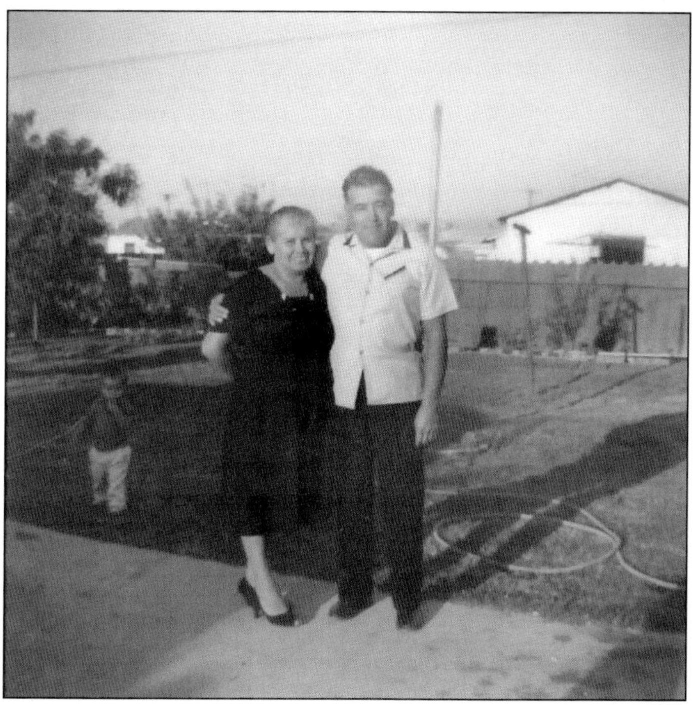

Soledad (Chole) Flores Grajeda was born in El Paso, Texas, and Miguel Grajeda was born in Chilchota, Mexico. Miguel came with his family from Mexico in 1917, and Soledad came with her father from Texas in 1919. Miguel worked for U.S. Steel; Chole worked for Torrance Laundry and Dry Cleaning. The couple, pictured here in the 1940s, had nine children. (Stella Gassett.)

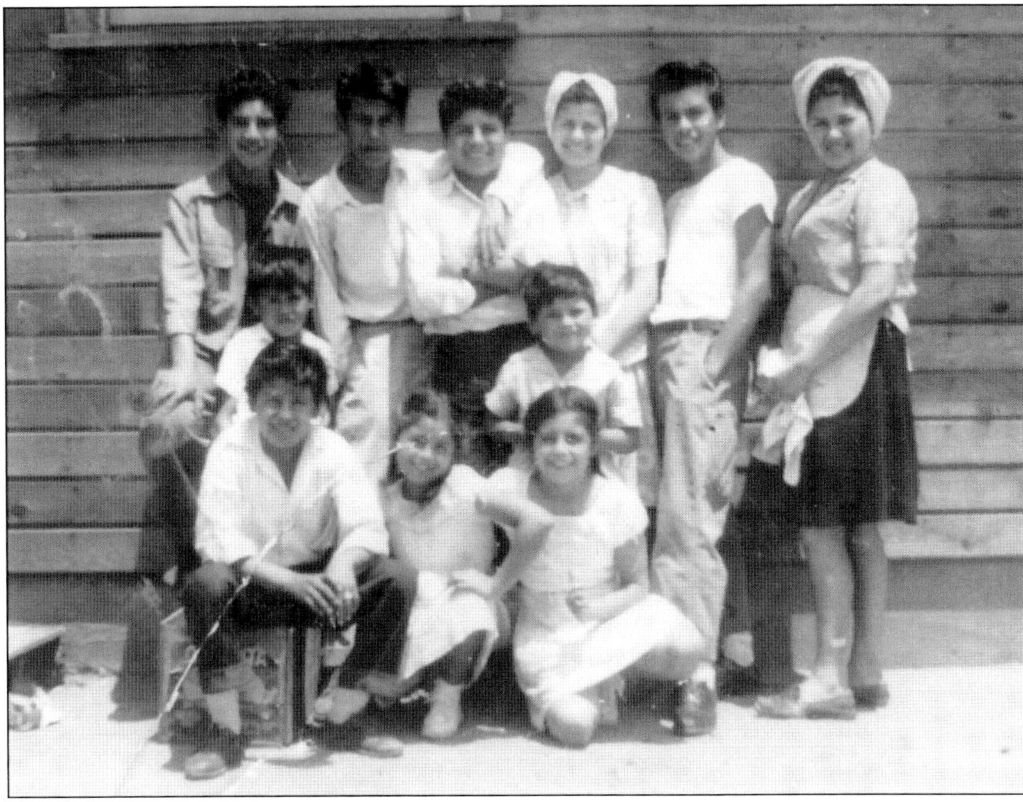

Miguel Grajeda finished constructing the building in the background in the 1940s. Pictured here are his children and relatives. They are, from left to right, (first row) Chino, Mellie, and Carmen Grajeda; (second row) Joe (Coni) Rodriquez, Rudy Flores, Mickey Grajeda, Conchita Grajeda, Benny Flores, and Dora Grajeda. Bobby and Frankie Grajeda are the two young boys standing between the rows. (Stella Gassett.)

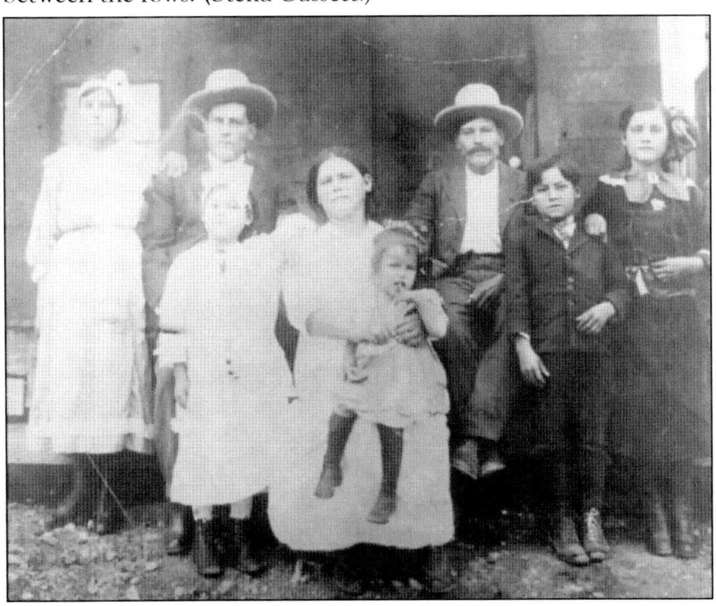

In the early years, photographers would go from house to house offering to take pictures of families. Rafael Grajeda had this picture of his family taken around 1919. The Grajedas were early settlers in La Rana, but the exact date of their arrival is unknown. From left to right are Jesusita, Rafael, Tula (in front of Rafael), Concepion (holding Celia), Don Rafaelito, Miguel, and Delfina. (Stella Gassett.)

Cruz Guerra came to La Rana at a very young age. He was married to Virginia Villegas, and they had three sons, Freddie, Robert, and John. Cruz lived his whole life in the community of La Rana. He was killed at a local bar over a card game. (Linda Ortiz.)

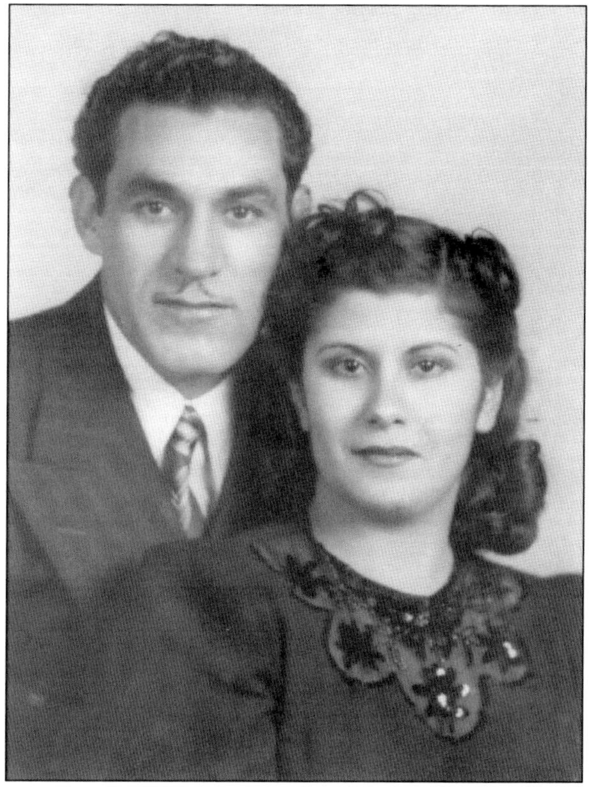

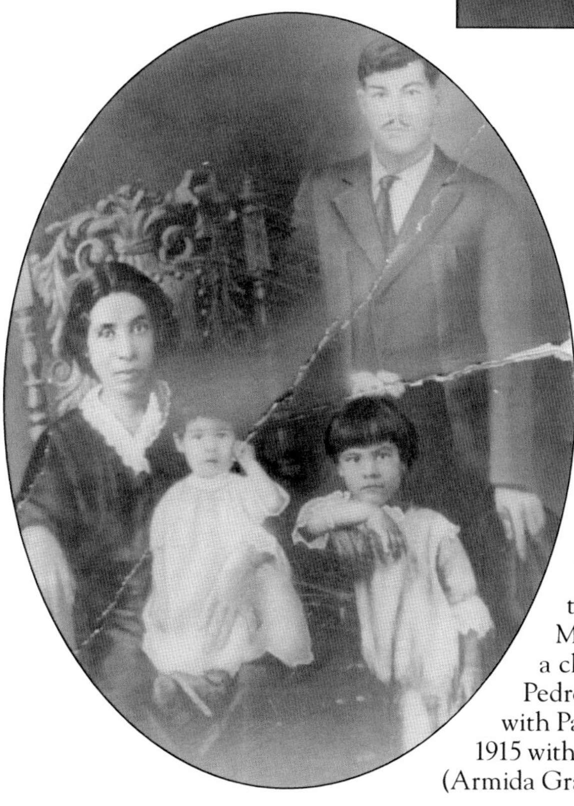

Pedro and Petra Gutierrez came to La Rana in the early 1920s. Petra worked tirelessly to raise funds to build St. Joseph's Mission. Pedro was instrumental in obtaining a church bell from U.S. Steel for St. Joseph's. Pedro fought during the Mexican Revolution with Pancho Villa. They are pictured here around 1915 with their two daughters, Delfina and Josephina. (Armida Grajeda.)

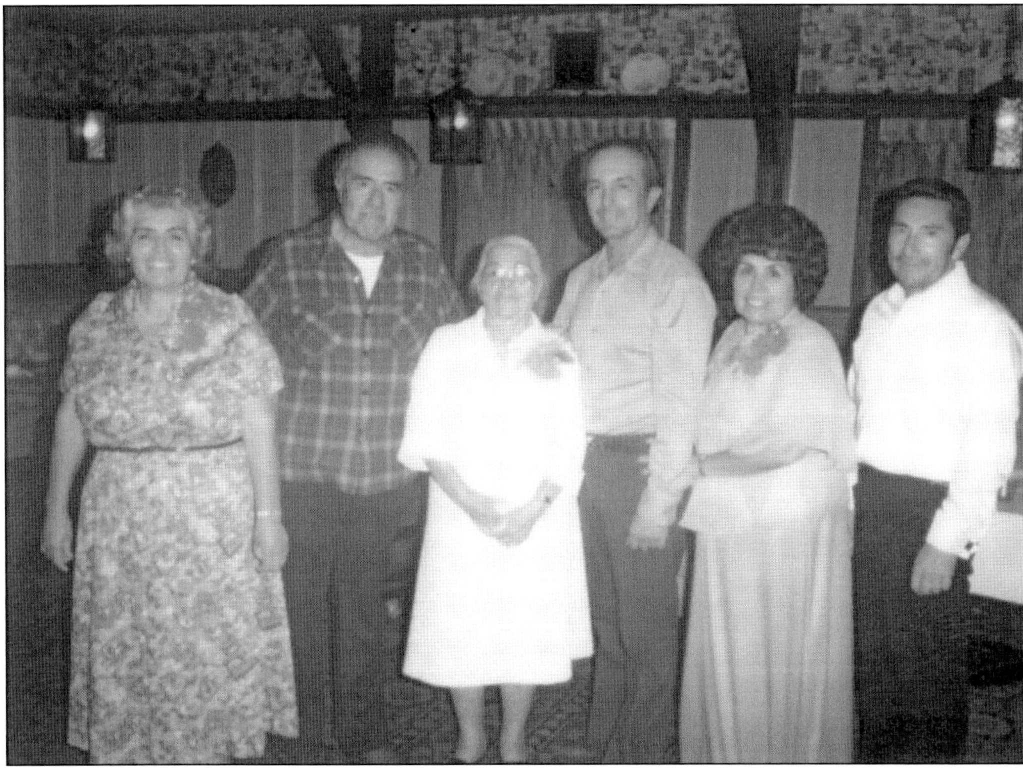

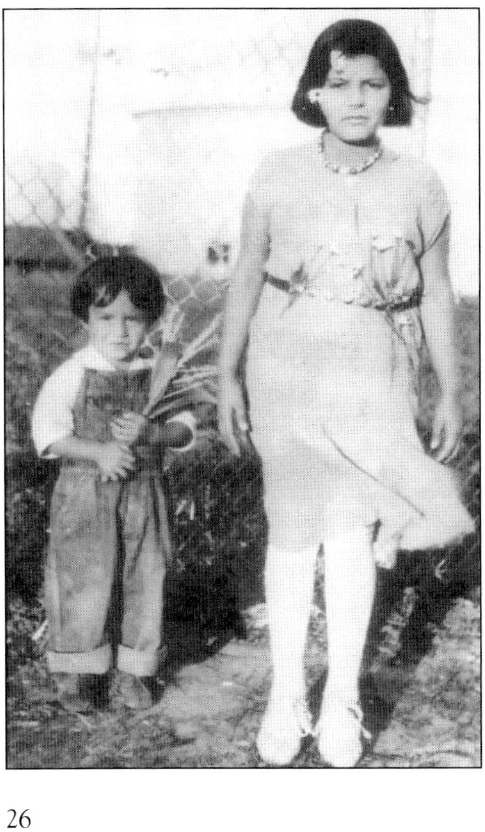

The Guzman family is pictured here in 1976. Esther Guzman was the pastor of the Pentecostal church in La Rana. Esther later became pastor of the Pentecostal church in Wilmington, California. From left to right are Eva Guzman, Tony Guzman, Esther Guzman, Armando Guzman, Esther Guzman, and Rudy Vega. (Rudy Vega.)

Eva Guzman was 12 and her brother Armando Guzman was 4 when this picture was taken in 1932. Eva was the second oldest of Dona Esther's children. In 1940, she became the first student from La Rana to graduate from Torrance High School. The tanks in the background are still part of La Rana's landscape. (Rudy Vega.)

Aleja Herrera was born in Zacatecas, Mexico, and came to the United States at age four. She came to La Rana from Colorado with five of her children in the early 1940s. Her eight children were Felix, Irene, Mary, Tony, Trini, Lollie, Socorro, and Fidel. (Irene Ordaz.)

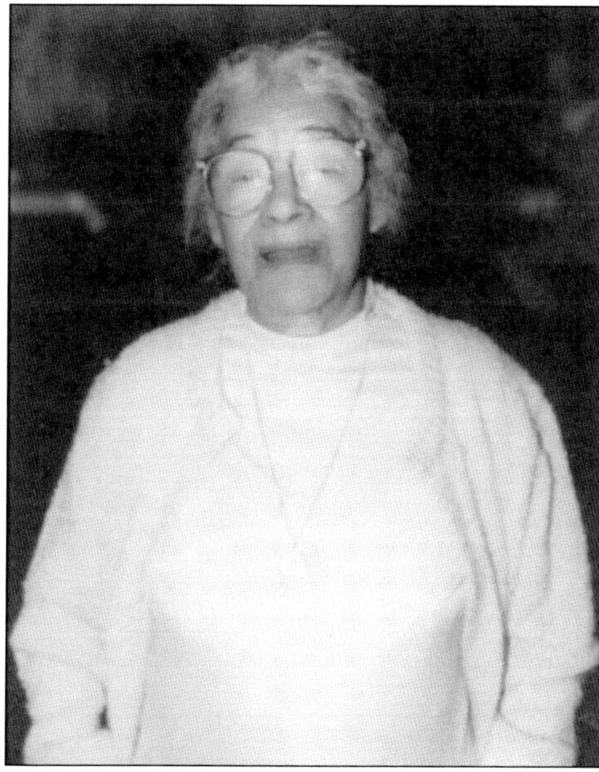

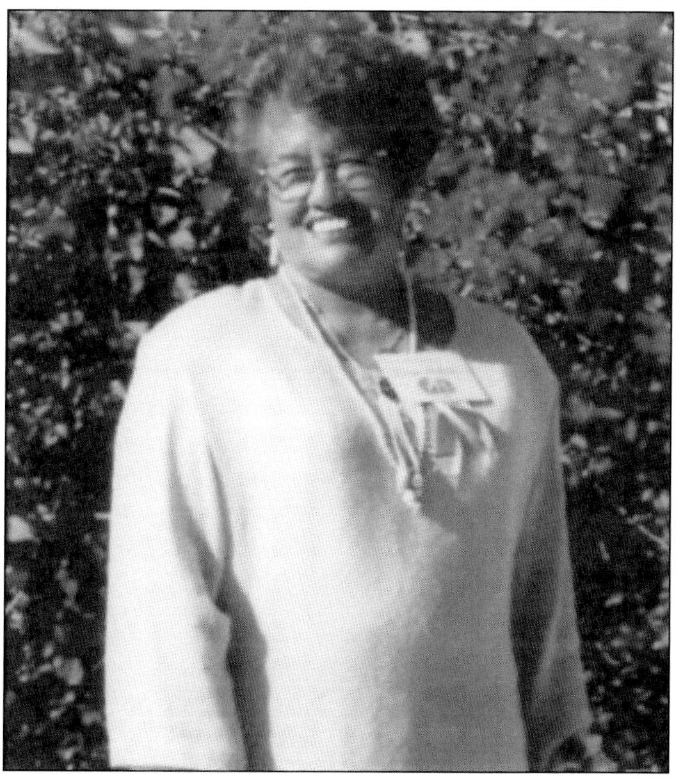

This is Irene Herrera Ordaz, a daughter of Aleja Herrera. Irene attended Torrance schools, married Ruben Ordaz, and had three children: Susan, Terrie, and Belen. In 1995, the City of Torrance honored Irene as Woman of The Year for her community work. (Irene Ordaz.)

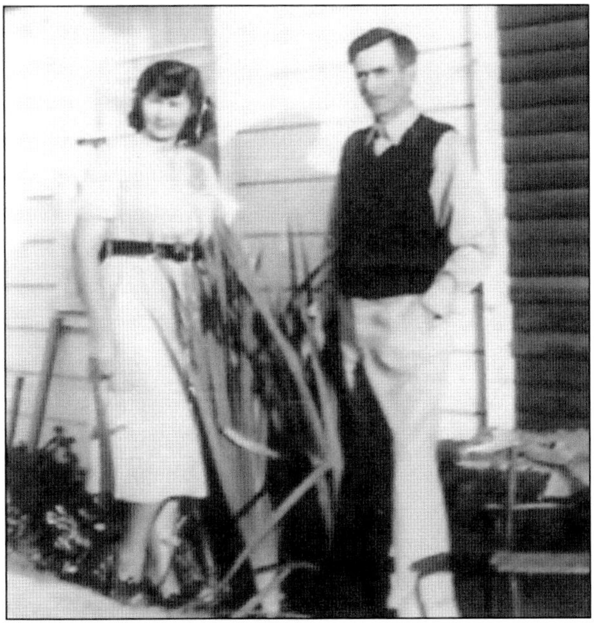

Juanita (Armenta) Iriarte was born in Sonora, Mexico. In 1945, she married Ramiro Iriarte, and they moved to La Rana in 1949. The Iriartes soon met many of the residents of La Rana and became involved in St. Joseph's Mission activities including annual fiestas. This picture of the couple was taken in front of their home in 1956. (Hector Molina.)

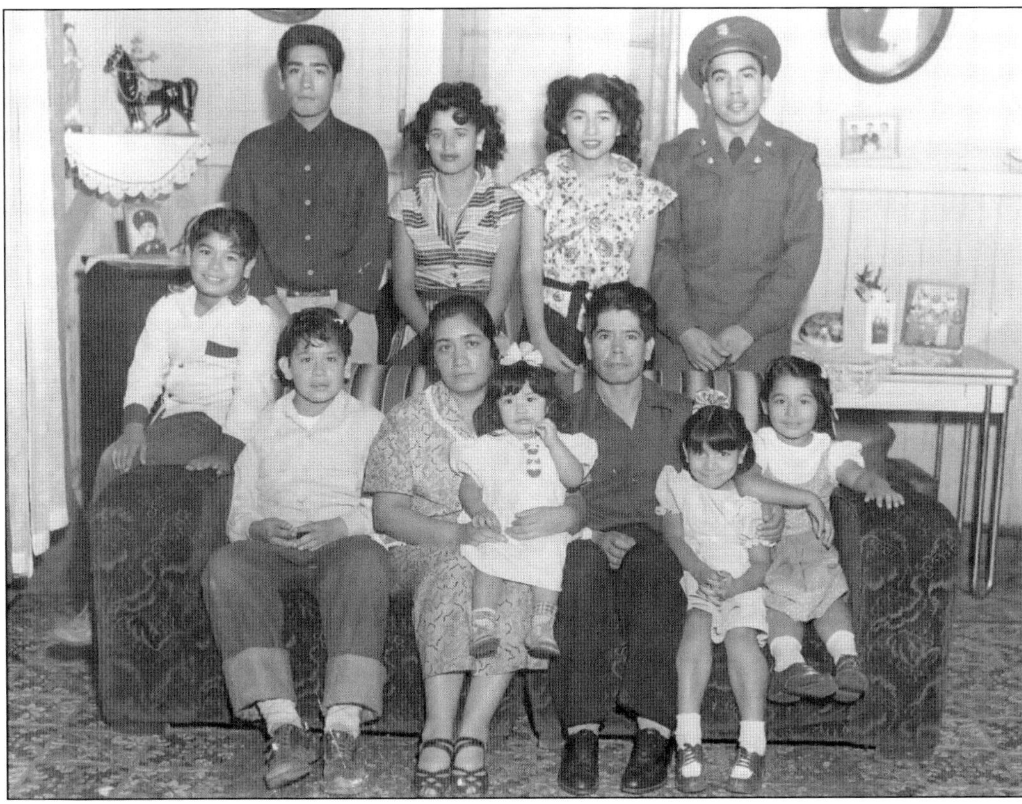

Antonio and Gabriela Martinez are pictured with their family in 1952. Their son Mike Martinez was on leave from the Korean War. From left to right are (first row) Louie, Paulo, Gabriela, Sara (Chuqi) on Gabriela's lap, Antonio Sr., Stella, and Manuela; (second row) Antonio Jr., unidentified, Dolores, and Mike. (Louie Martinez.)

Maria Martinez married Pedro Martinez in Purépero, Michoacán, Mexico, in 1923 and came to La Rana shortly after their marriage. They had six children: Josie, Angie, Artie, Ramiro, Alice, and Velia. Maria died at an early age. Artie said, "Our mother died when we were very young. The neighbors in La Rana looked after us." (Artie Martinez.)

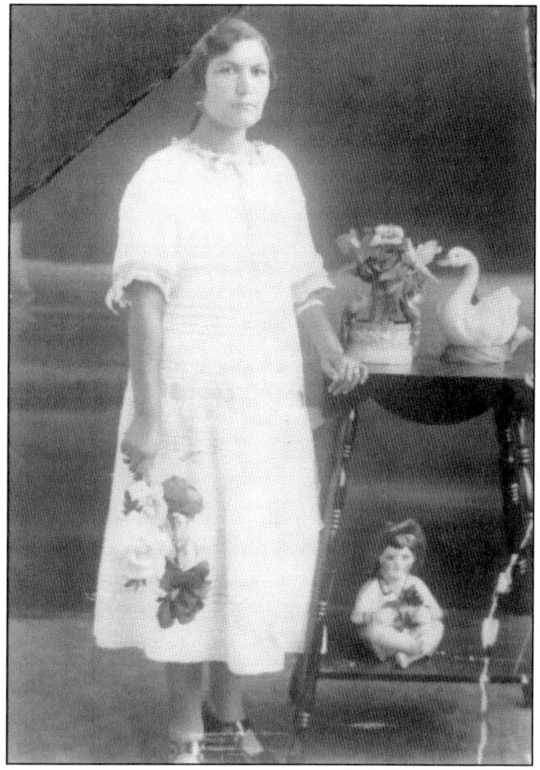

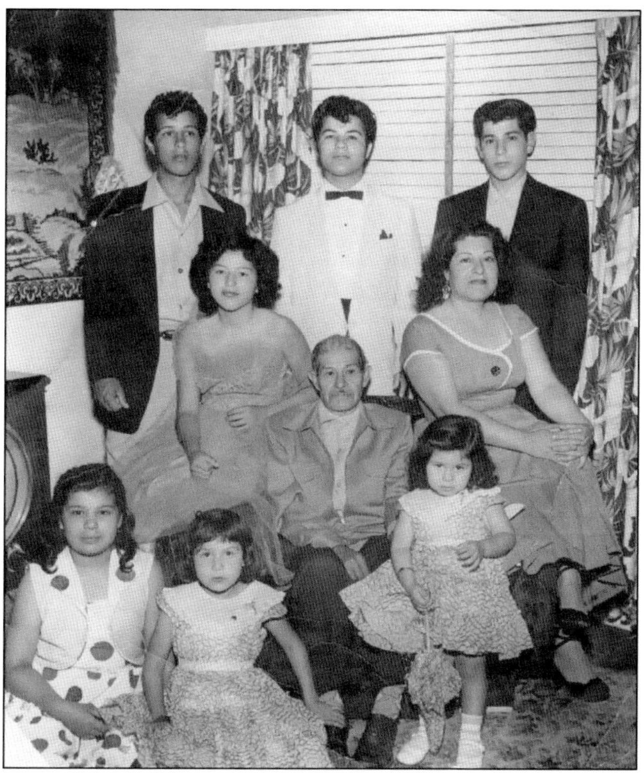

The Delfina Molinar family and their grandfather Pedro Gutierrez are pictured at a family gathering in 1955. Delfina is the daughter of Pedro. From left to right are (first row) Stella, Alice, and Dolores; (second row, seated) Armida, Don Pedro, and Delfina; (third row, standing) Henry, David, and Valente. (Armida Grajeda.)

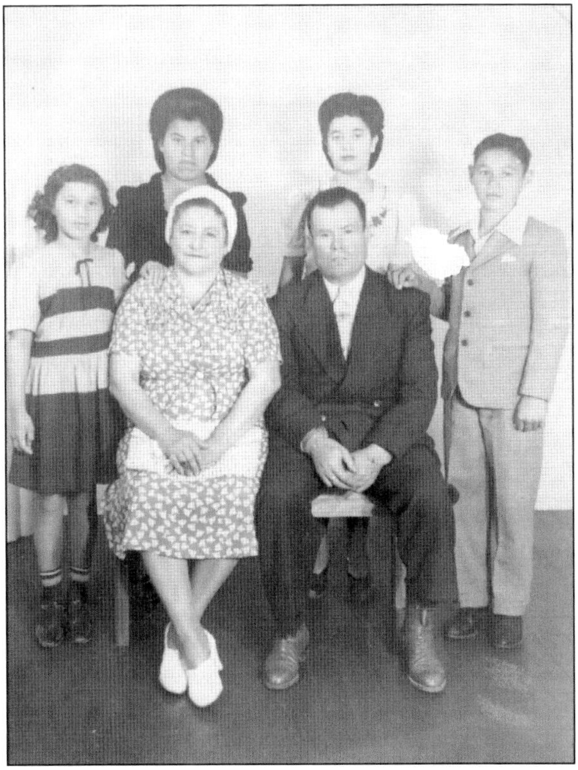

Florencio Mora came from Jalisco, Mexico, to La Rana in 1919. He was employed by U.S. Steel and was very active in the community. The Mora children all attended Torrance High School. Pictured here in 1944 are, from left to right, (seated) Chavela and Florencio; (standing) Anita, Dorothy, Trindad, and Frankie. (Dorothy Medina.)

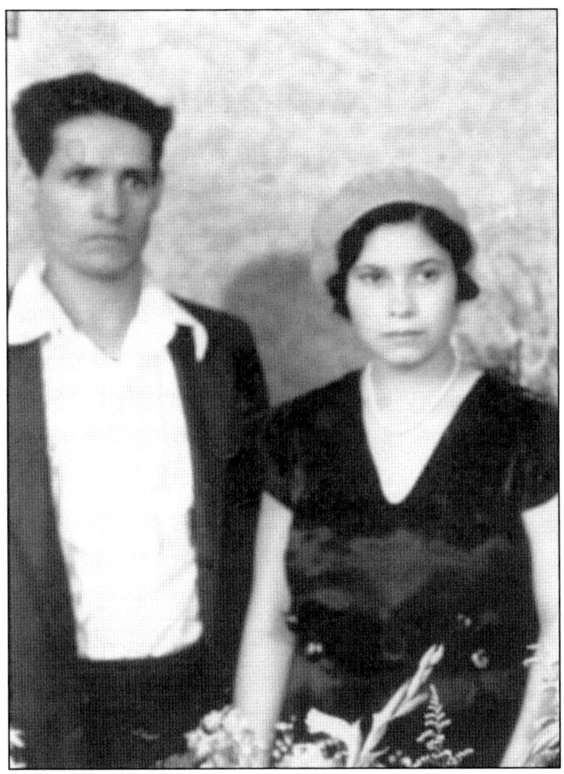

Antonio Moreno (1905) and Maria Alvarez (1915) were both born in Purépero, Michoacán, Mexico. Antonio came to La Rana in the early 1920s, Maria arrived in 1931, and they married and had 15 children. Antonio worked at Columbia Steel. This photograph was taken in 1933. Antonio died while he was at work. (Alice Duarte Solis.)

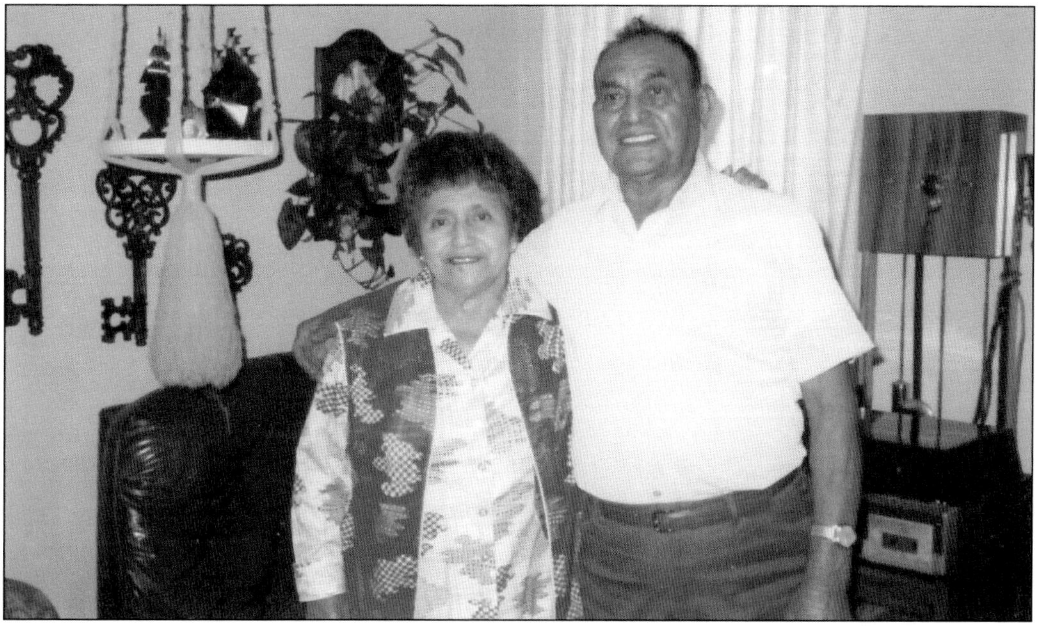

Pilar Olvera was born in Redlands, California, in 1899 and came to La Rana in 1930. He worked at U.S. Steel for 36 years. Pilar is pictured here at his 50th birthday celebration with his wife, Pauline, in 1949. Pauline Murillo Olvera was born in Guanajuato, Mexico. The Olveras had four children. (Maggie Olvera.)

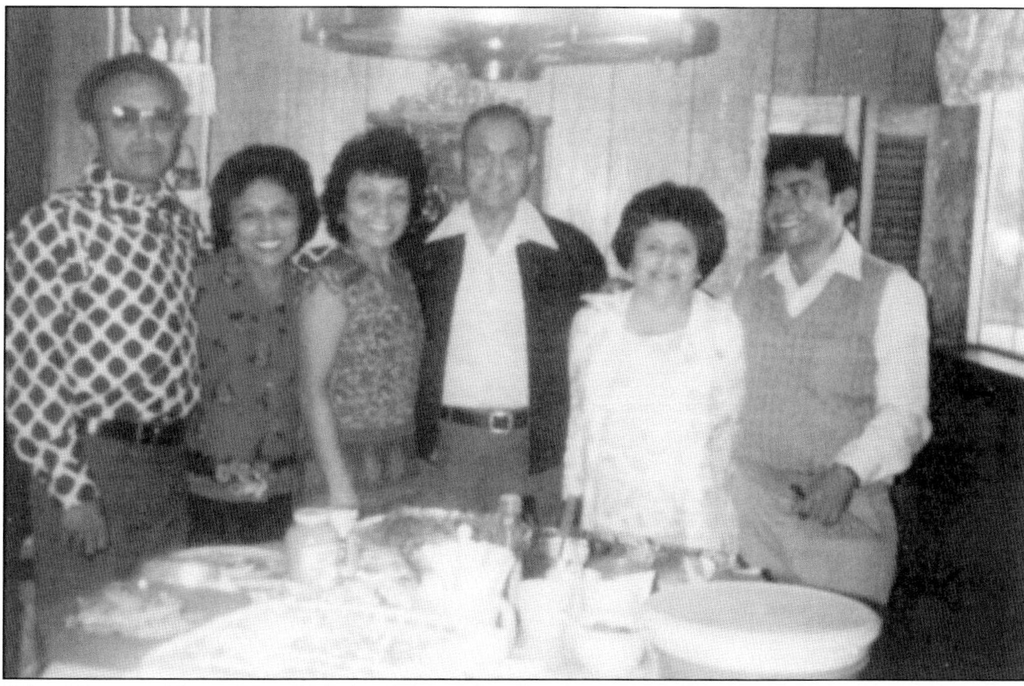

Pilar Olvera celebrated his 80th birthday at his daughter Lucy's home in 1979. Pictured here are, from left to right, Billy, Lucy, Maggie, Don Pilar, Pauline, and Bobby. Lucy passed away in 2009, leaving behind a husband and five children. Bobby passed away in 1989, leaving behind four children. (Maggie Olvera.)

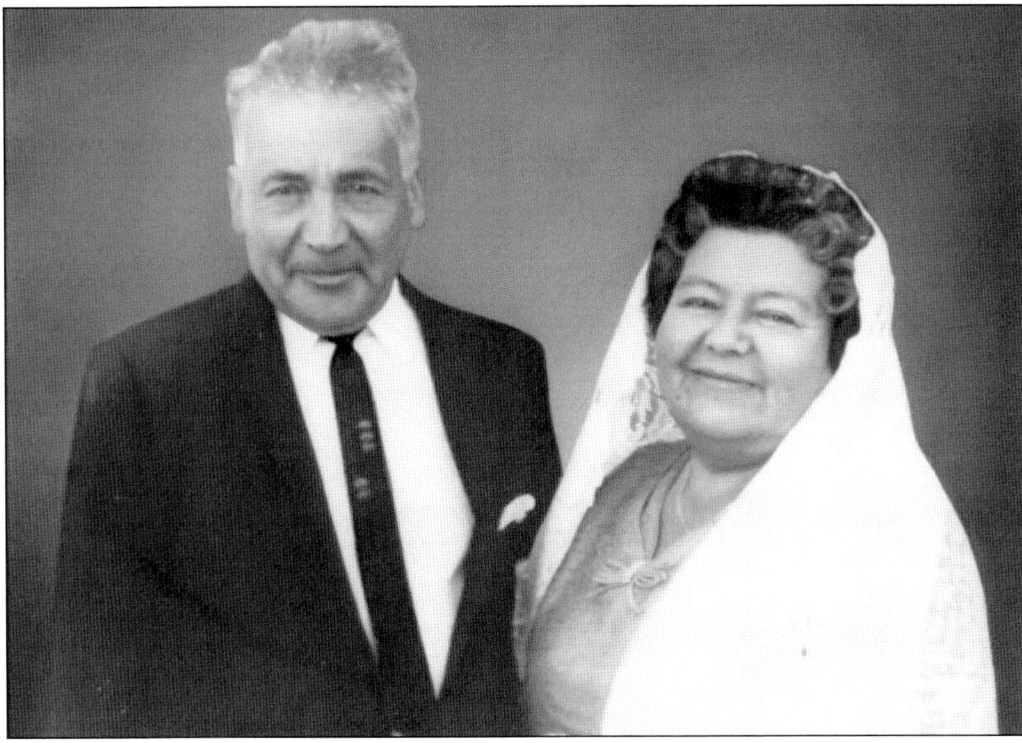

Ruben Ordaz was born in Purépero, Michoacán, Mexico, in 1904. Tula Ordaz was born in Chilchota, Michoacán, Mexico, in 1907. Both came to La Rana in 1920. They had seven children. This picture was taken in Tijuana, Mexico, when their marriage was blessed by the Catholic Church on an unknown date. (Stella Gassett.)

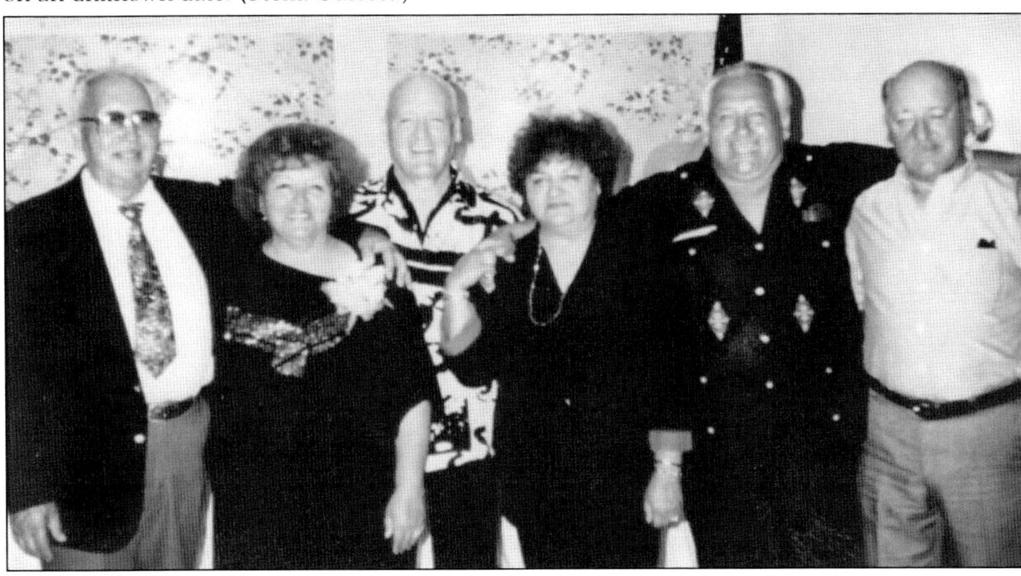

Stella Gassett celebrated her 50th birthday at Del Conte's restaurant in Torrance in 1989. Pictured from left to right are Ruben Jr., Stella, Alfonso (Ponchi), Maura, Tony, and Victor. Genaro is not pictured. Stella is married to Tony (Zapata) Gassett, and they are the parents of three children. (Stella Gassett.)

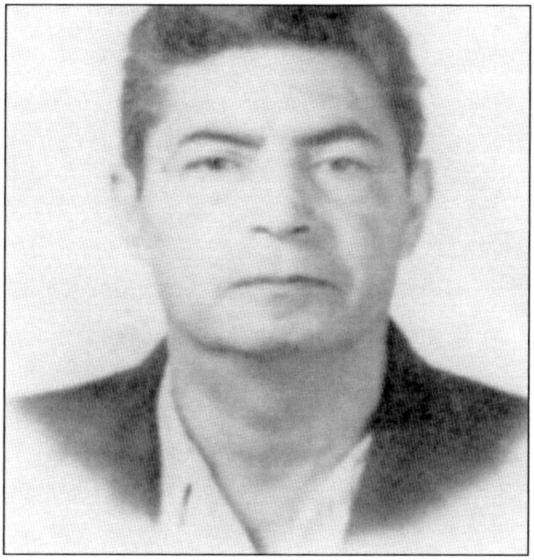 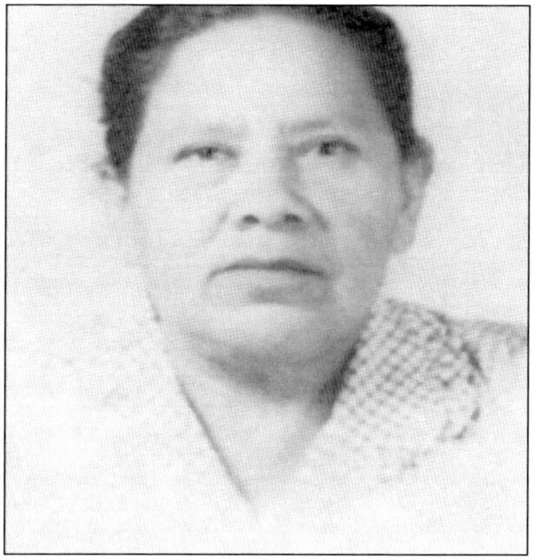

Luis and Dona Carmen Ordaz came to La Rana in 1919. Ordaz had four children: Mary Louisa, Ramiro, Edmundo, and Jessie. These are passport pictures taken in 1940. The processions for Our Lady of Guadalupe on December 12 always started in front of the Ordaz home. They were known for making beautiful decorations for these celebrations. (Jessie Valencia.)

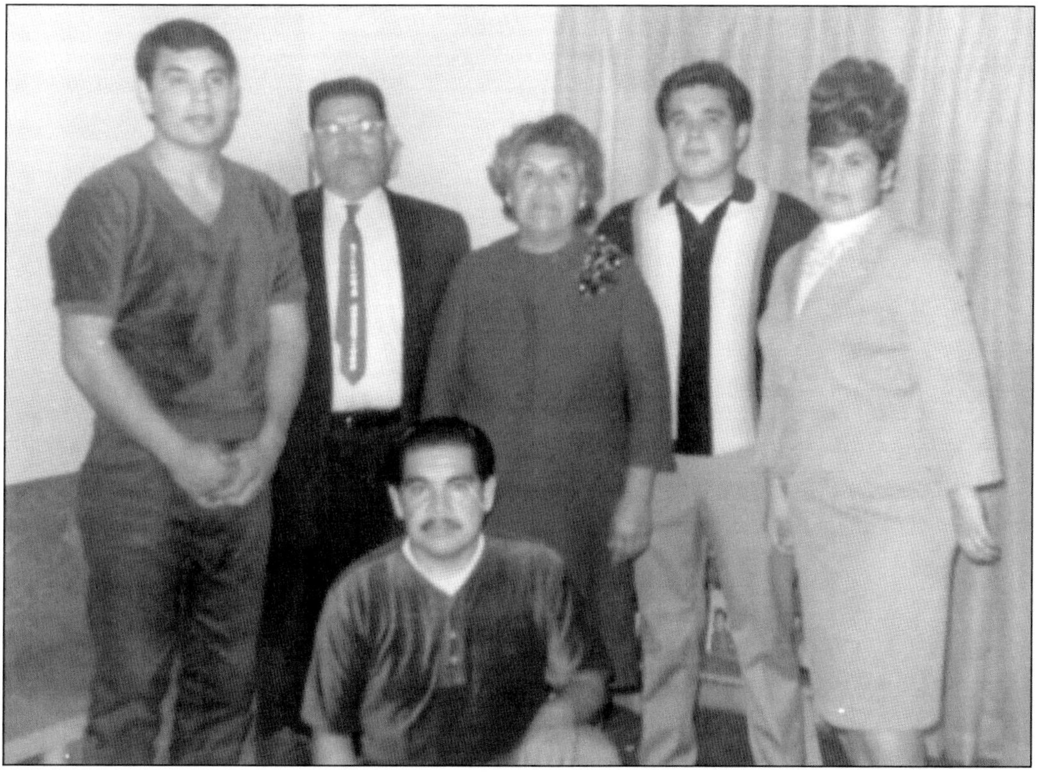

Jose Olloque was born in Jiquilpan, Michoacán, Mexico, in 1902 and came to La Rana in the early 1920s. Juanita Mendez Olloque was born in Mexico and raised in Redondo Beach. Jose worked at U.S. Steel. This family picture was taken in 1954. From left to right are Manuel, Jose, Juanita, Jose Jr., Pilar, and Johnnie (kneeling in front). (Manuel Olloque.)

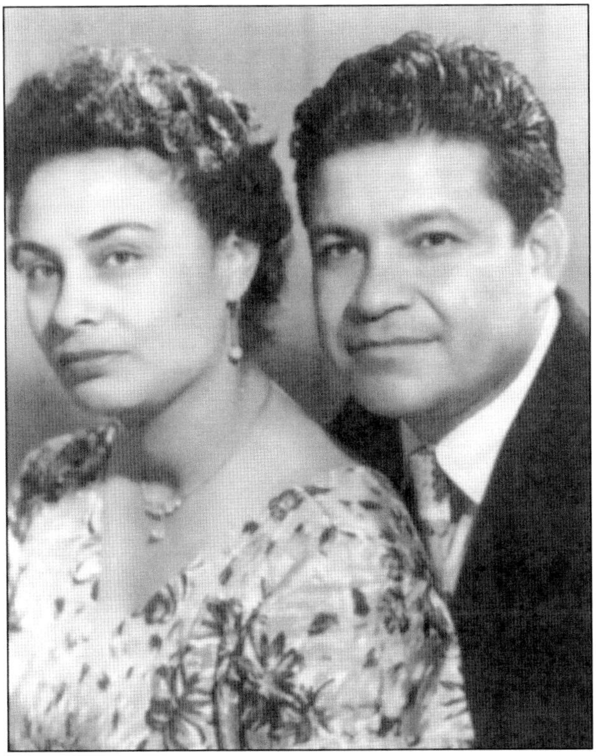

Tony Razo was born on November 22, 1920, in Torrance. The Razo family moved back to Irapuato, Guanajuato, Mexico, when Tony was an infant. He returned to the United States in 1947 and married Margaret Romero. Tony and Margaret are pictured at the celebration of their 50th wedding anniversary in 1954. The Razos had three children: Tony, Rachel, and Sally. (Sally Bernal.)

The Razo children took this photograph as a Mother's Day gift for Margaret Razo in 1991. From left to right are Sally, Tony Jr., Rachel, and Michelle Grajeda (seated), a beloved neighbor. Michelle was like a daughter to Margaret and Tony. (Sally Bernal.)

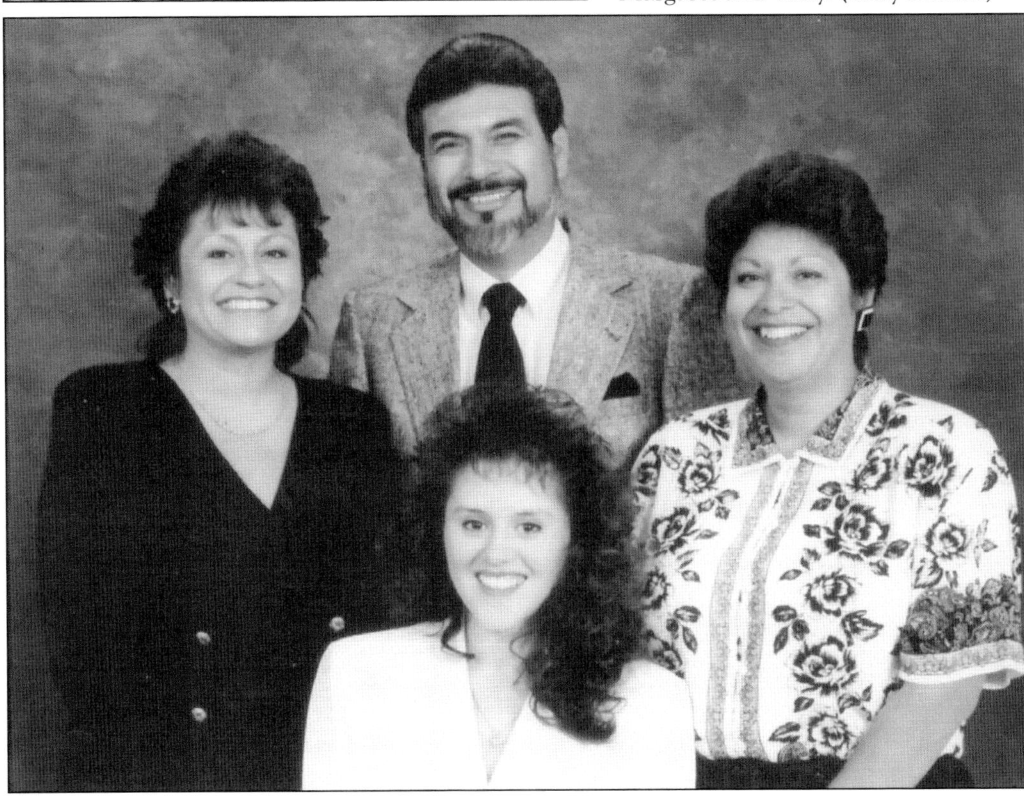

Jennie Reyes is pictured here in 1940. She was the mother of Dora, Nellie, John, Josie, Judy, and Tony. Jennie was born in Mexico City in 1906 and came to La Rana in 1925. She was known for helping members of the community with translating from Spanish to English. (Judy Ybarra.)

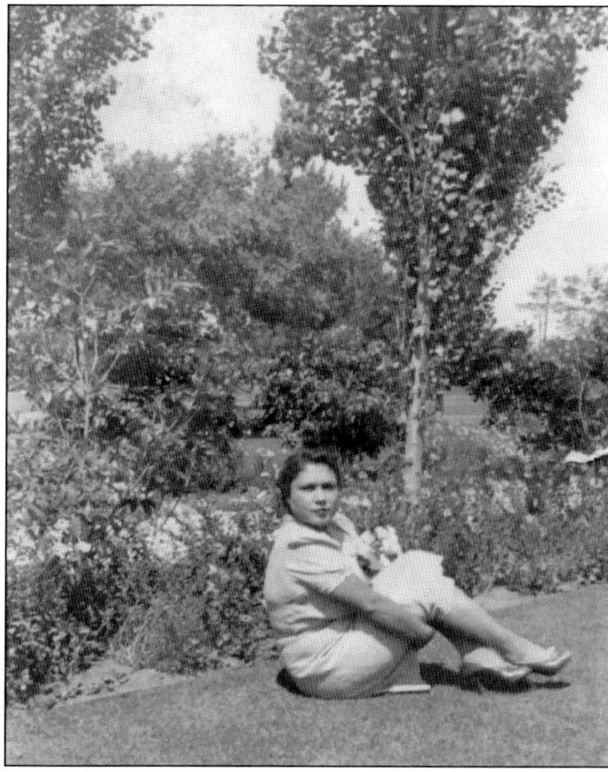

The Rafael Solis family came from Douglas, Arizona, to La Rana in 1933. During World War II, the family owned a farm on Spencer and Amy Streets. Rafael was later employed at U.S. Steel. This photograph was taken on Easter Sunday in 1958; from left to right are, (first row) Connie, Juanita, Rafael, and Virginia (the child in front); (second row) Augie, Fred, Ralph Jr., and Joe. (Alice Duarte Solis.)

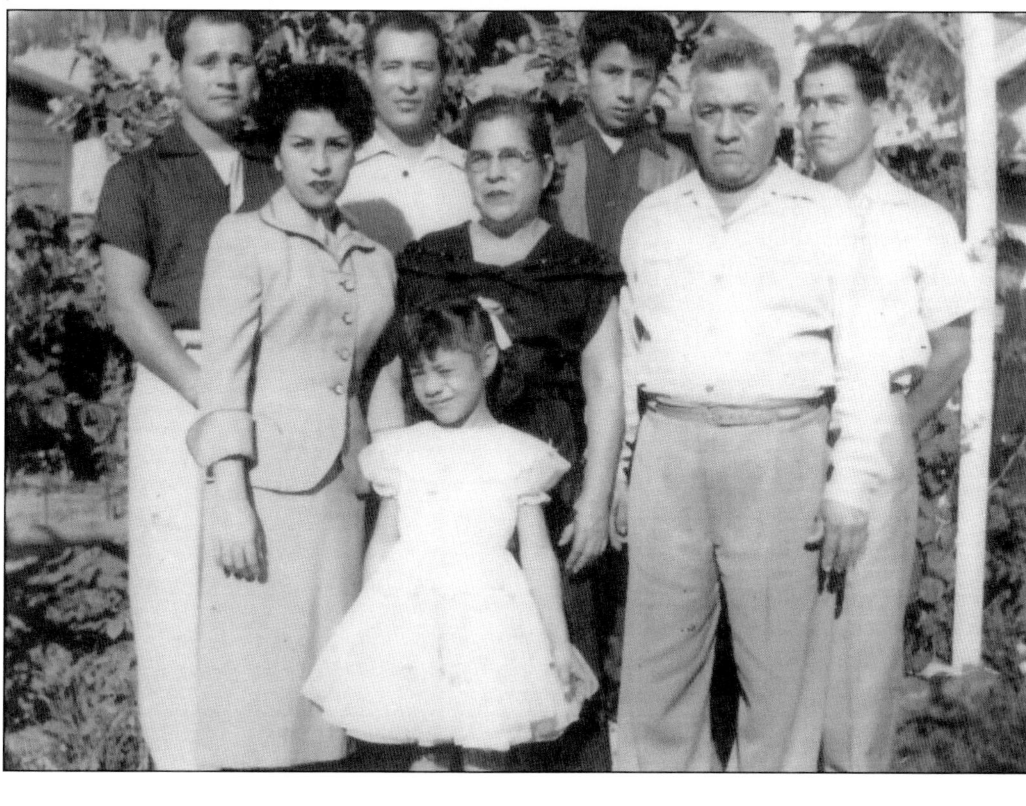

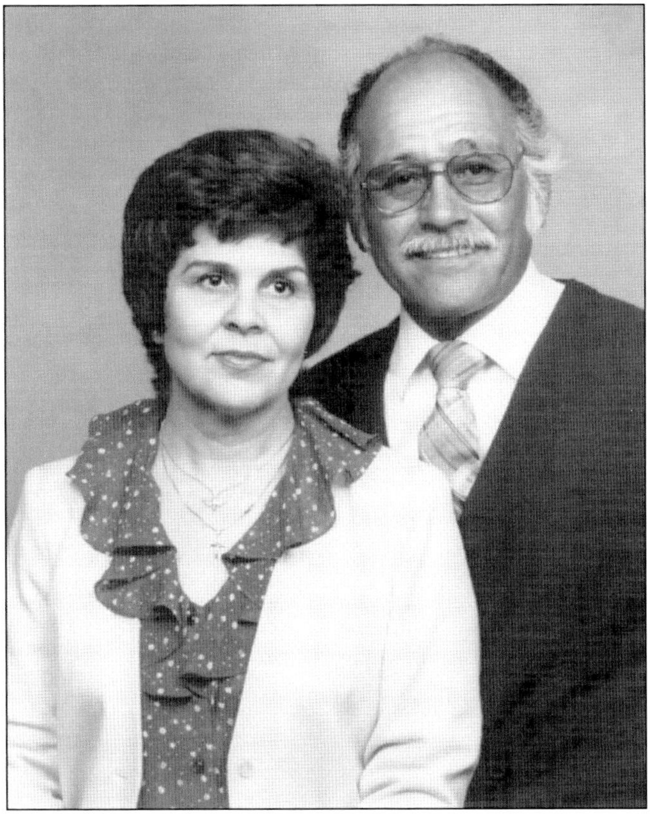

Augustine (Augie) Solis was born in Douglas, Arizona, on May 5, 1930. Alice Duarte Solis was born in Van Nuys, California, on September 15, 1930. Augie was a tree-trimmer for the City of Torrance for 33 years. Alice owned and operated a beauty salon for 46 years. Both attended Torrance High School. (Alice Duarte Solis.)

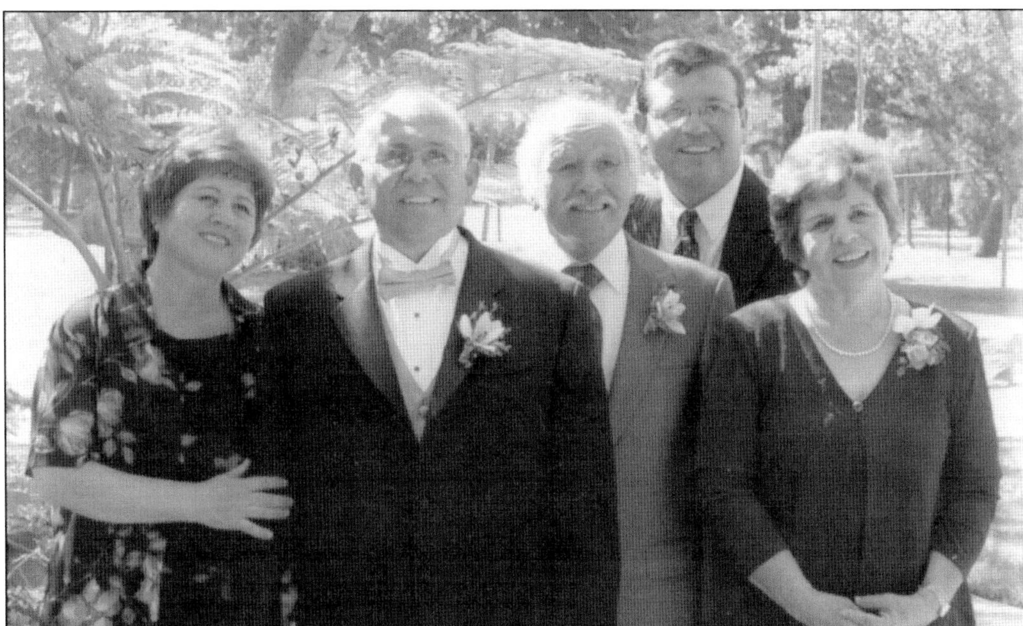

In 2005, Laura Jean, John, Augie, Mark Anthony, and Alice Solis pose at a wedding in Glendale. The Solis family continues to live in Torrance. Alice's family came to La Rana in 1917, and Augie's family arrived in 1933. All of their children attended Torrance schools. (Alice Duarte Solis.)

Tony Rios was born in Guadalajara, Mexico, in 1908. Rebecca Rios was born in Chihuahua, Mexico, in 1908. The Rios family came to La Rana in early 1908. This picture was taken in the early 1940s. Tony was employed by U.S. Steel and was very active in community activities. They had four children: Nellie, Paul, Clara, and Joe. (Clara Rios.)

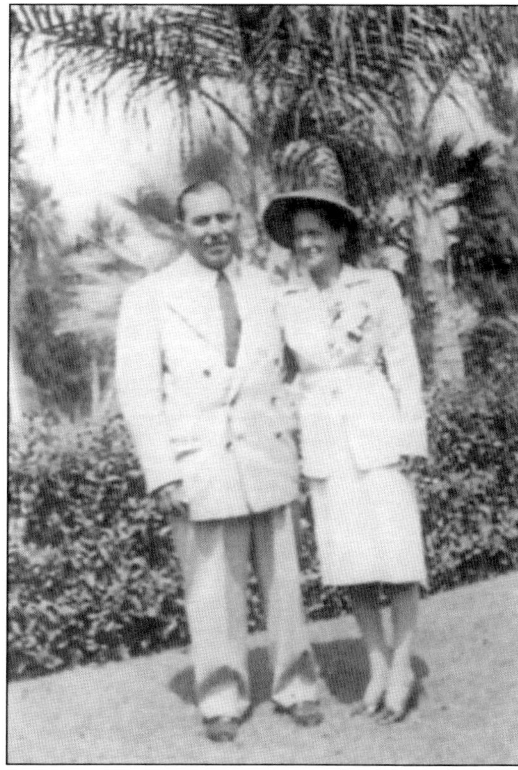

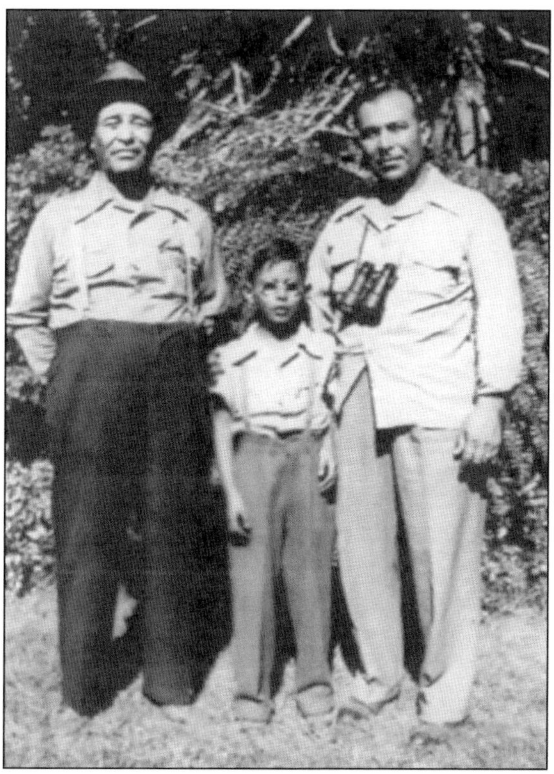

From left to right, Silviero, Paul, and Tony Rios are pictured around 1944. Silviero was Tony's father and Paul's grandfather. Silviero was born in Guadalajara, Jalisco, Mexico, in 1882. He and his wife, Petra, were some of the very first settlers in La Rana. (Clara Rios.)

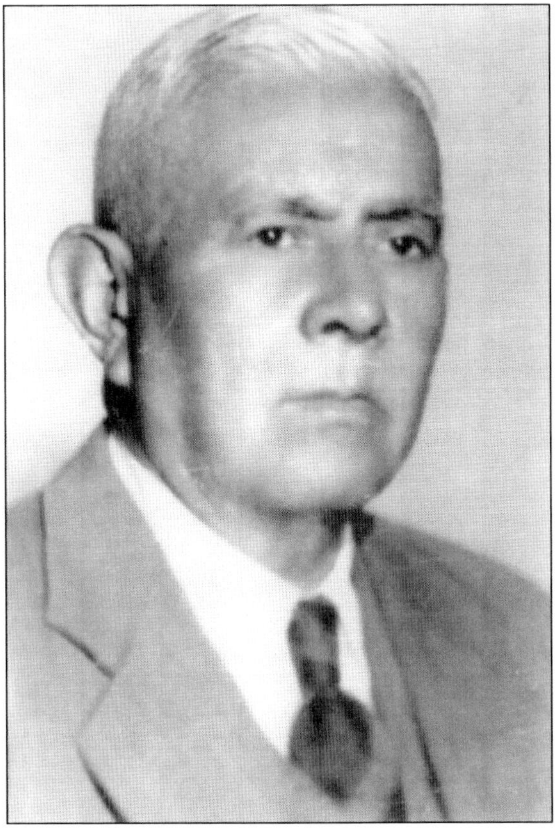

Lauro (Lalo) Torres was born in Purepéro, Michoacán, Mexico, in 1882 and came to La Rana after fleeing the Mexican Revolution in 1917. He had been a shoemaker and leather tanner in Zamora, Michoacán. In 1930, he opened the La Michocana grocery store in La Rana, and operated it until 1944. He was father to Carmen, Lauro, Aurora, Antonia, Angelina, Carlos, Dolores, and Consuelo. Lauro was a World War I veteran. (Alice Duarte Solis.)

Mauro Torres was born in Zacatecas, Mexico, and came to La Rana in 1945. Angelina Torres was born in Mexicali, Mexico. This picture was taken in Tijuana, Mexico, in 1960. From left to right are (first row) Gloria, Angelina, and Mauro; (second row, standing) Jose (Pepe) and Julieta. (Gloria Salce.)

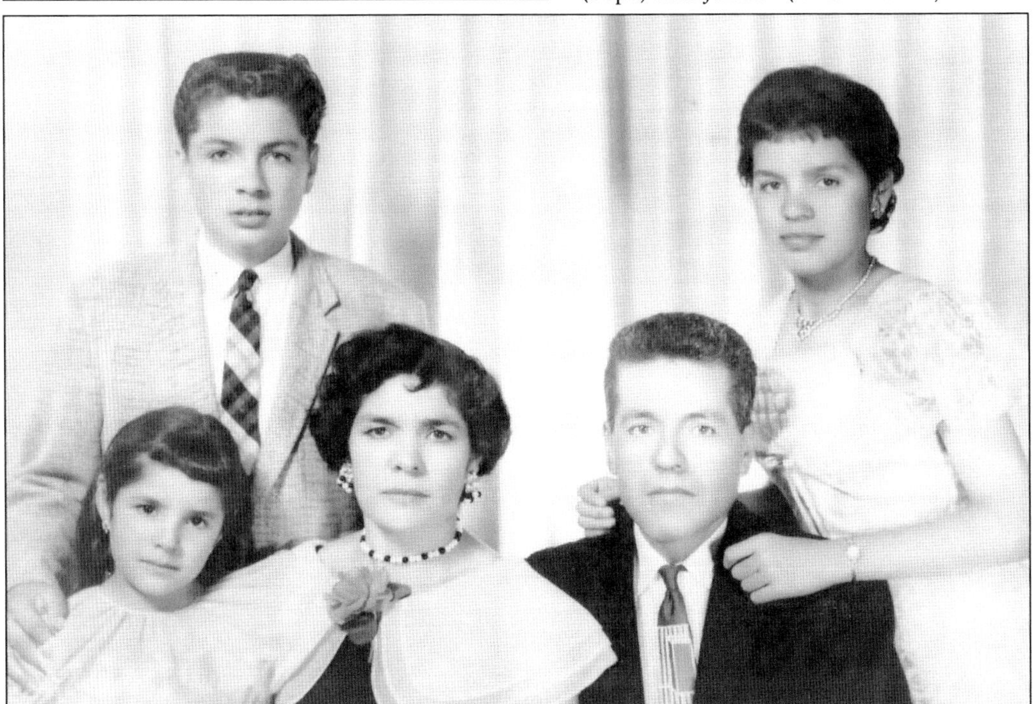

Manual and Irene Valdez are shown here in 1951. In the early 1940s, Irene came to La Rana from Arizona with her father, Agustin Hermenegildo, and her brothers Tony and Richard. Manual Valdez and his brother Tony and mother, Rosalia, came from Colorado. Irene was very involved with the social clubs of La Rana. (Dora Camou.)

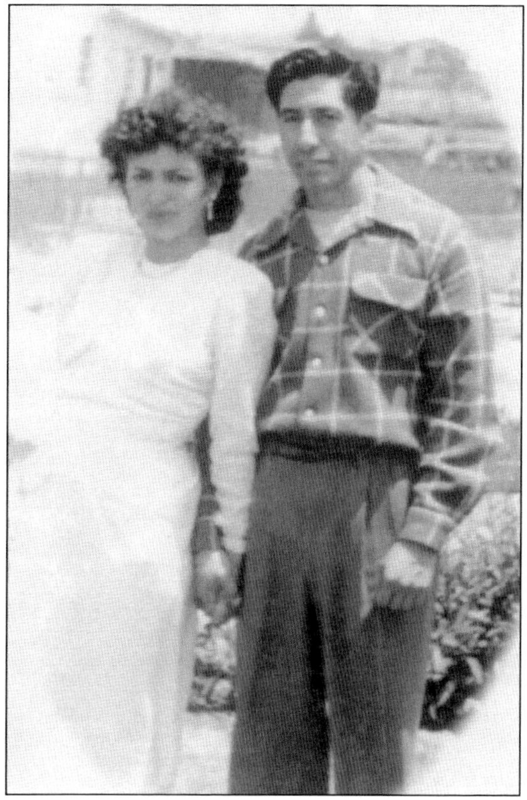

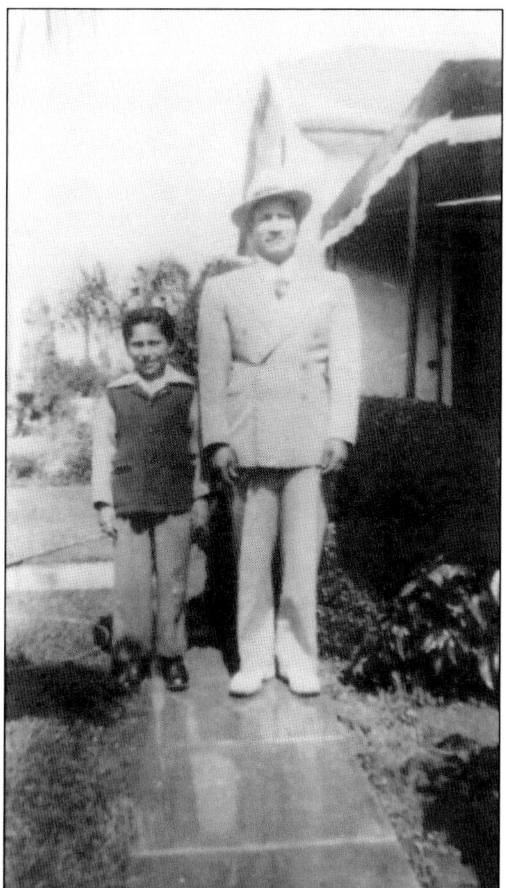

Francisco (Pancho) Vega was born in Purepéro, Michoacán, Mexico, in 1903 and came to La Rana in 1920. He was employed by U.S. Steel for 38 years. Rudy's mother was Dona Esther Guzman, pastor of the Pentecostal church in La Rana. Francisco is pictured with his son Rudy Vega in 1947 in Gardena, California. (Teresa Vega.)

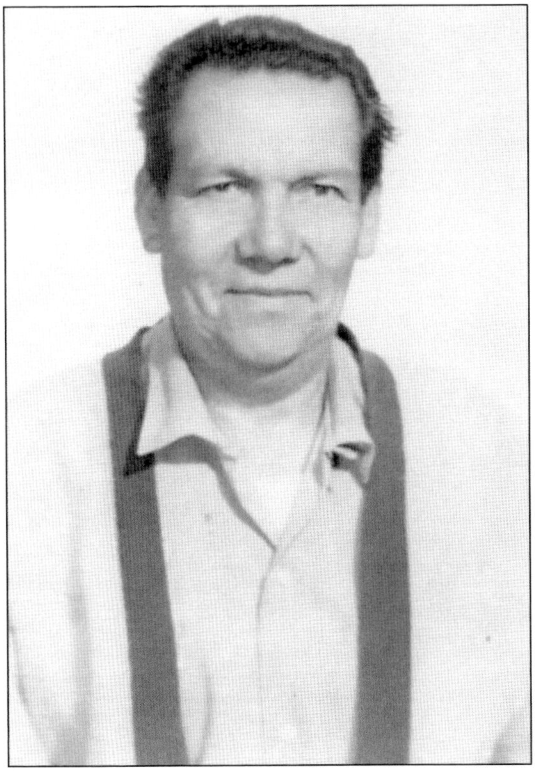

Reyes Ybarra Sr. came from Douglas, Arizona, to La Rana in the early 1940s. He was employed by U.S. Steel and was also the sacristan for St. Joseph's Mission. In 1976, Ybarra died after he was hit by a car while walking home from church. (Eleazar Ybarra.)

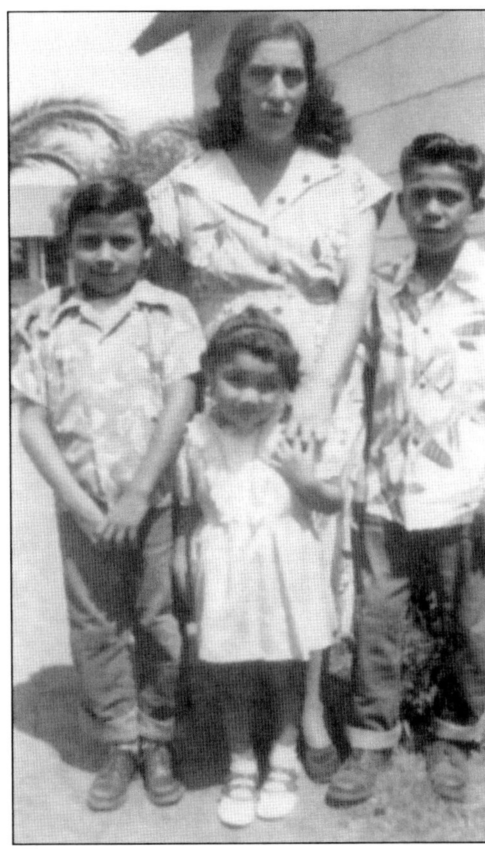

The Reyes Ybarra family came to La Rana from Agua Prieta, Sonora, Mexico, in 1945. Pictured here in 1950 is Elena (Reyes' wife) with her sons Eleazar (left) and Ignacio. The young girl in the front is Silvia Chires, Elena's granddaughter. (Eleazar Ybarra.)

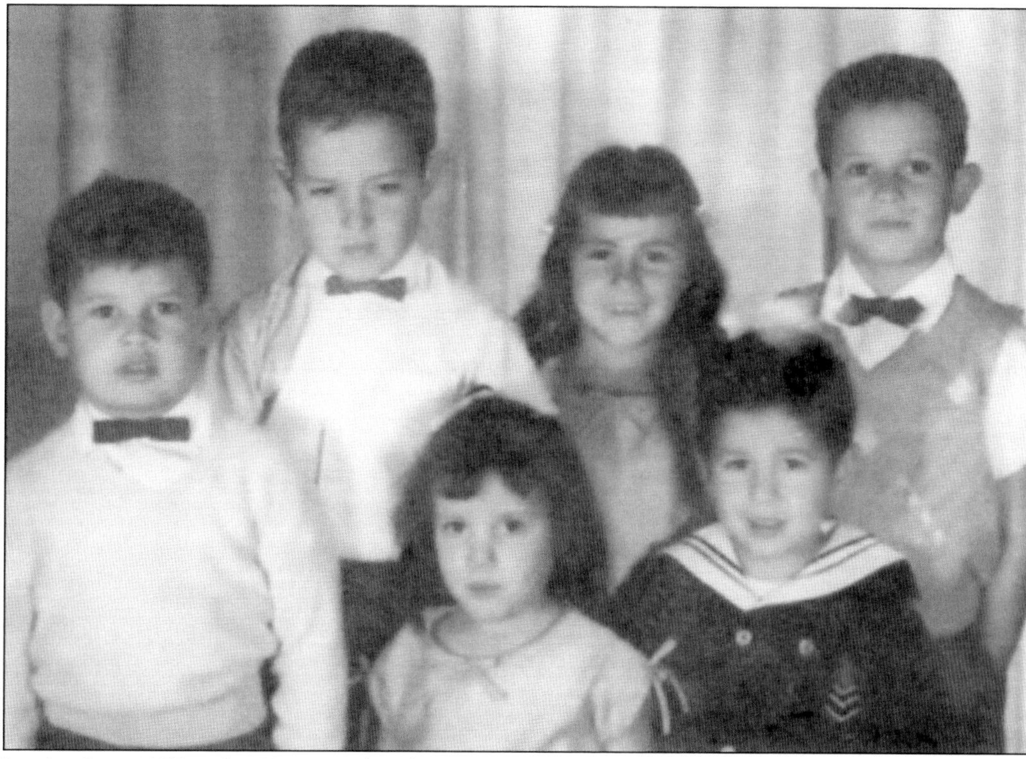

In the late 1950s, the Yniguez family moved to La Rana from the Keystone area, another neighborhood in Torrance near the present-day area of Torrance Boulevard and Main Street. The Yniguez children are pictured in 1962. From left to right are (first row) Randy, Cindy, and Tommy; (second row) Ricky, Jennie, and Bobby. (Randy Yniguez.)

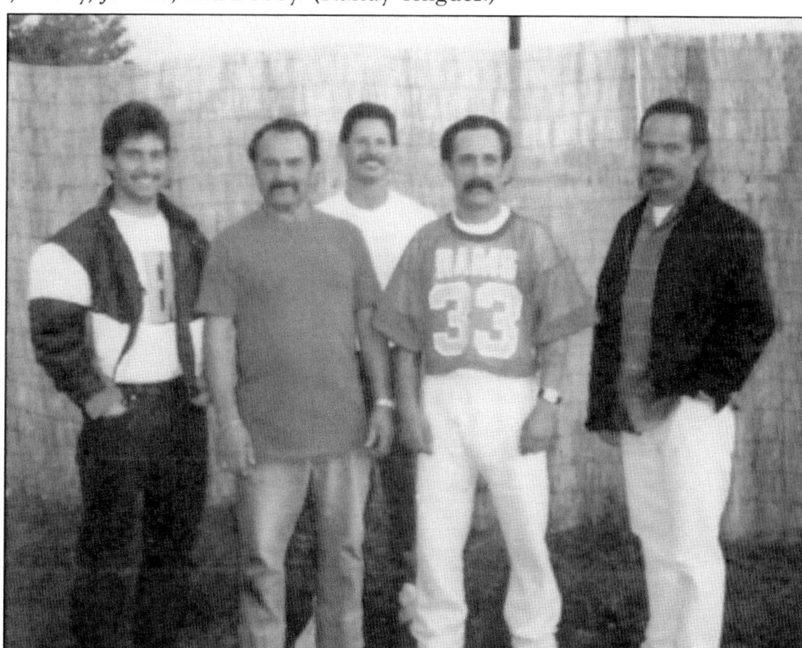

The Yniguez sons are shown here visiting their father Pete in Wilmington, California, in 1979. Randy still lives in La Rana and is a well-known handyman in the area. From left to right are Rusty, Pete, Randy (Magoo), Bobby, and Ricky. (Randy Yniguez.)

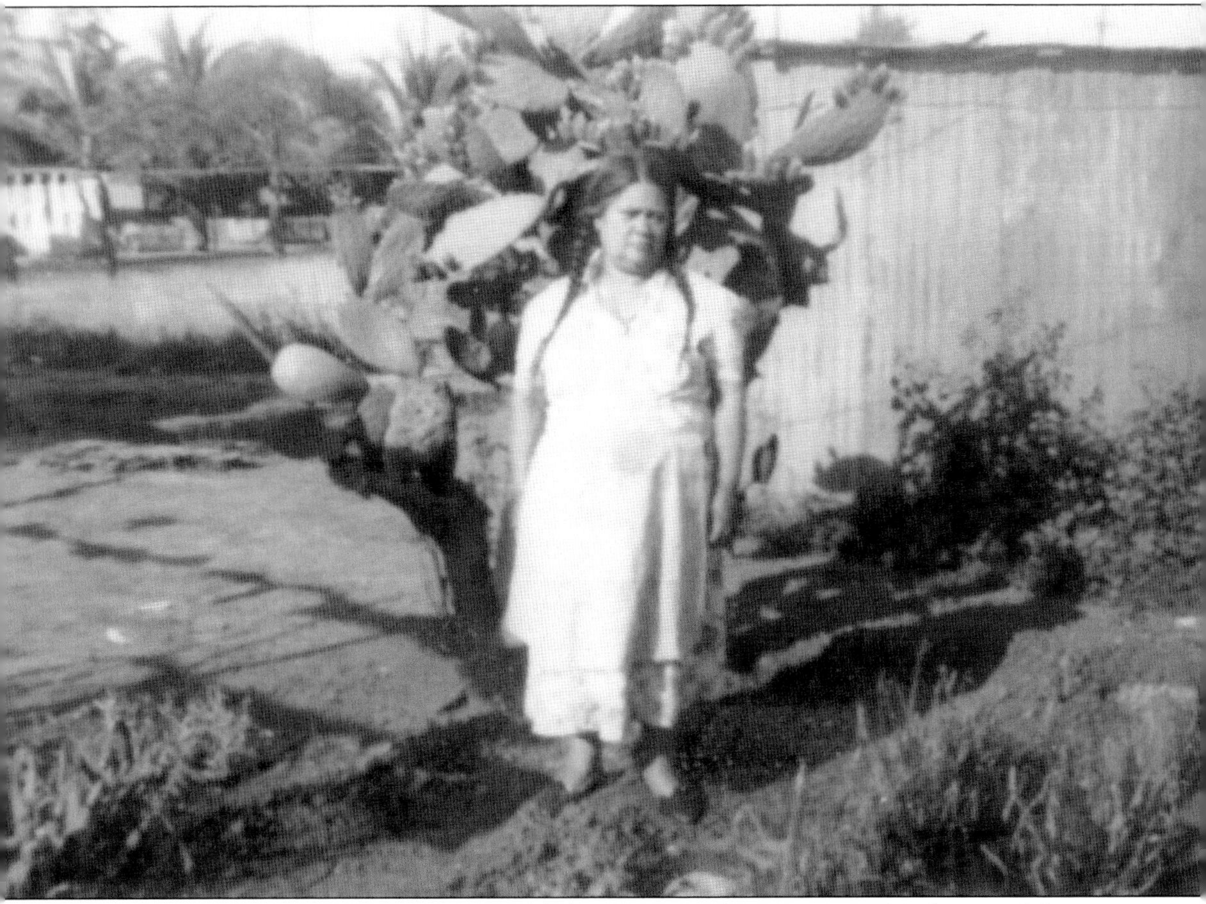

Anita Robledo was married to Jose Robledo. Jose came from Purépero, Michoacán, Mexico, to La Rana in the early 1920s. He met Anita, and they married in Torrance. He worked at local farms, and she was a housewife. They spent their entire married life in the community of La Rana. (Virginia Camou.)

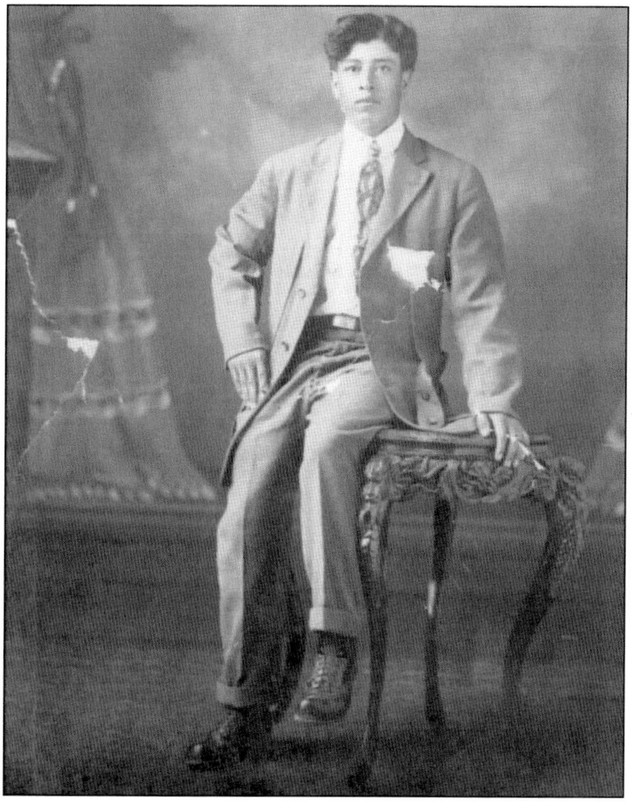

Beatrice Villa Hernandez (below) was born in Zacalecas, Mexico, in 1905. She came to the United States in 1920 and married Alfonso Hernandez (left), who was born in Jalisco, Mexico, in 1900. Alfonso was the son of Qirina Calvillo and Alberto Hernandez. The Calvillo family were owners of land taken by the federal government in the Gadsden Purchase of 1854 (now the southern part of Arizona and New Mexico). Alfonso and Beatrice are parents to Esther, Hortencia, Dolores, Sophia, Alice, Molly, Josie, Stella, Lupe, and Joseph. All of their children attended Torrance schools. Alfonso was a talented guitar player who would sing and play the guitar with his friends Efrein and Constantino Vega. In 1942, the Hernandez family moved to Lomita, California. (Albert Hernandez.)

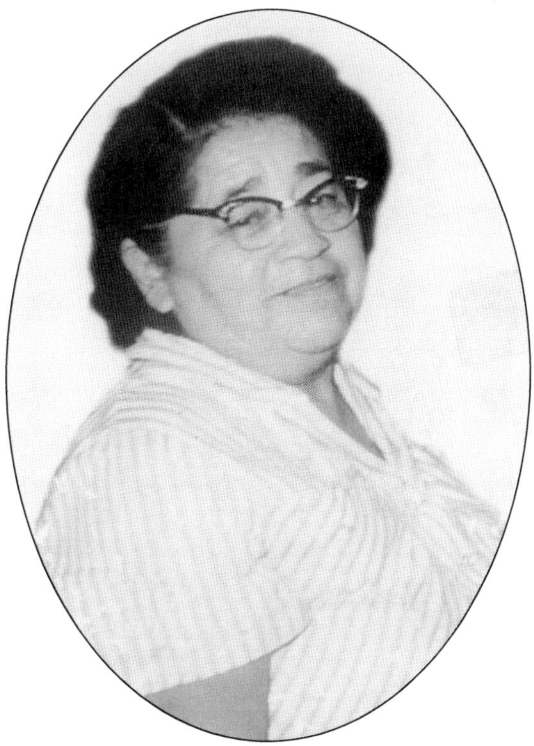

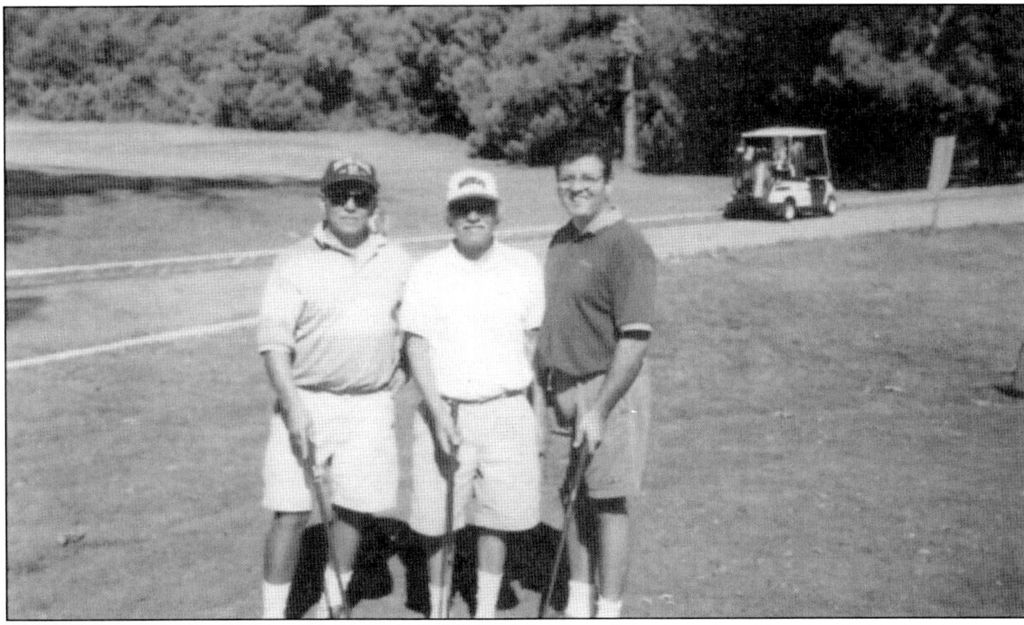

From left to right, John, Augie, and Mark Solis are pictured at Griffith Park Golf Course in 2005. This family spent most of their lives in La Rana and remained close to the people in the neighborhood. They were avid golfers and regularly golfed together until Augie's health made it impossible for him to continue playing. (Alice Duarte Solis.)

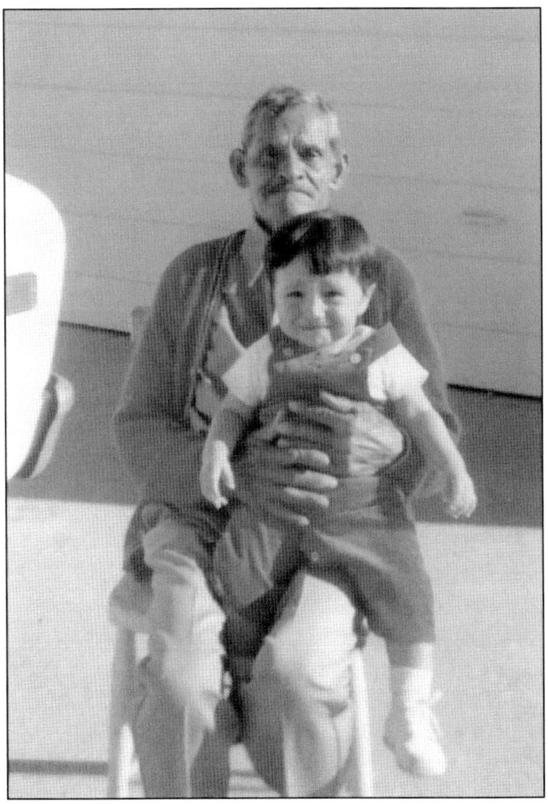

Jose Ayala is holding Matthew Vega, son of Rudy Vega. Don Jose was the husband of Dona Juanita Ayala, the mother of Dona Ester Guzman, pastor of the Pentecostal church of La Rana. They came to La Rana in 1926. He was the *sobador* (masseur) of the street. When people had an ache in part of their body, he would help cure them with his massages. (Rudy Vega.)

Phillip (left) and Bonifacio (Boni) Olivarez were the sons of Eloisa Castillo and Ismael Olivarez and the brothers of Kate, Helen, Henry, Leo, and Beatrice Castillo. The two boys were born and raised in La Rana and remained here their entire lives. Both attended Torrance schools. (Beatrice Castillo.)

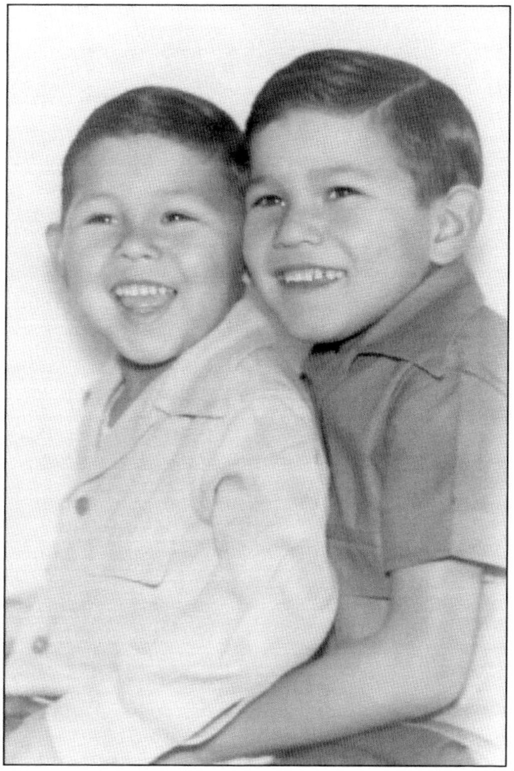

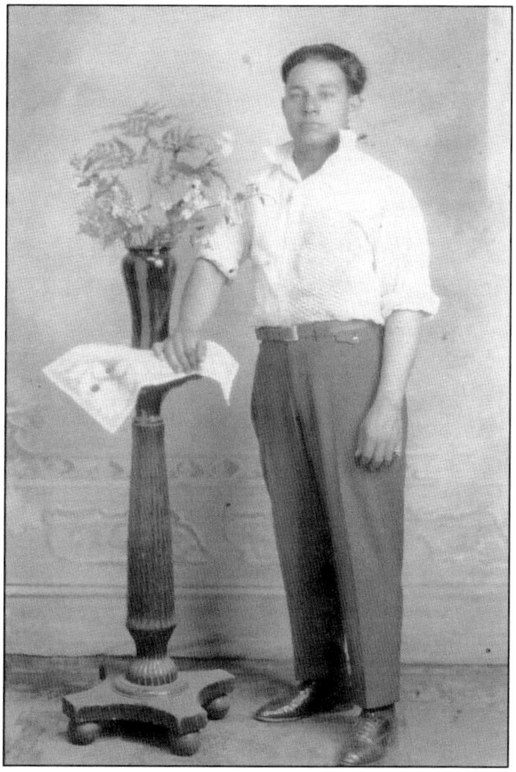

Ismael Olivarez arrived in La Rana in the early 1920s. He fled the Mexican Revolution that had taken over his hometown of Purépero, Michoacán, Mexico. He worked for U.S. Steel for 35 years. He was a baker in Mexico before coming to the United States. He married Eloisa Castillo and was the father of Bonifacio and Phillip Olivarez. (Beatrice Castillo.)

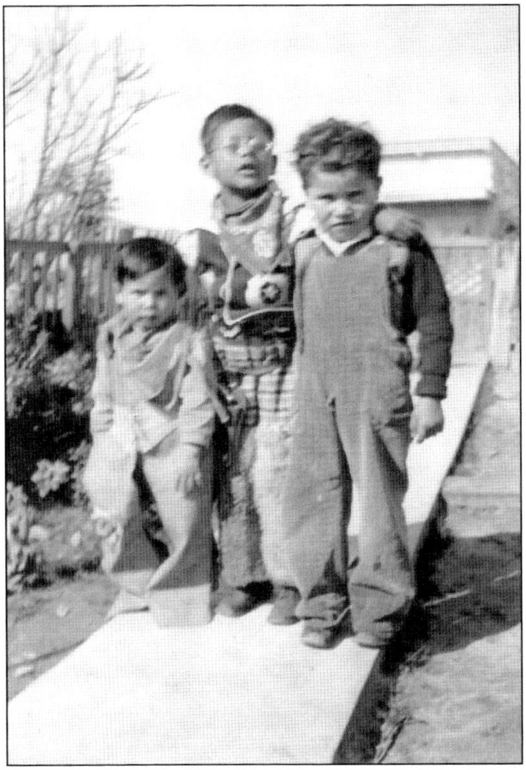

From left to right, Freddie Escobar, Paul Rios, and Andy Escobar are pictured in front of Tony and Rebecca Rios's home around 1938. Freddie and Andy were the sons of Lupe and Herman Escobar. The family eventually moved to Redondo Beach and Andy later became a professional boxer. (Clara Rios Guana.)

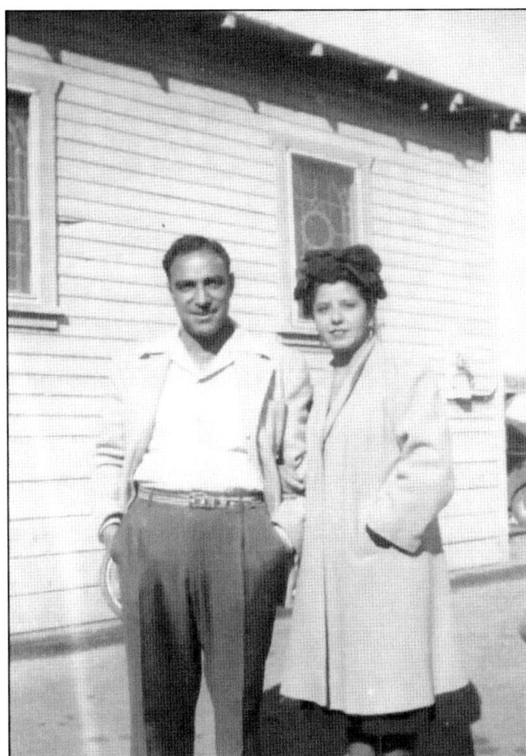

Gilbert and Rose Atencio are shown standing by the side of St. Joseph's Mission. Gilbert is a veteran of World War II. He and his wife arrived in La Rana in 1939 from Santa Monica. Gilbert and Rose have one son, Phillip. Rose is the daughter of Don Regino and Dona Soledad Villegas. (Langa Alvarez.)

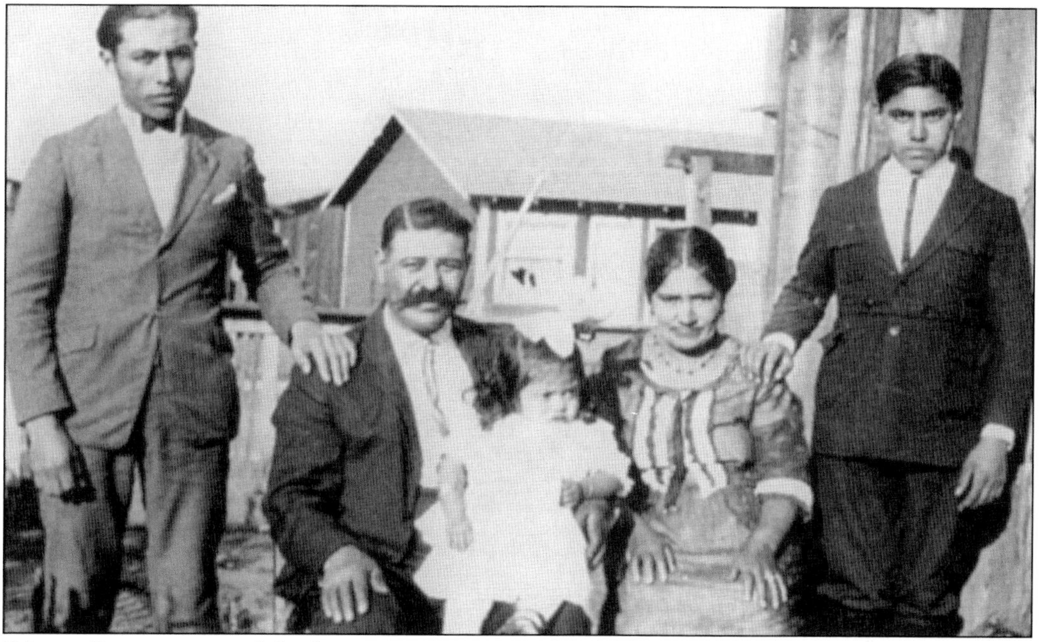

Silverio Rios was one of the first immigrants to arrive at La Rana. He arrived with his family in 1908. Pictured here from left to right are Tony, Silverio with Kata on his lap, Petra, and Peter. Upon their arrival, they were forced to live in tents, since no homes were yet available. Silverio took part in the naming of the local Catholic church. He suggested the name "Guadalupe," but the priest in charge said St. Joseph was a better name. St. Joseph is the patron saint of workers, and this was reflected in the hardworking people of La Rana. (Langa Alvarez.)

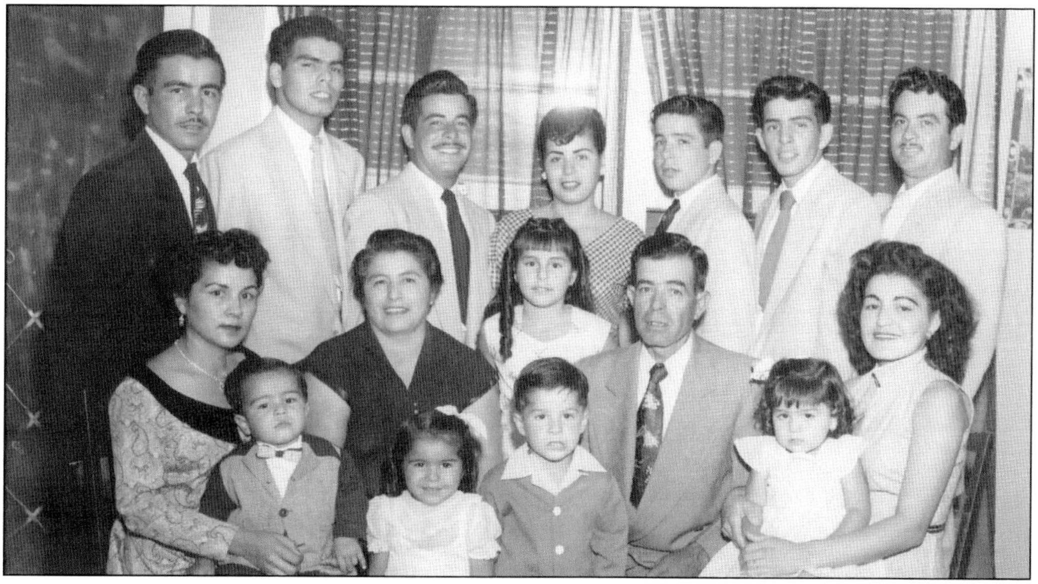

Pictured here in 1955 are Alfred and Bertha White with all their children and grandchildren at the time. The Whites had eight children and many grandchildren. The family came from Texas in 1940. In 1950, they bought their first home on the street of La Rana. Alfred was a carpenter by trade and worked at Todd shipyard in San Pedro. He was also a handyman for St. Joseph's Mission. (David White.)

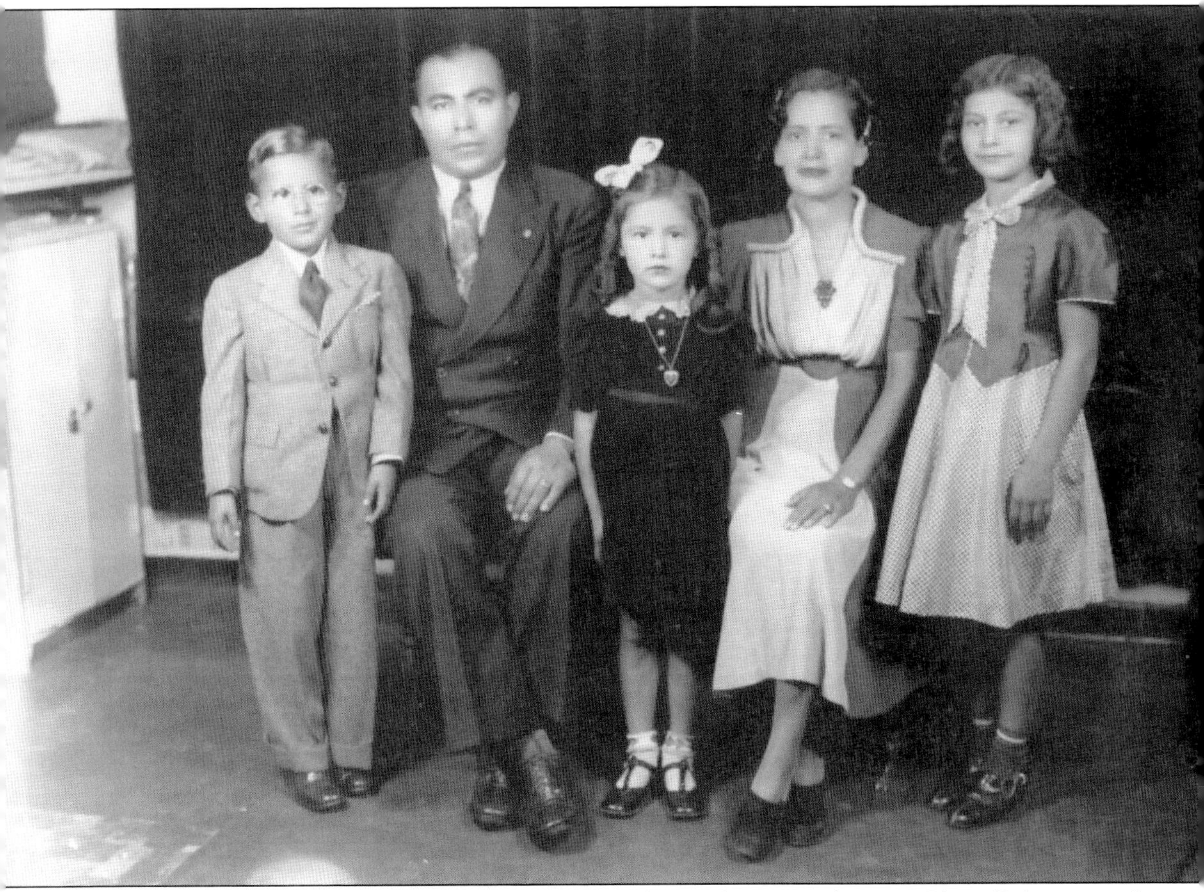

The Rios family is pictured here in 1938. From left to right are Paul, Tony, Clara, Rebecca, and Nellie. The Rios family was one of the first to arrive in La Rana. When they arrived, Tony was nine months old. Housing was unavailable, and the family lived in tents. Two other Rios children, Pete and Kate, were born in La Rana. (Clara Rios.)

Two

Social Life

The families that lived on the street of La Rana were very close and united. They celebrated all traditional holidays, including Mother's Day, Father's Day, and Mexican Independence Day (September 16). Many of the traditions they celebrated originated in Mexico. Men and women would gather at the church hall to plan and prepare for all social events. It was not uncommon for women to spend all day preparing Mexican food for the celebrations. They cooked tacos, pork tamales, refried beans, and rice, while men set up booths and stages. The Hispanic community that lived and worked in farms all over Torrance and Redondo Beach would come and join the festivities. These were family-oriented events with 300 or more attendees. The celebrations offered the La Rana residents a chance to socialize and enjoy one another's company.

Some of the families would celebrate their daughters' 15th birthdays with a *quinceañera*—a common Mexican tradition that marks a young woman's passage into adulthood. It is considered both a religious and social event that unites friends and families.

Funerals were very sad for the residents of La Rana. Artie Martinez stated, "If one hurts, we all hurt." When a citizen of La Rana passed away, the services were always well attended no matter where they were held. Many of the former residents of La Rana still keep in touch, even though some have moved away.

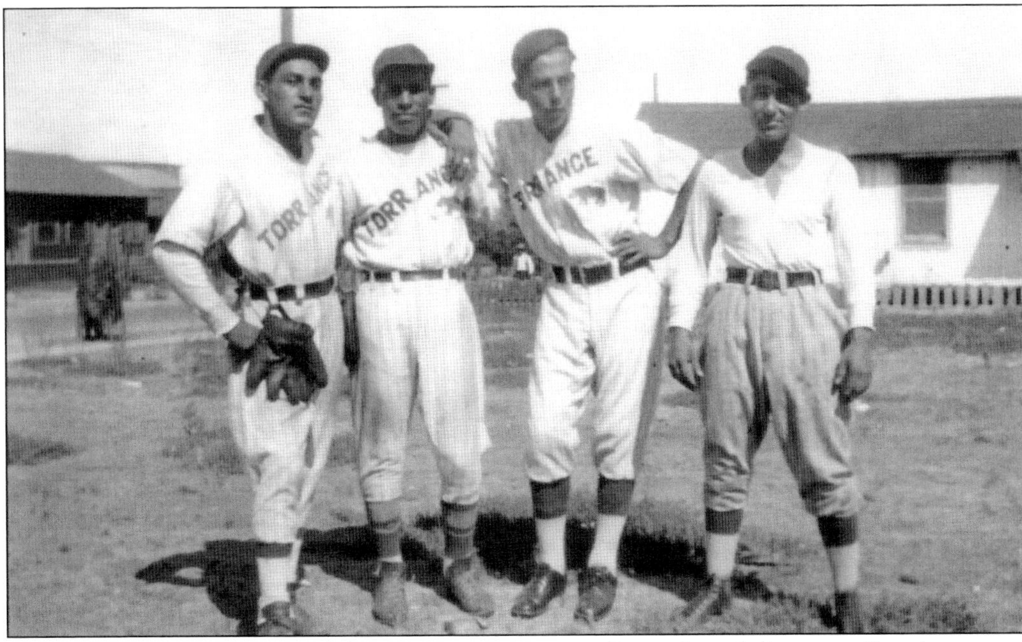

There was vacant land west of the La Rana community. Boys cleared the area of brush to create a baseball field. Today, this area is the southeast corner of Crenshaw and Del Amo Boulevards. The boys would form teams and play regularly. Pictured here in 1935 are, from left to right, Cruz Guerra, Jose Olloque, Angel Molinar, and unidentified. (Armida Grajeda.)

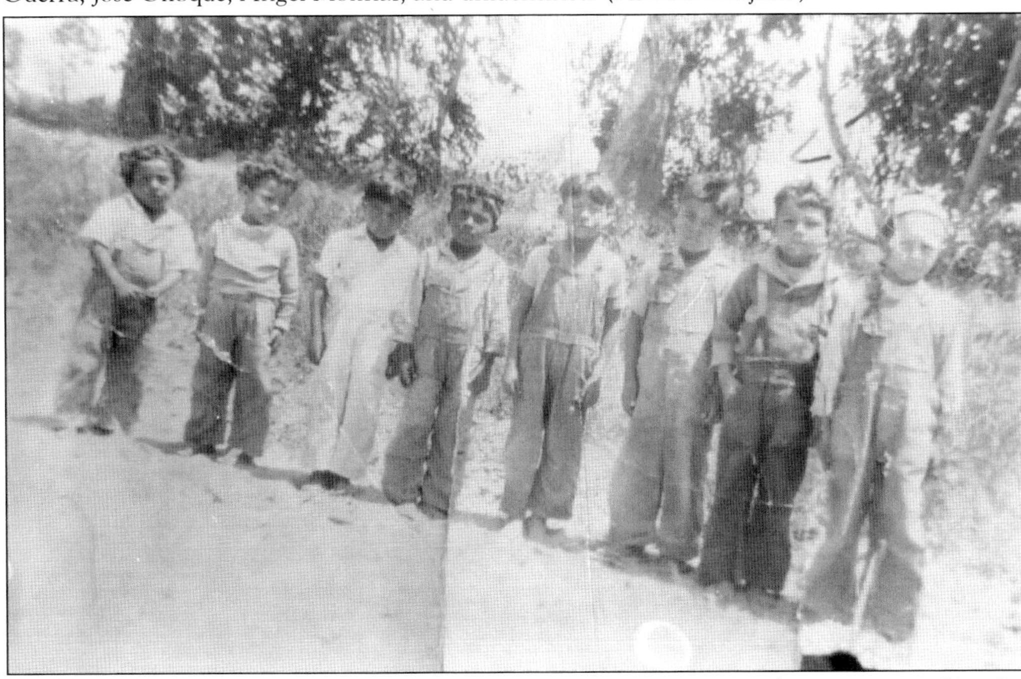

This 1936 picture features a group of young boys between the ages of six and ten. Many would gather together to play on what is now the area near the corner of Crenshaw and Del Amo Boulevards. From left to right are Billy Olvera, Ralph Escobar, Robert Contreras, Bobby Olvera, Freddie Solis, Henry (Chato) Castillo, Gabriel Mendez, and Armando Guzman. (Alice Solis.)

In 1941, Margaret Romero Razo and her mother, Josefa Barrega, traveled to Purepéro, Michoacán, Mexico. They lived in Purepéro for one year and returned to La Rana in 1942. In this picture, 14-year-old Margaret is wearing a traditional costume for a Mexican Independence Day celebration on September 16, 1941. (Sally Bernal.)

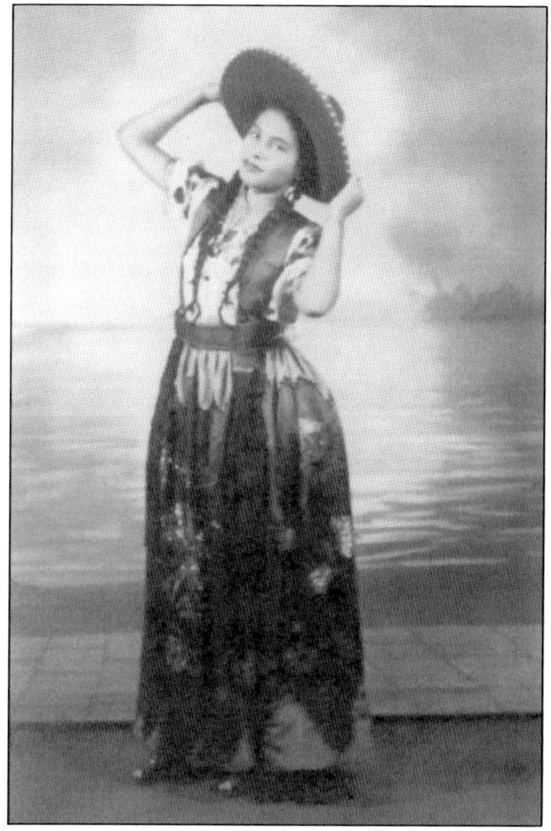

Children played in the street in the small community of La Rana. Dario Duran gathered these children and seated many of them on his car for this picture in 1940. From left to right are (first row) Frankie Mora, Billy Olvera, Gilbert Duran, Dora Duran, Beatriz Castillo, and Raul Chavez; (second row) five unidentified, Katie Chavez, and Connie Alvarez. (Dora Duran.)

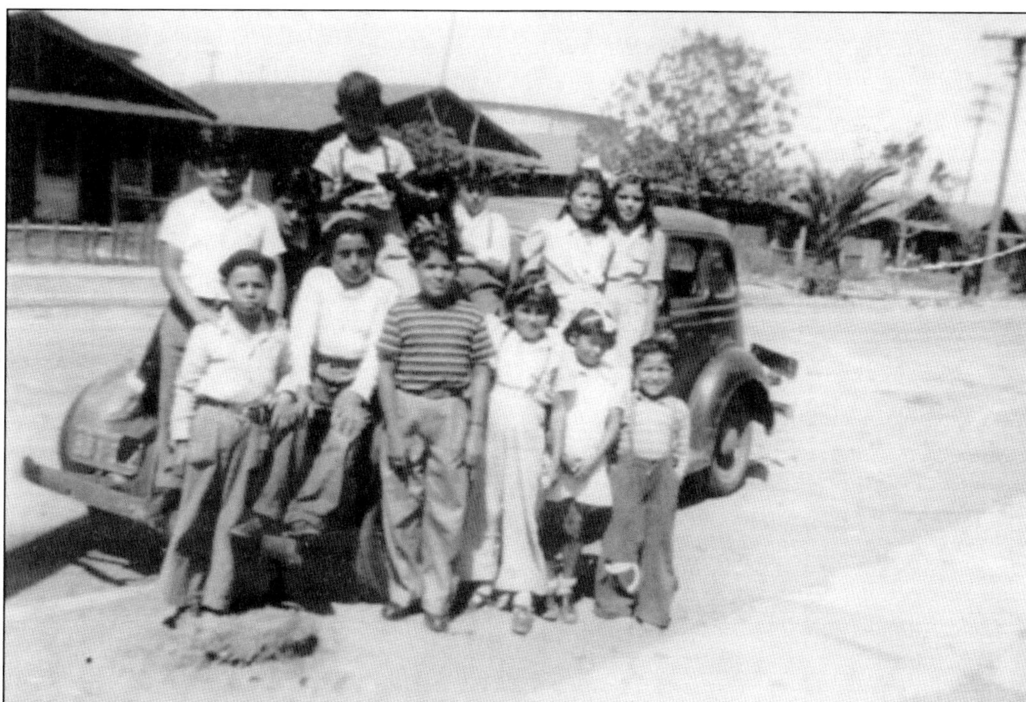

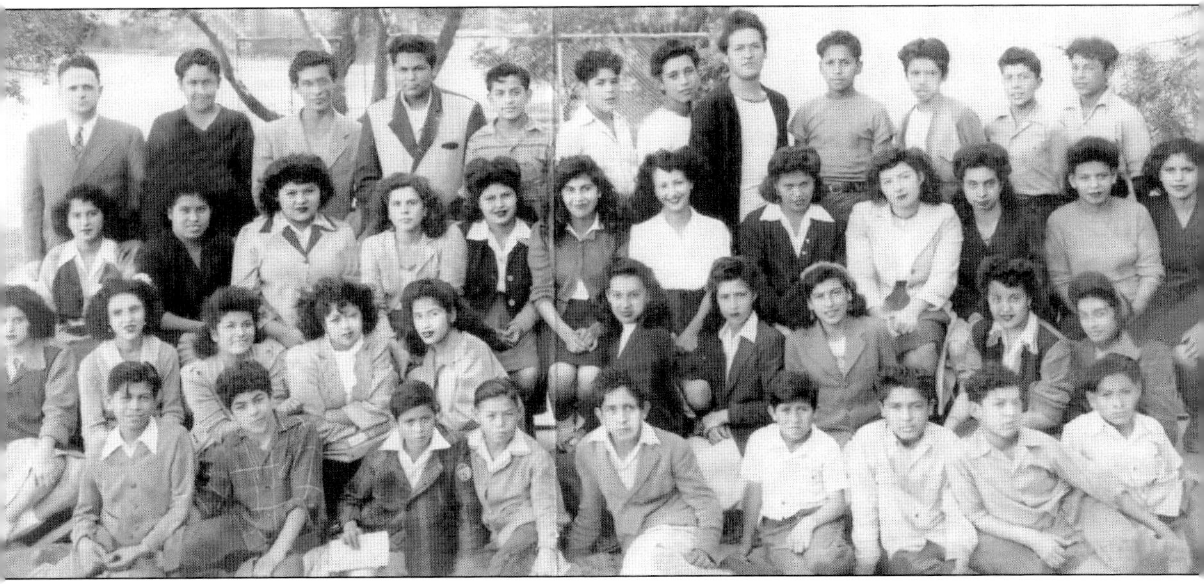

This picture of Torrance High School's Aztec Club was taken in the spring of 1944. Mr. Green, a Torrance High teacher, formed this club to unite the Mexican-American students of the campus. The students pictured here were in grades 7 through 12. From left to right are (first row) Rudy Flores, Leo Castillo, Leo Alvarez, Frankie Mora, Alfonso Barrera, Jessie Delgado, unidentified, Ralph Estalano, and unidentified; (second row) Esther Sanchez, unidentified, Artie Martinez, Elisa Hernandez, Lola Valencia, Jessie Ordaz, unidentified, Virginia Camou, Sadie Velaquez, and Alice Martinez; (third row) Ramona Delgado, Dorothy Mora, Dora Grajeda, Alicia Duarte, Carmen Garcia, Gloria Flores, Lupe Escobar, Pearl Olloque, Gloria Lucero, Olia Fernandez, Josephine Bustillos, and Connie Alvarez; (fourth row) Mr. Green, unidentified, Fred Solis, Victor Quionez, Tommy Torres, Gilbert Duran, Augie Solis, Alfonso (Ponchi) Ordaz, "Fuzzy" Hernandez, Joe Rojas, Miguel Duarte, and Richard Hermenegildo. (Gloria Flores Castaneda.)

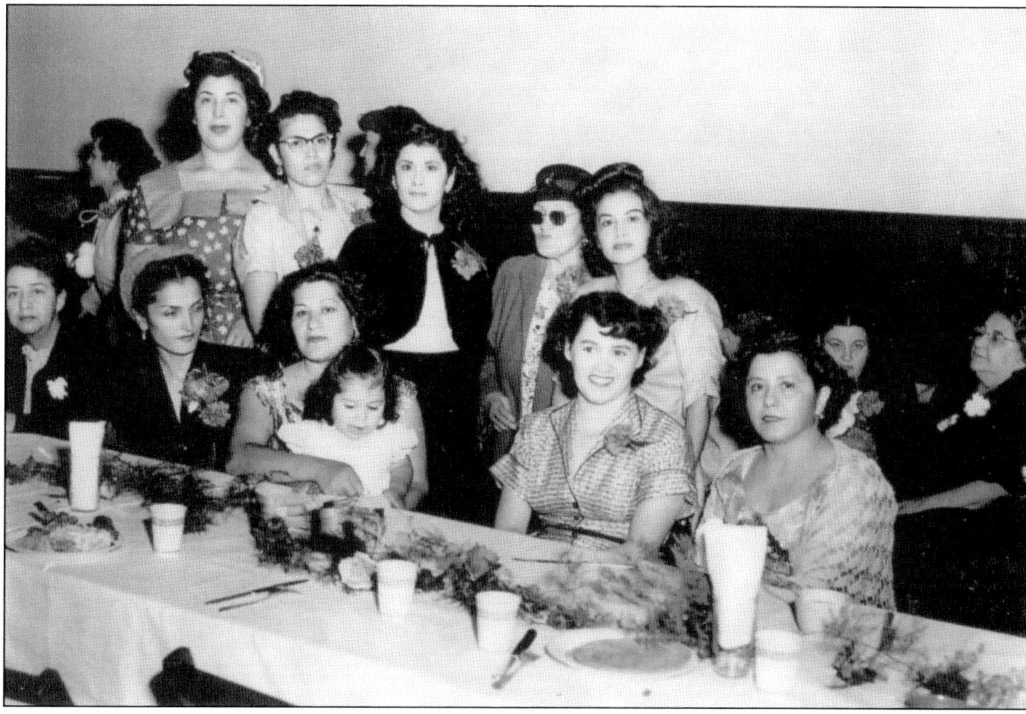

This photograph was taken during a Mother's Day celebration in 1950. From left to right are (first row, seated) Lucy Villegas, Della Molinar holding Dolores, Isabel Villegas, and Rose Villegas Atencio; (second row) unidentified, Pearl Olloque, Virginia Guerra, Dona Soledad Villegas, and Peggy Villegas. In the background at far right are Rosario (left) and Lupe Molinar. (Lucy Villegas.)

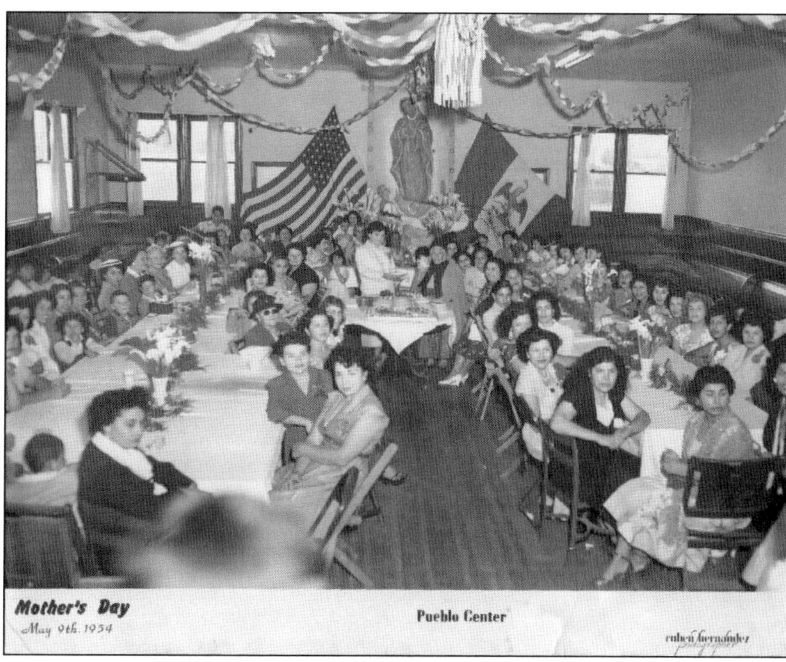

The fathers of La Rana honored the mothers of the community on Mother's Day in 1954. The oldest and youngest mothers were recognized. This was an important annual event for the community and was always held in the St. Joseph's Mission hall. (Lucy Villegas.)

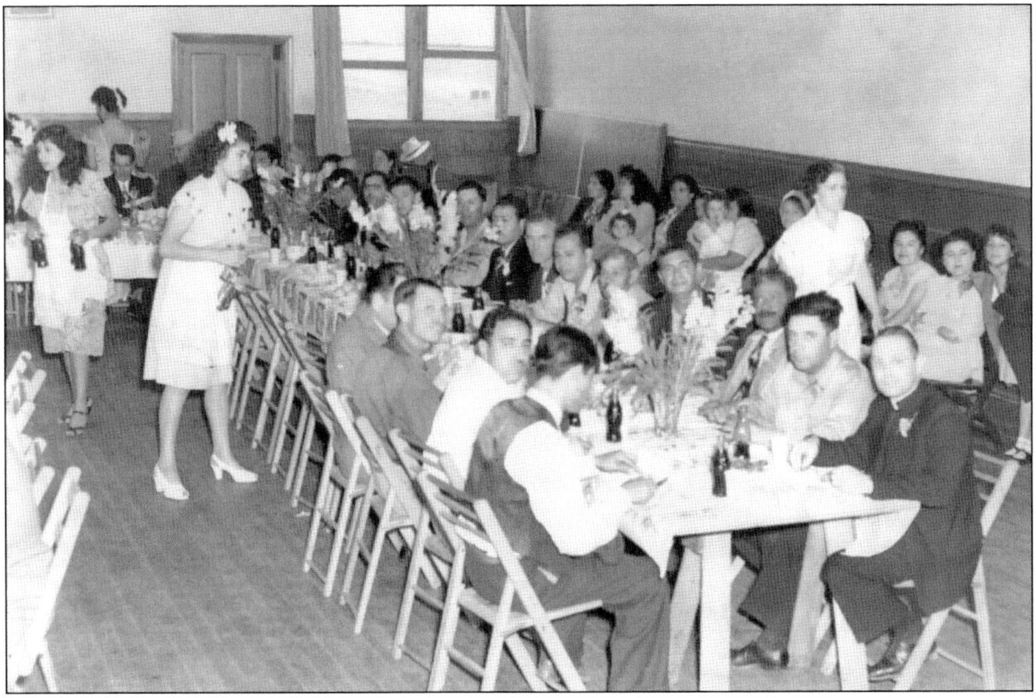

This picture was taken in the 1940s during a Father's Day celebration in the church hall. Mothers would honor the fathers of La Rana in this important annual event. Father Cyrial Wood (far right, seated at the table) was responsible for building the church hall and seeing that both the hall and church were upgraded with electrical service in the 1940s. The church hall was the gathering place for many community social events. (Alfonso Ordaz.)

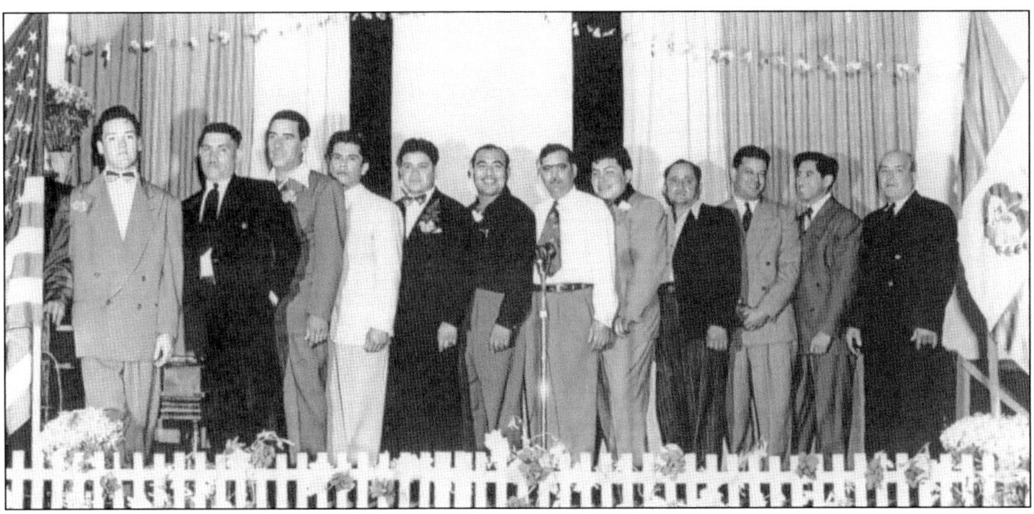

The Men's Club was formed to support the community and plan church functions. The club helped to keep the neighborhood together by planning church fiestas and other social events. Pictured from left to right are Alfonso Ordaz, Jose Olloque, Ricardo Quiones, Andy Alvarez, Tony Razo, Tony Rios, Jose Quiones, Salomon Vidal, Felipe Villa, Jose Rojas, Manuel Valdez, and Henry Camou. (Alfonso Ordaz.)

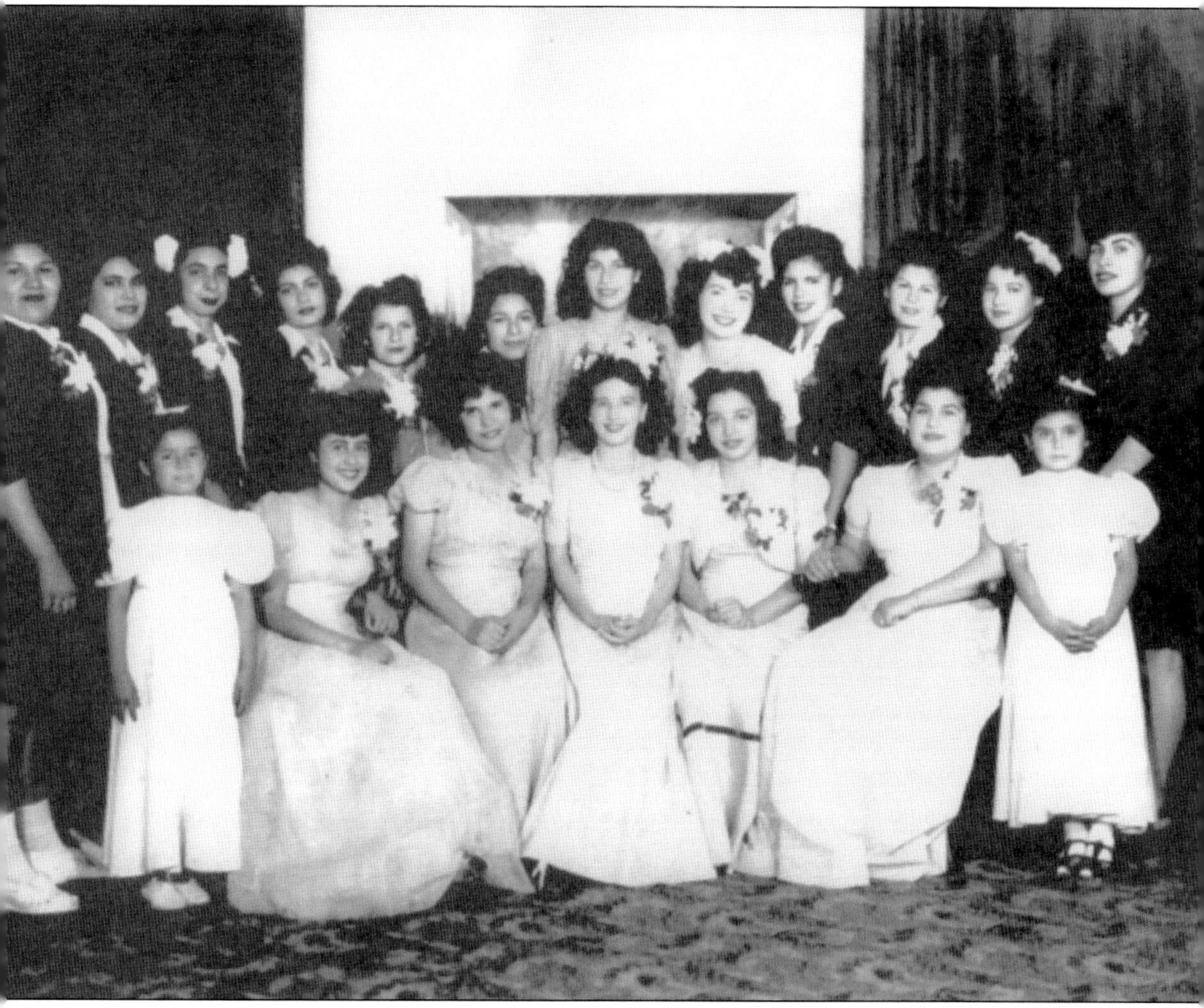

La Rana's Social Club is pictured here around 1944. From left to right are (first row) Mellie Grajeda, Dora Torres, Pearl Olloque, Lupe Escobar, Irene Hermenegildo, Margaret Duran, and Carmen Grajeda; (second row) Dora Grajeda, Francis Alvarez, Olia Fernandez, Julia Alvarez, Josie Martinez, Angie Martinez, Gloria Flores, Gloria Lucero, Connie Alvarez, Conchita Grajeda, Josie Zamora, and Mary Flores. (Gloria Flores.)

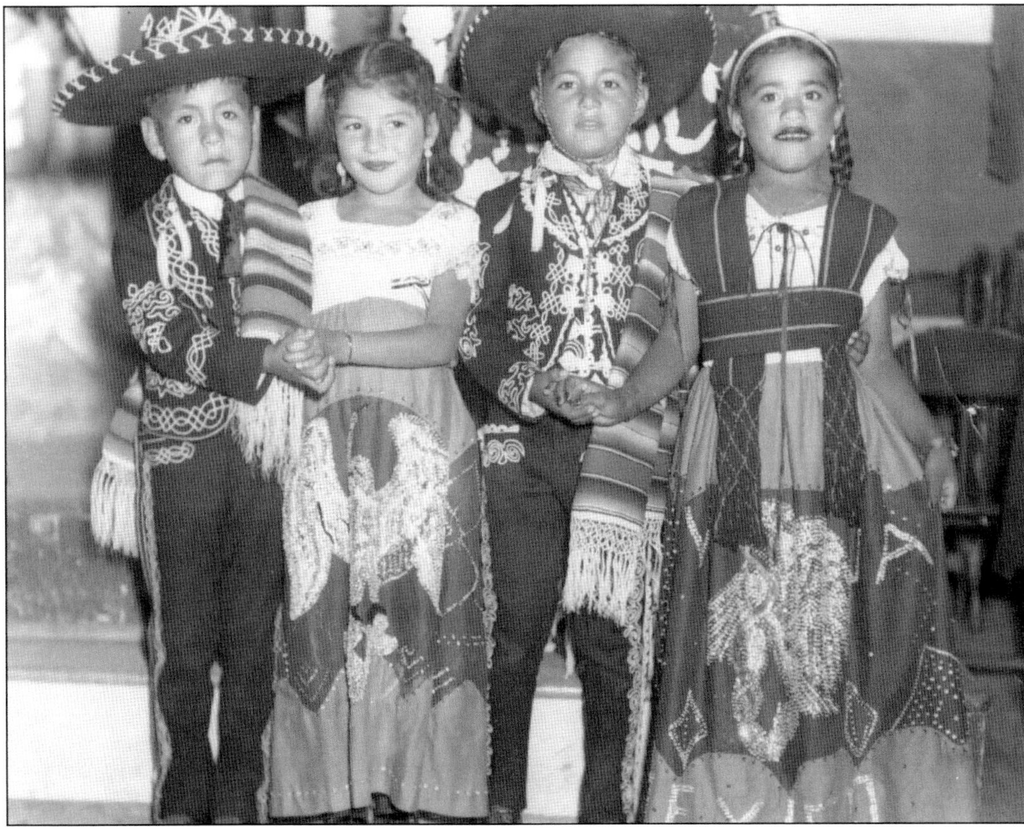

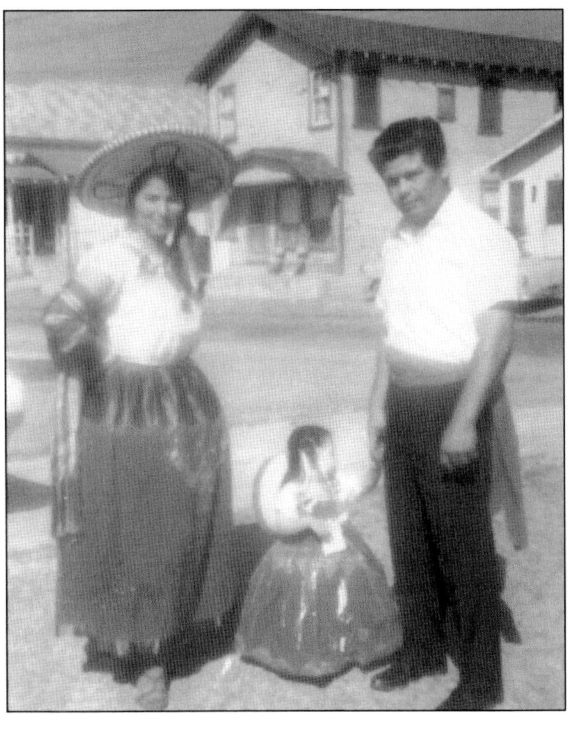

Children performed traditional dances in costume on Mexican Independence Day (September 16) in 1946. Armida Molinar would dance and sing with her father, Angel, as he played the guitar. Pictured from left to right are Ralph Solis Jr., Armida Molinar, Joe Rios, and Mary Quiones. (Armida Molinar Grajeda.)

Armida and Bobby Grajeda and their one-year-old daughter Michelle are dressed in traditional costume for Mexican Independence Day on September 16, 1980. In the background are the Baca home, Cruz Lucero's grocery store, and Dona Ester Guzman's home. Armida would sing at all the events. Today, Armida is the choir director of the Spanish Mass at St. Margaret Mary Church in Lomita. (Armida Grajeda.)

Armida Grajeda formed a youth group that sang at St. Joseph's Mission services on Sundays. The group would also visit retirement and convalescent homes to entertain and bring joy to the residents. The group is pictured here in 1981. From left to right are (first row) Mikey Grajeda, Jamie Torres, and Stephanie Ybarra; (second row) Michelle Grajeda, Denise Torres, Annette Ybarra, Armida Grajeda, and Lisa Ybarra. (Armida Grajeda.)

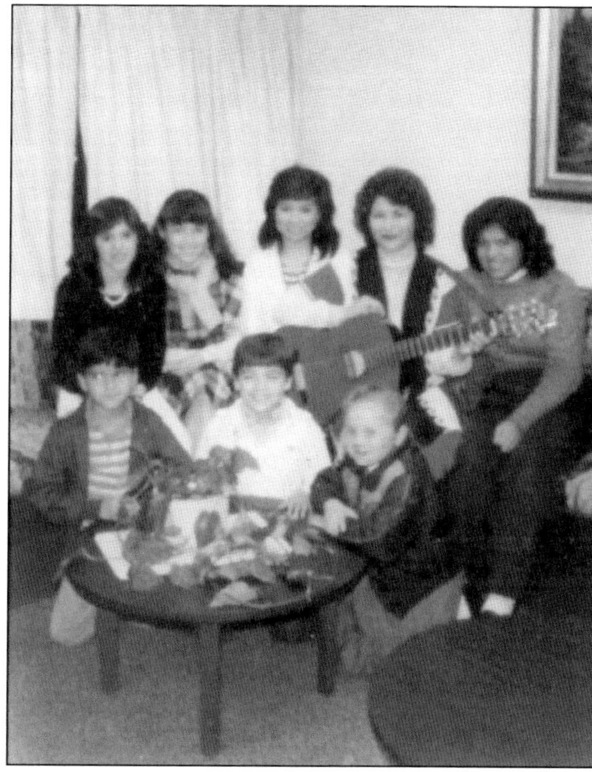

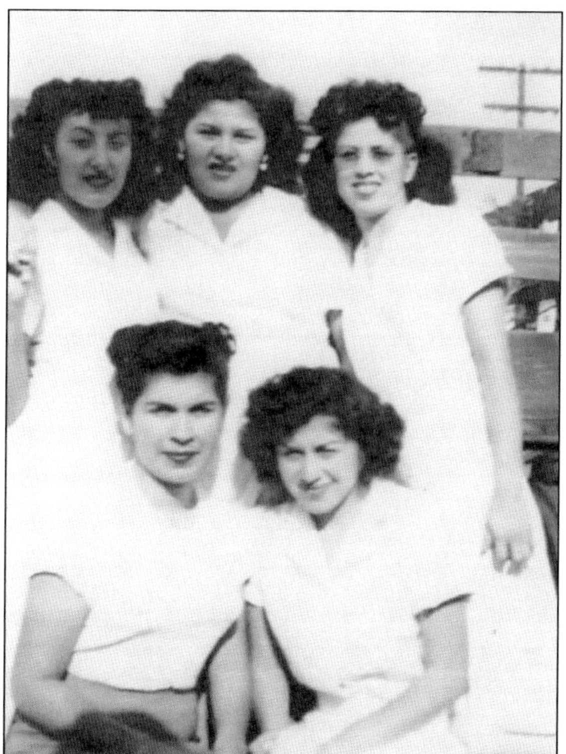

The women at Torrance Laundry are pictured on their lunch break in 1952. Torrance Laundry was located on Carson and Border Streets and employed many young women of La Rana. From left to right are (first row) Mary Flores and Dolores Hernandez; (second row) Sadie Velasquez, Dora Grajeda, and Sophie Hernandez. (Gloria Castanedo.)

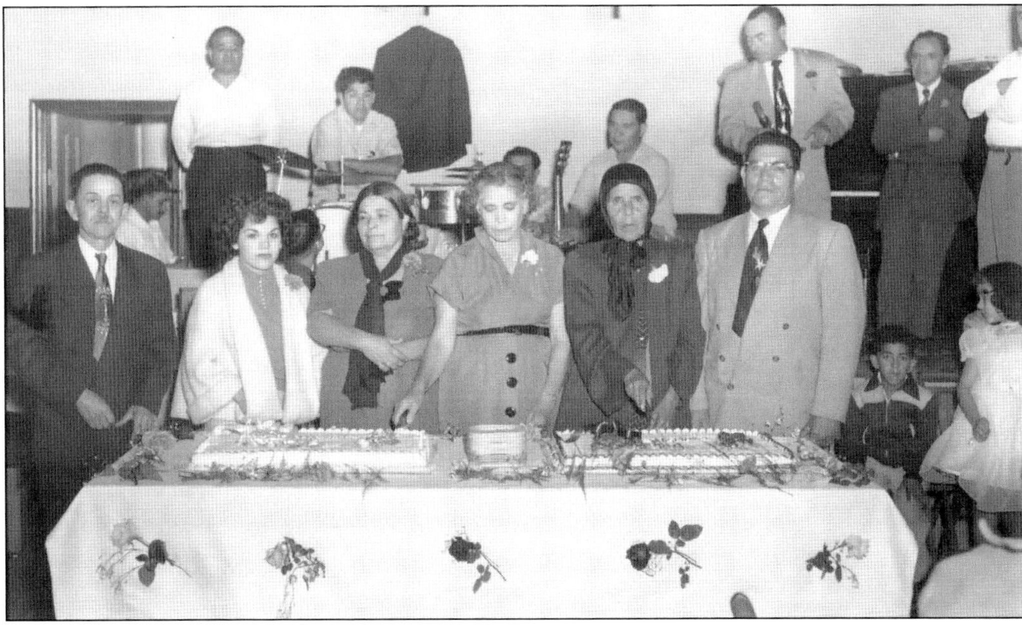

Agapita Alvarez and Petra Banda are cutting a Mother's Day cake in 1950 in honor of the oldest mothers of La Rana. In the background, Tony Alvarez is with his band. Tony would play for dances at the church hall. The Mother's Day celebration would start with a Mass, followed by a late lunch and then a dance. (Longa Alvarez.)

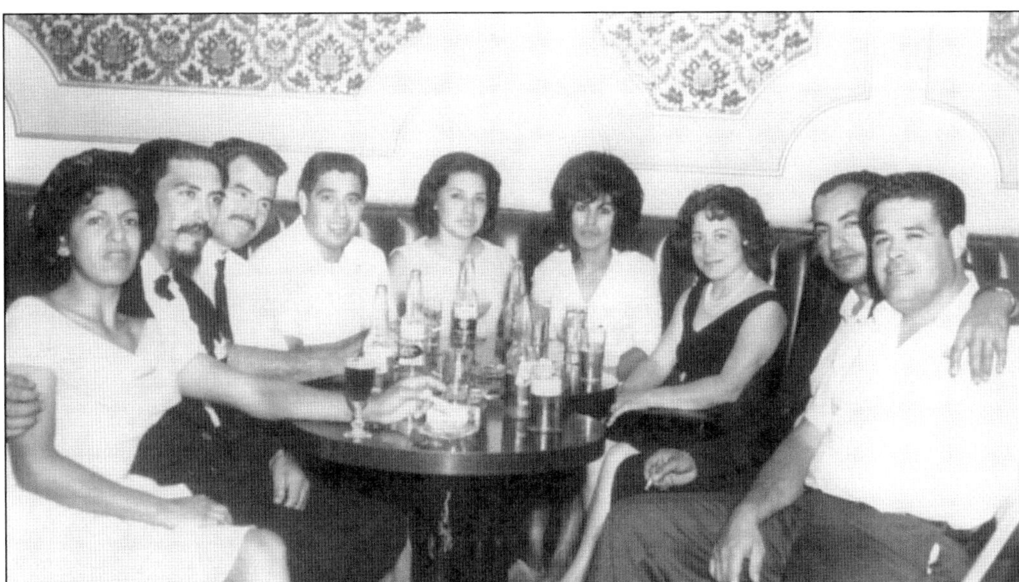

This group attended the wedding of Manuel and Rosa Olloque during Labor Day weekend in 1951. Rosa was from Jiquilpan, Michoacán, Mexico, and came to marry Manuel in Tijuana, Baja California, Mexico, in 1951. Seated from left to right are Josie Reyes Duran, Tommy Grande, Clemente Camou, Manuel Valencia, Jessie Ordaz Valencia, Dora Arelleno Camou, Mollie Ornelas Flores, Louie Flores, and Gilbert Duran. (Dora Camou.)

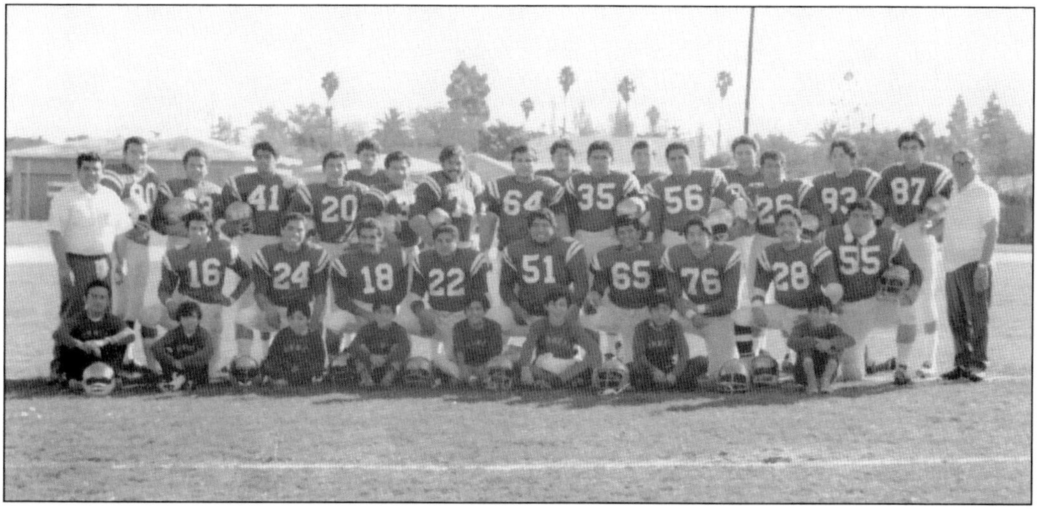

The La Rana Hornets football team was organized by Fred Solis in 1968, creating community pride and keeping the young boys of La Rana busy. The Hornets played other local teams in the area. Nellie Solis, Fred's wife, would make candied apples to sell; along with other fundraising events, this raised money for uniforms and football equipment. (Raymond Vidal.)

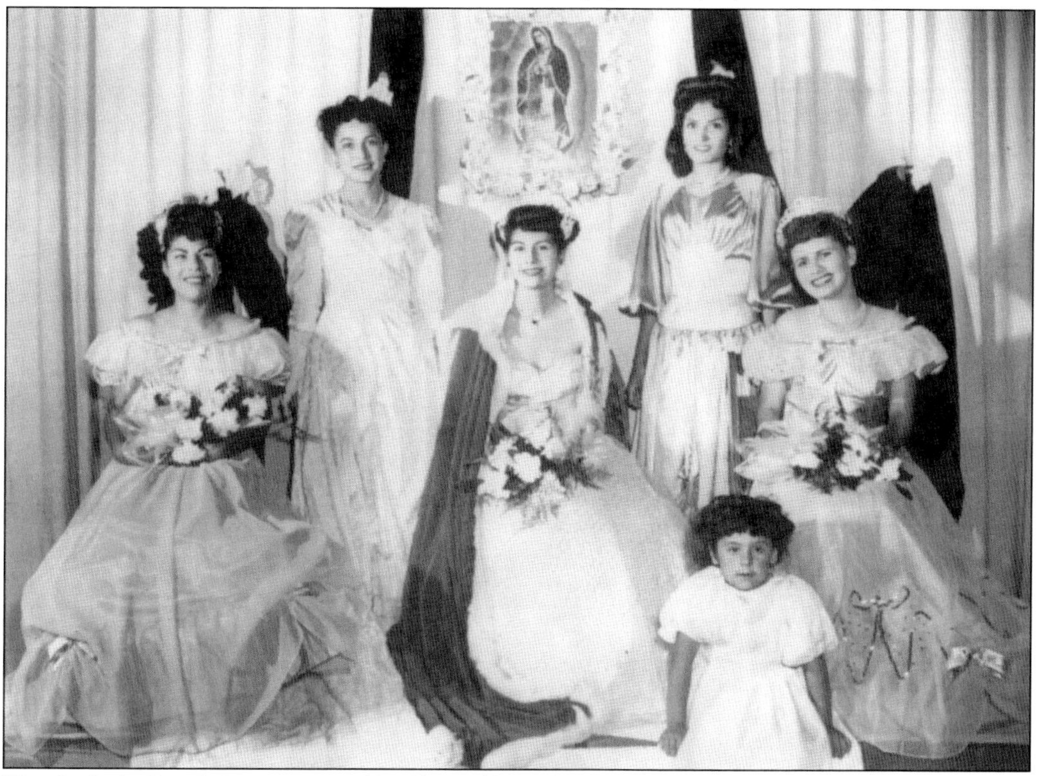

The Catholic Youth Organization (CYO) would conduct fundraising efforts to support CYO events. One of the fundraising activities involved naming a queen and her court based on the number of tickets sold for the organization. Gloria Flores Castaneda was named queen in 1947. Pictured from left to right are Aurora Arellano, Ofelia Duarte, Gloria Flores Castaneda (queen), Lucy Villegas, and Hermelinda Alvarez. The little girl is Judy Grajeda. (Gloria Flores Castaneda.)

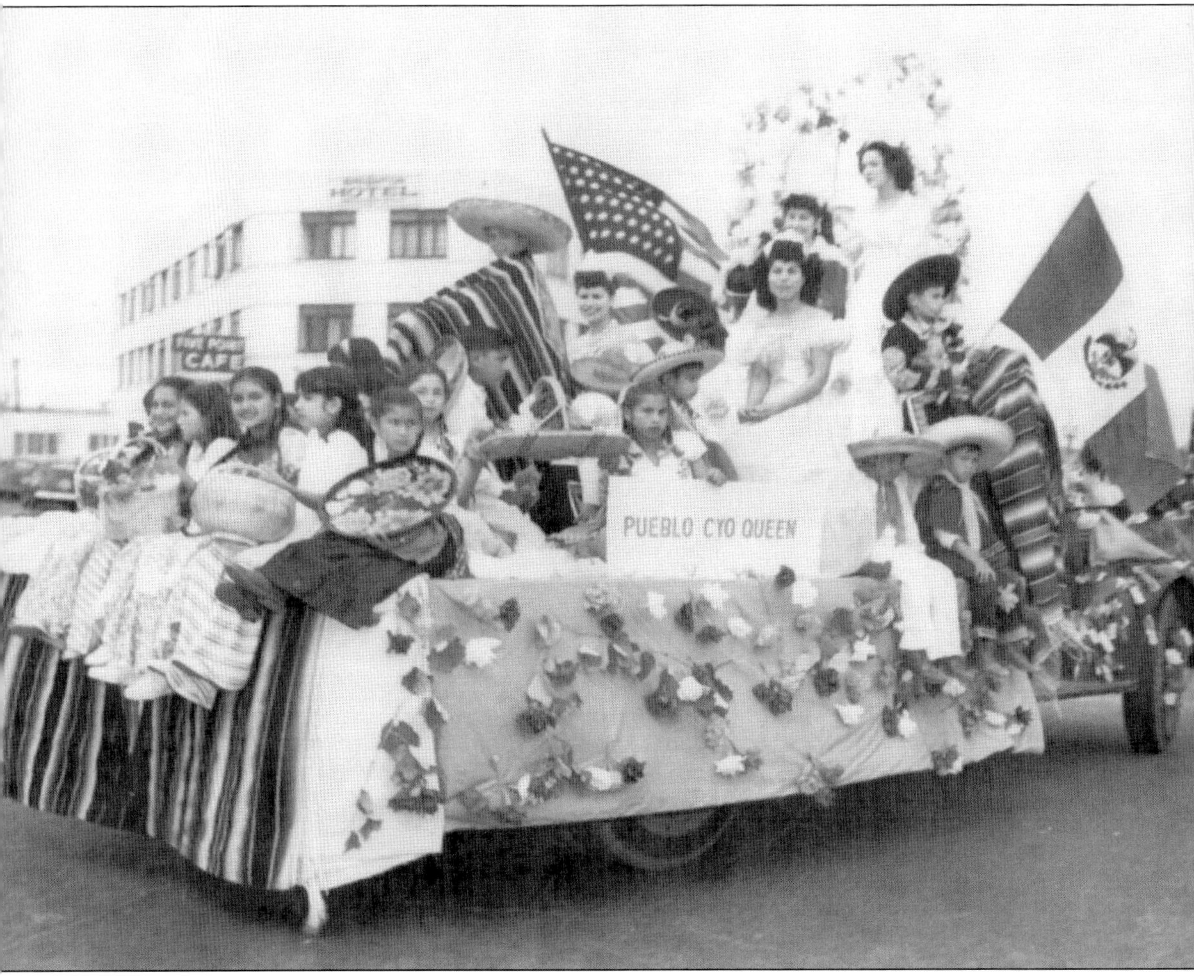

These churchgoers are celebrating Mexican Independence Day on September 16, 1947. The float, pictured in downtown Torrance where the parade began, was built by the men of La Rana and used in the annual parade that would travel down Del Amo Boulevard (La Rana). The CYO queen and her court would ride on the float along with other notable community members. (Gloria Castaneda.)

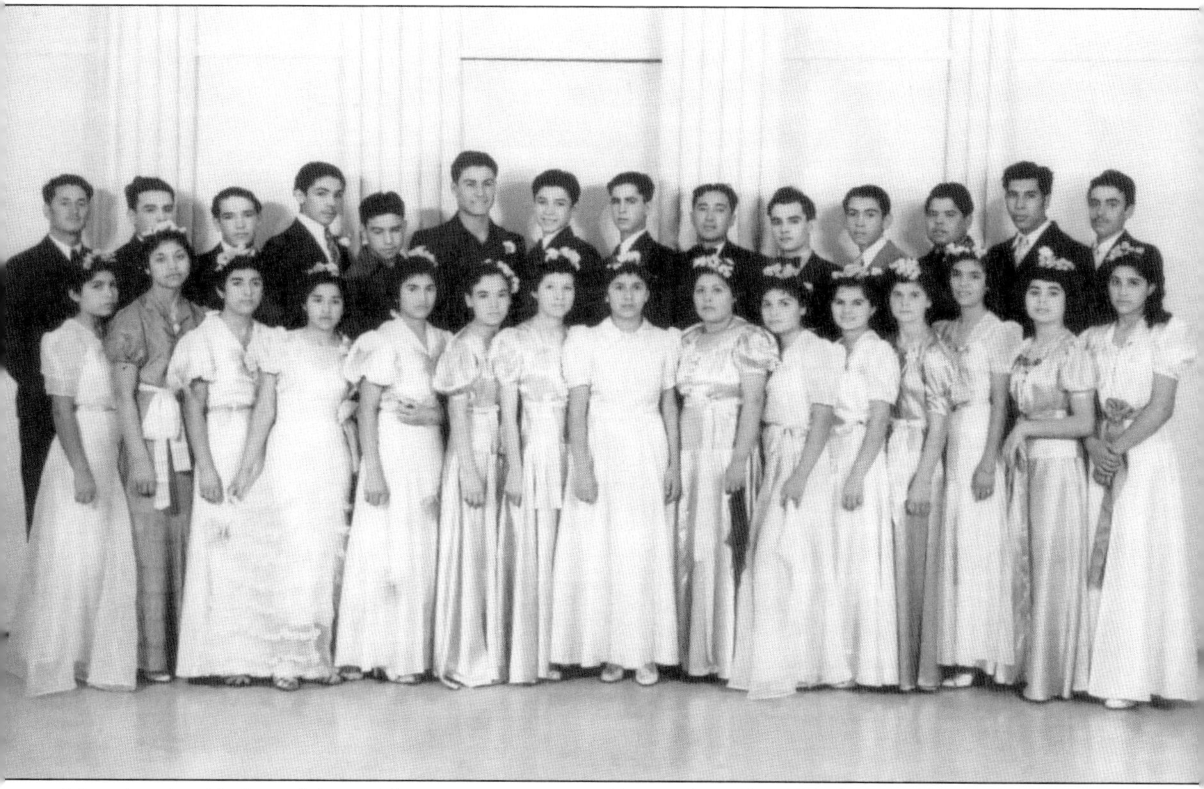

Mary Louise Ordaz celebrated her quinceañera on September 19, 1937. Quinceañeras are one of the many traditions Mexican immigrants brought from Mexico. Pictured from left to right are (first row) Nellie Reyes, Kate Rios, Helen Grande, Vera Ortega, Ernestina Grande, Artemisa Castillo, unidentified, Maria Louisa Ordaz, Esther Guzman, Dora Reyes, Emelia Espinosa, Magdalena Avalos, unidentified, Helen Castillo, and Socorro ?; (second row) Benny Flores, Gerald H. Castillo, Jason Castillo, Benny Mendez, Nicholas Ortega, unidentified, Tony Ortega, Avelino Gonzales, two unidentified, Nestor Flores, Francisco Garcia, Manuel Gutierrez, and Toby Reynaga. Mary Louise later married the young man who was her partner at this event. (Jesse Ordaz Valencia.)

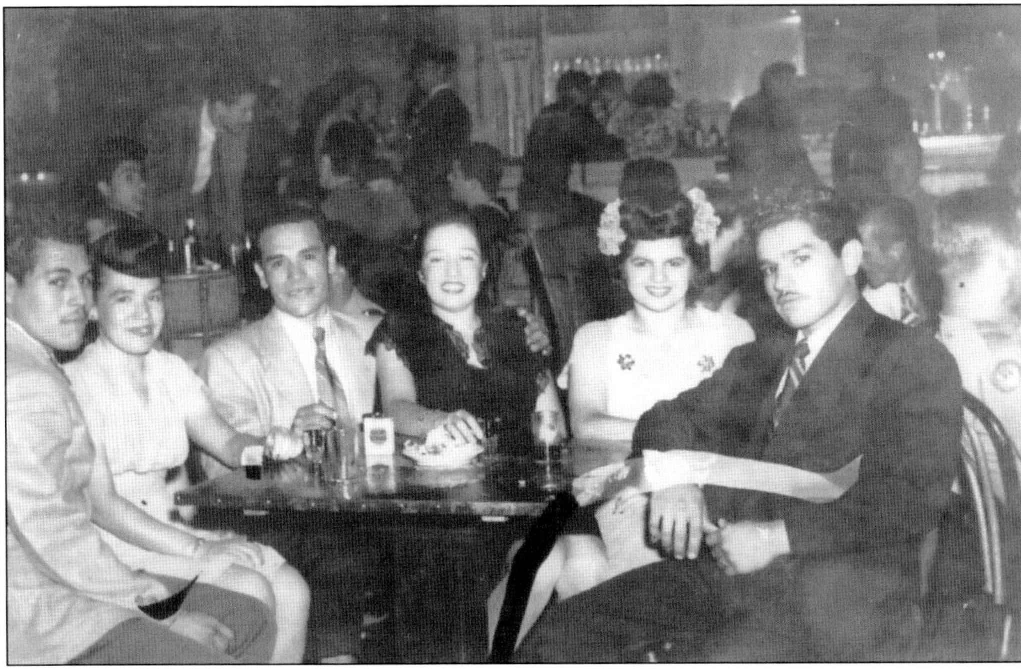

The Castillo brothers and sisters are pictured here socializing at a dance club in the early 1950s. From left to right are Joe Solis, Artemisa Castillo Solis, Gerald H. Castillo, Ofelia Castillo, Amelia Espinosa Castillo, and William H. Castillo. (Amelia Espinosa Castillo.)

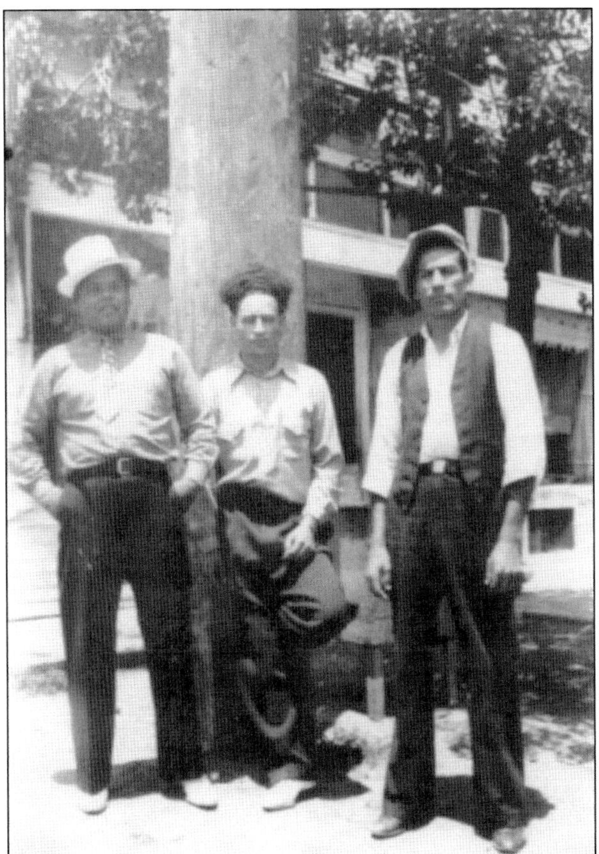

Pictured here from left to right are Francisco (El Gordito) Garcia, Jesus Escobar, and Dario Duran, the first settlers of La Rana. There is no information about Garcia except that he was always seen at La Rana. This picture was taken in the evening in front of Cruz Lucero's grocery store. Escobar was the husband of Sebastiana Cisneros. Duran was the husband of Antonia Duran. (Linda Ortiz.)

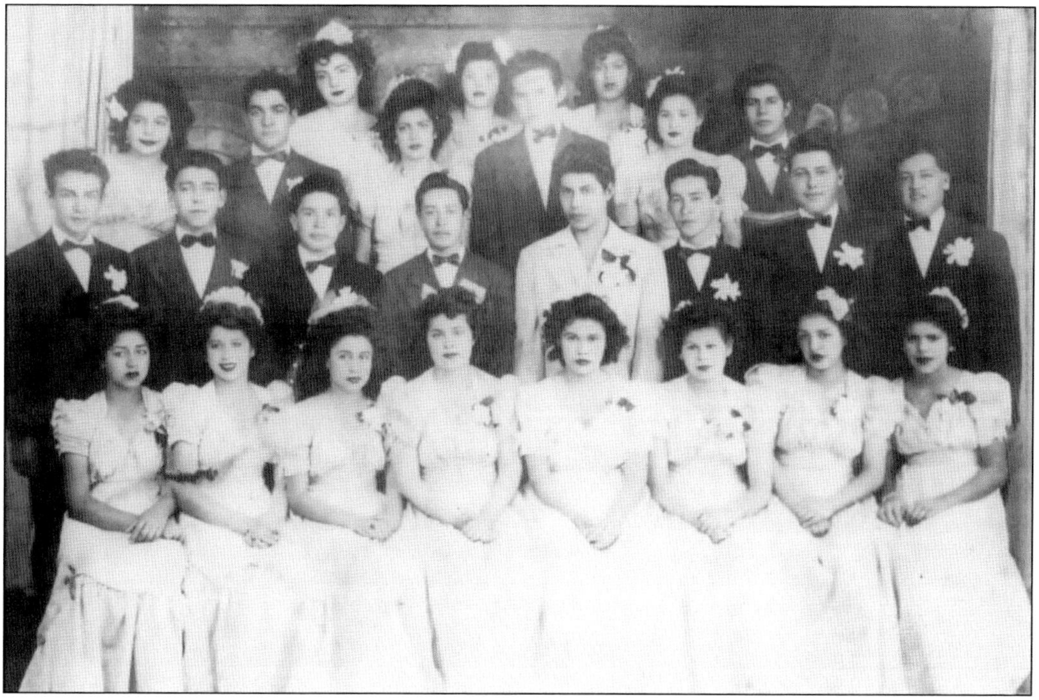

Pearl Olloque celebrated her quinceañera in 1943. Pictured here are, from left to right, (first row) Alice Hernandez, Sofie Hernandez, Aurora Torres, Stella Tapia, Pearl Olloque, Conchita Grajeda, Irene Hermanegildo, and Consuelo Alvarez; (second row) Aurora Banda, Henry Castillo, Julia Alvarez, Reyes Ybarra, Josie Zamora, and Felix Hernandez; (third row) Armando Guzman, Frank Bustillos, Tony Hermenegildo, Ramiro Ordaz, Freddie Solis, Ruben Ordaz, and Alfonso Ordaz; (fourth row) Gloria Lucero, Doris Villa, and Josie Reyes. (Conchita Grajeda.)

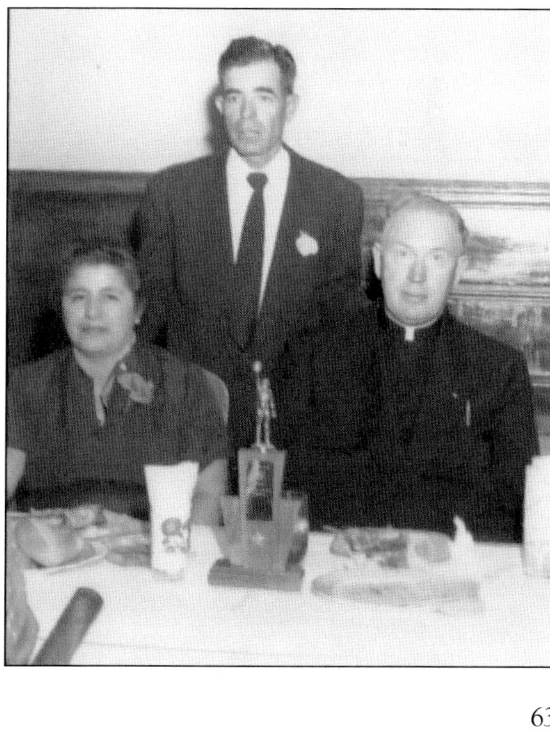

Alfredo and Bertha White are pictured with Father McGinnis, who was very active in the community along with the White family. Alfredo, the handyman at St. Joseph's Mission, constructed the roof tower of St. Joseph's and did the exterior plastering of the building. This photograph was taken during a Mother's Day celebration. (Stella Gassett.)

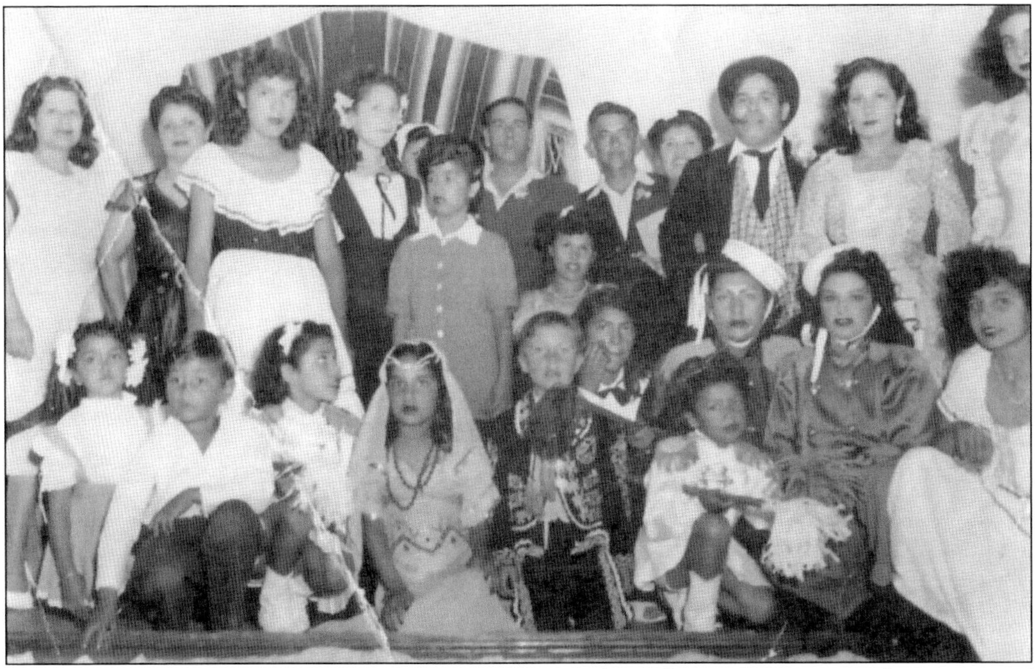

These community members are celebrating Mexican Independence Day in 1948. This was one of many traditions that Mexicans who immigrated from Mexico celebrated each year. The celebration consisted of participants singing, dancing, and performing skits for entertainment at the events in the church hall. (Connie Molina.)

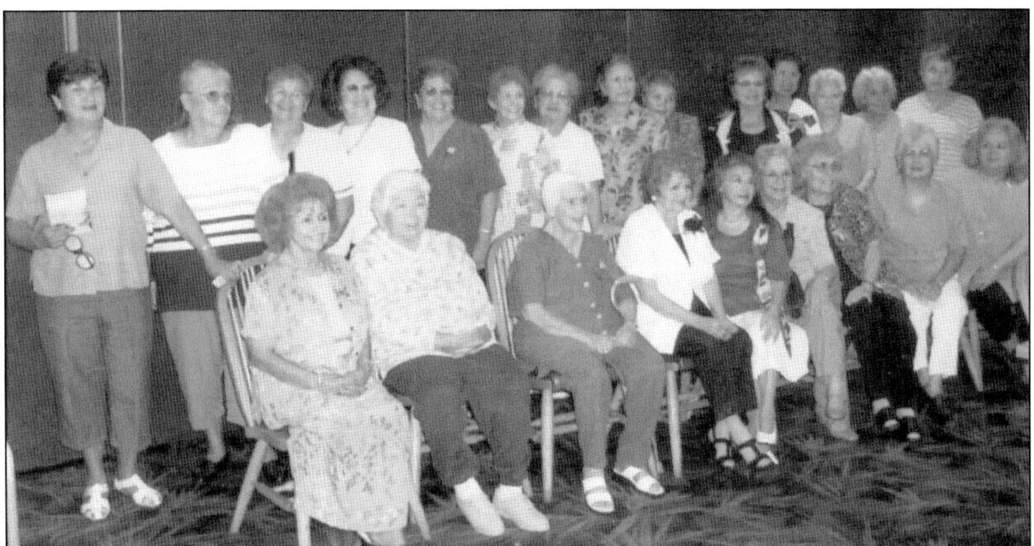

Esther Muro gathered many of the women who lived in La Rana for regular reunions. In 1970, the reunion was held at the Sizzler in Torrance. Pictured here are, from left to right, (seated) Virginia Duarte, Eva Guzman, Luz Duarte, Mellie Castillo, Peggy Villegas, Esther Muro, Esther Guzman, Mary Flores, and Luisa Rodriguez; (standing), Virginia Camou, Pearl Olloque, Conchita Grajeda, Sophie Hernandez, Irene Hermanegildo, Anita Duarte, Mollie Espinosa, Ernie Castillo, Jessie Escobar, Dolores Hernandez, Virginia Acosta, Ruth Torres, Josie Torres, and Lucy Villegas. (Lucy Villegas.)

This 1950 photograph features Miguel Duarte (left) and Joe Rodriguez when Duarte was on military leave. Soon after this picture was taken, he was sent to Hawaii and then Korea, where he made his first jump with the 187th Airborne on October 20, 1950. He lost his life on February 15, 1951. Duarte attended Torrance High School and would have graduated in 1950—instead, he joined the Army. (Alice Solis.)

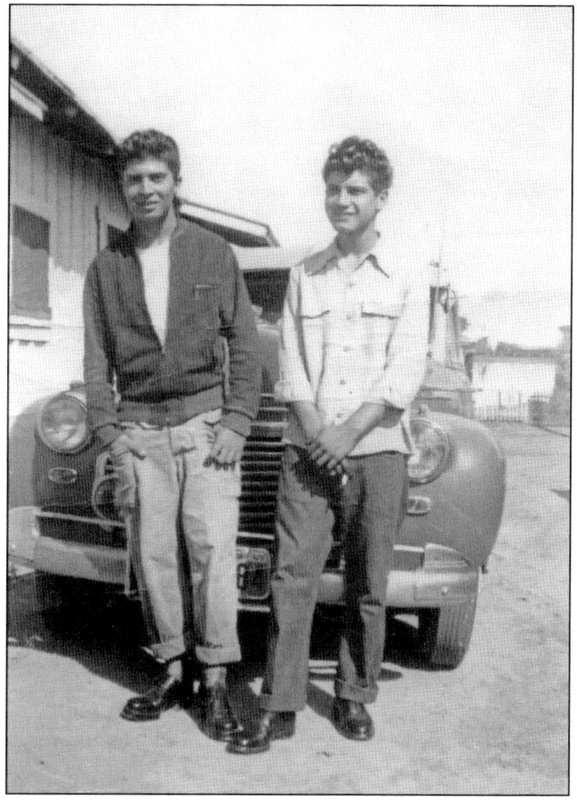

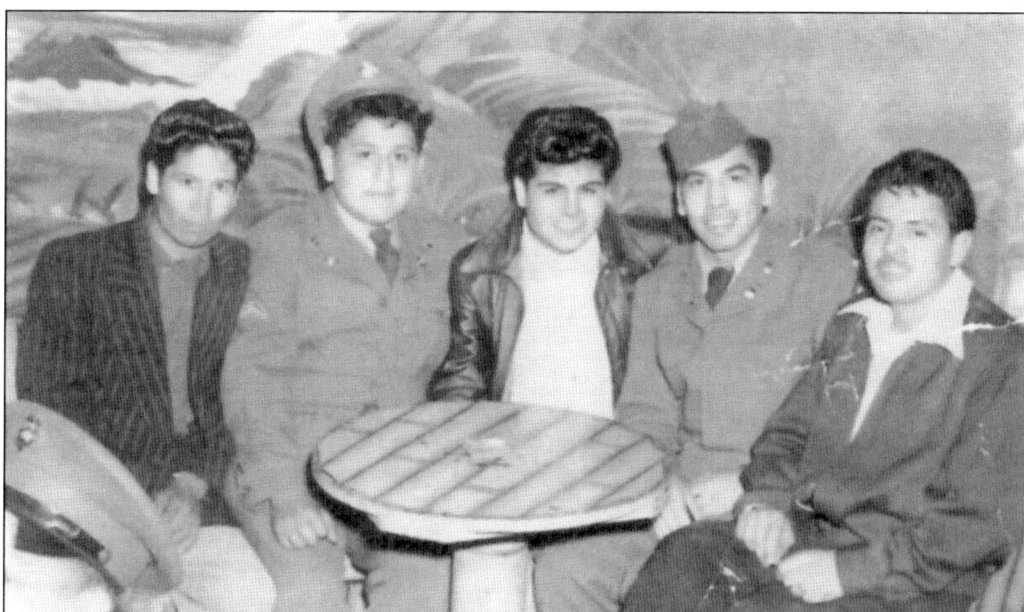

Mike Martinez and Willie Guadiana were both on military leave during the Korean conflict in 1952. Pictured here are, from left to right, Serafin Suniga, Willie Guadiana, Mike Grajeda, Mike Martinez, and Senon Grajeda. Mike Grajeda's family, one of the first families to arrive in La Rana, came from Chilchota, Michoacan, Mexico. (Armida Grajeda.)

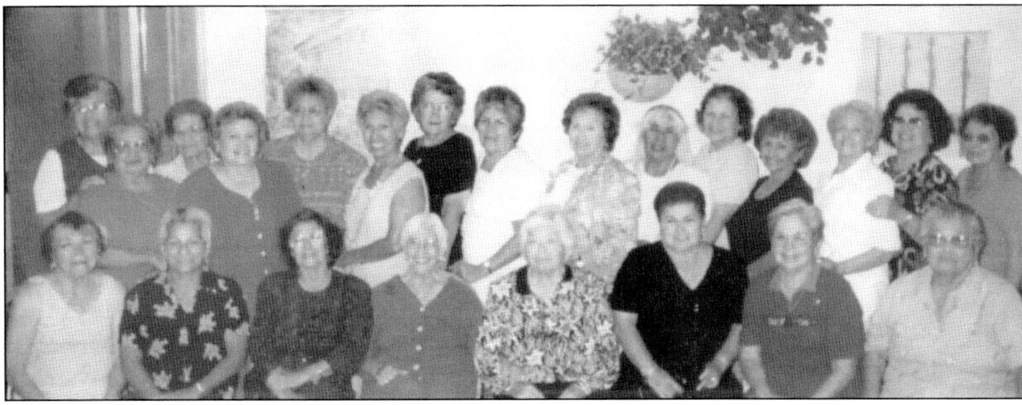

Pictured around 1974 is a reunion of friends who lived in La Rana in their youth. Esther Muro would gather a lunch meeting at the Sizzler in Torrance. From left to right are (first row) Francis Alvarez, unidentified, Virgina Acosta, Luz Duarte Ordaz, Esther Guzman, Erma Vargas, Esther Hernandez Muro, and unidentified; (second row) Gloria Flores Castanda, Molly Espinoza, two unidentified, Margaret Razo, Dorothy Mora, Lucy Villegas, Connie Alverez, Dolores Hernandez, Dora Arellano, Ernestina Castillo, Virgina Duarte Casado, Anita Duarte Martinez, Sophia Hernandez, and Irene Hermenegildo. (Lucy Villegas.)

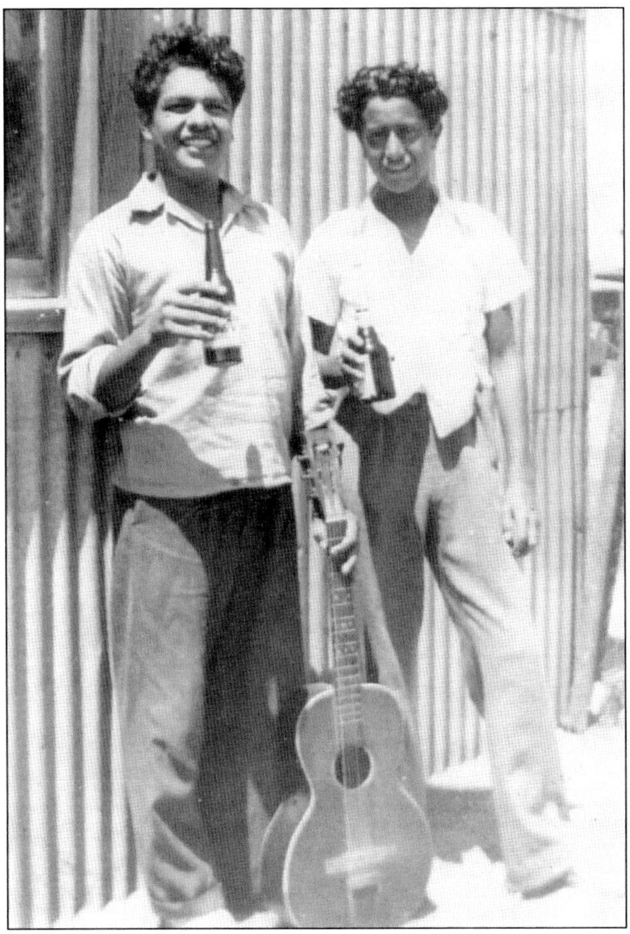

Robert Alverez (left) and Charlie Villegas are pretending to drink beers near the side of the Tortilleria in the late 1930s. These two good friends lived across the street from one another. Robert was the son of Agapita and Andres Alverez, and Charlie was the son of Don Regino and Soledad. (Longa Alverez.)

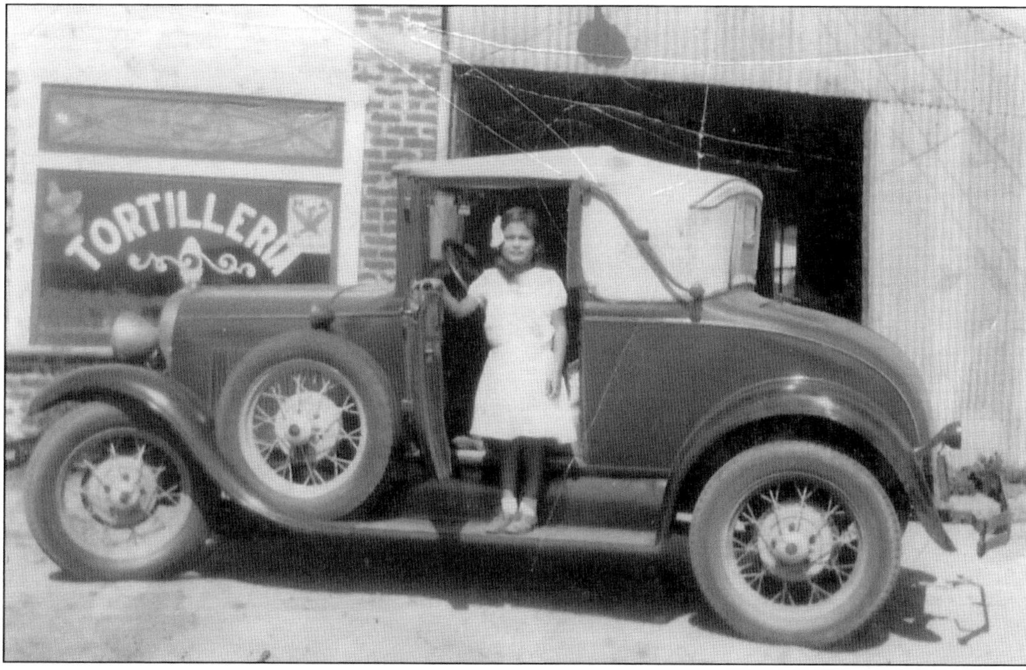

In this 1933 photograph, Francis Alvarez poses in front of the Tortilleria owned by Luis and Lupe Moreno. The Tortilleria later became a pool hall owned by Jose Olloque. Francis is the daughter of Agapita and Andres Alvarez; the Alvarez family lived across the street from the Tortilleria. (Longa Alvarez.)

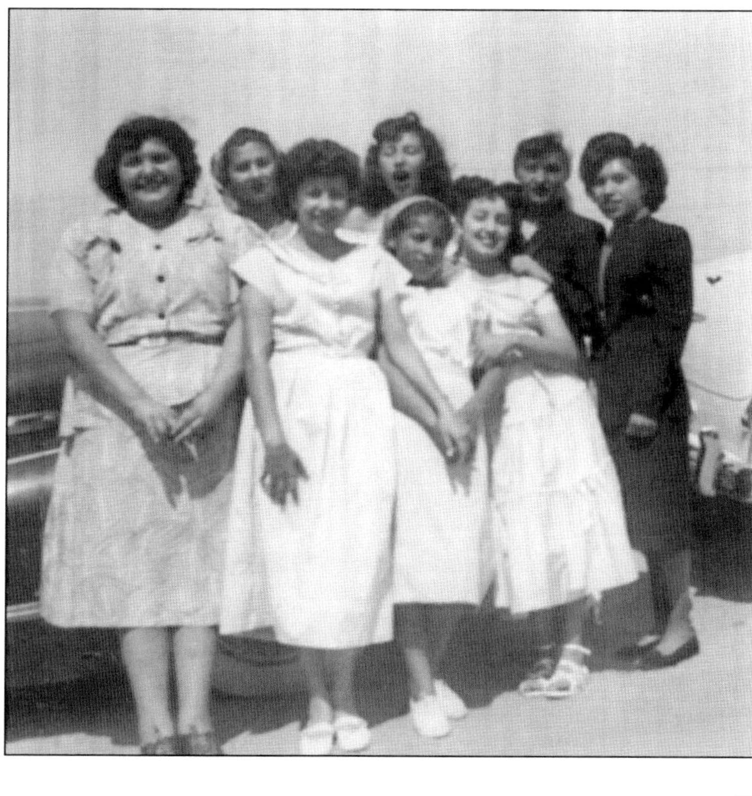

These ladies were getting ready to go to the movies and dancing in Redondo Beach on a Sunday afternoon in 1953. They are, from left to right, (first row) Delia Alvarez, Rachel Alvarez, Sadie Velasquez, and Dorothy Mora; (second row) Rosa Rodriguez, Gloria Montejano, Jessie Ordaz, and Jessie (Cucu) Gonzales. (Virginia Camou.)

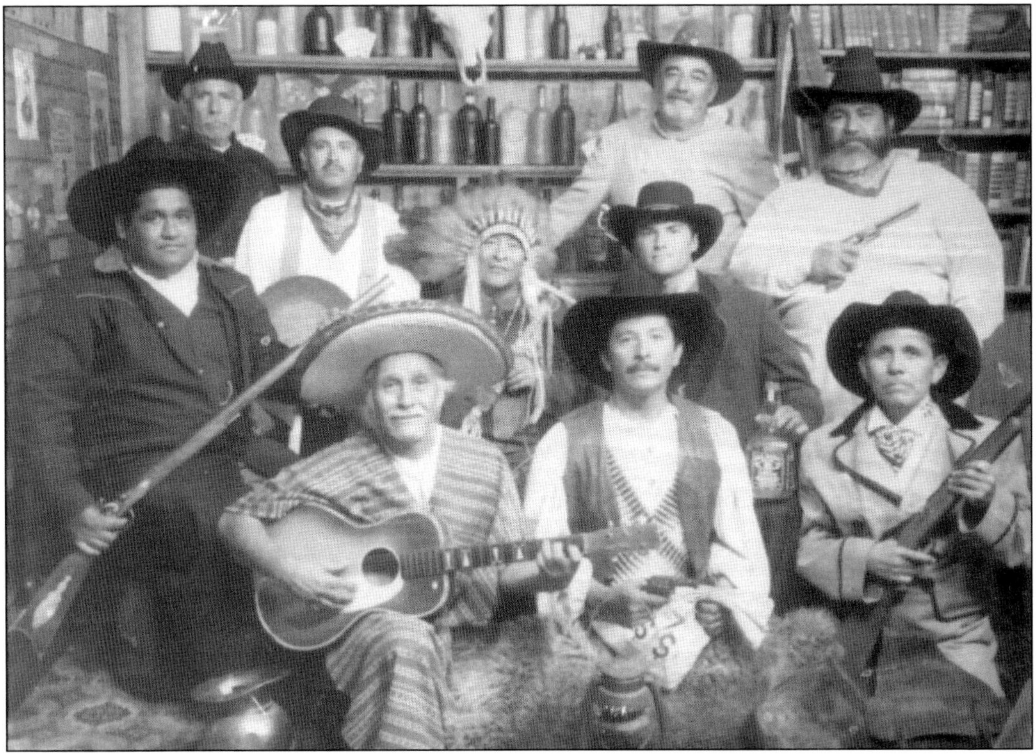

In the mid-1990s, the Solis family and friends went to Virginia City, California, and went to a place that took fun pictures. Pictured here are, from left to right, (first row) Augie Solis, Eddie Solis, and John Solis; (second row) Raymond Vidal Jr., Fred Solis, and Richard Camou Jr.; (third row) Eleazar Ybarra, Tony Ordaz Jr., Richard Camou Sr., and Raymond Vidal Sr. (Alice Solis.)

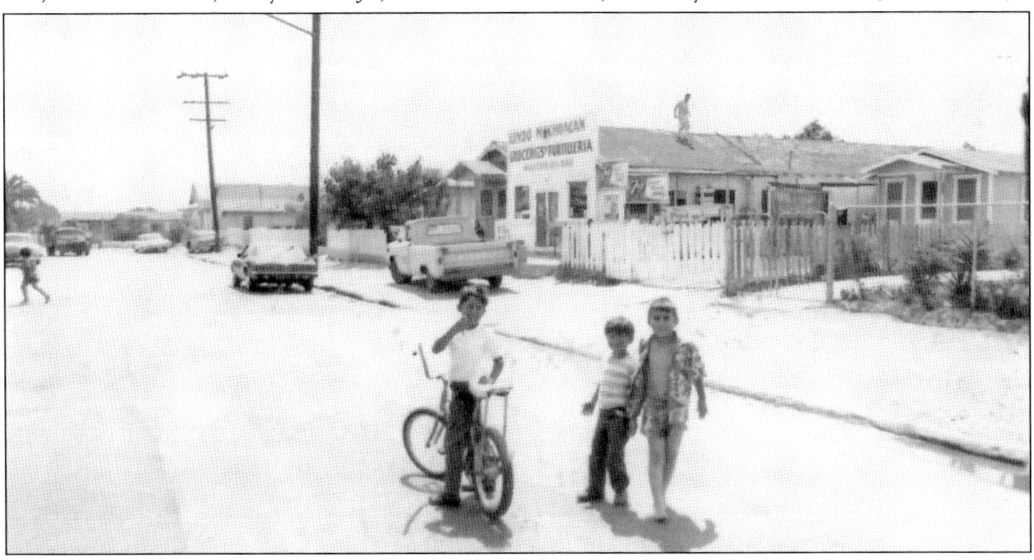

Artemio and Dolores Duarte opened up Linda Michoacán Grocery and Tortilleria in 1946. Their children helped with the store. The Duarte family operated the store for 30 years. Pedro Alonzo took over the business in 1976 and kept the little grocery store open for three more years. Pictured here on the bicycle is Kito Ybarra, and next to him are Larry and Alex Villalobos. (Longa Alvarez.)

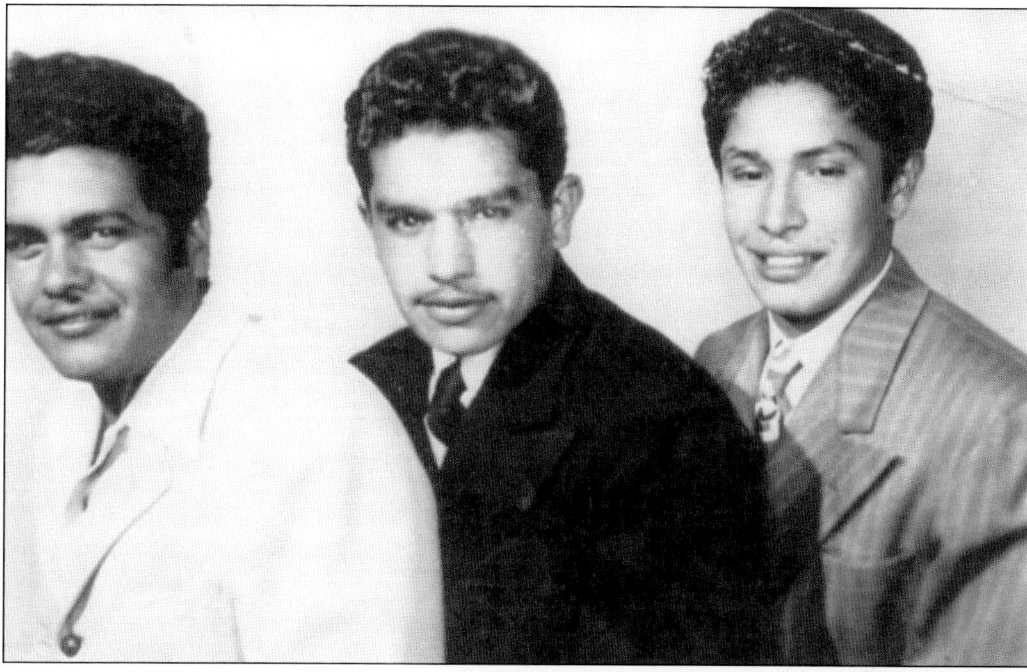

From left to right, Robert Alvarez, William Castillo, and Joe Escobar were good friends and neighbors. Alvarez played the guitar, and Escobar played the trumpet. They would play guitar and sing on the porch for the neighborhood to enjoy. Tony Alvarez had a band that played at celebrations. Escobar played a trumpet in the band, and Castillo became the manager of a furniture store in Los Angeles. (Longa Alvarez.)

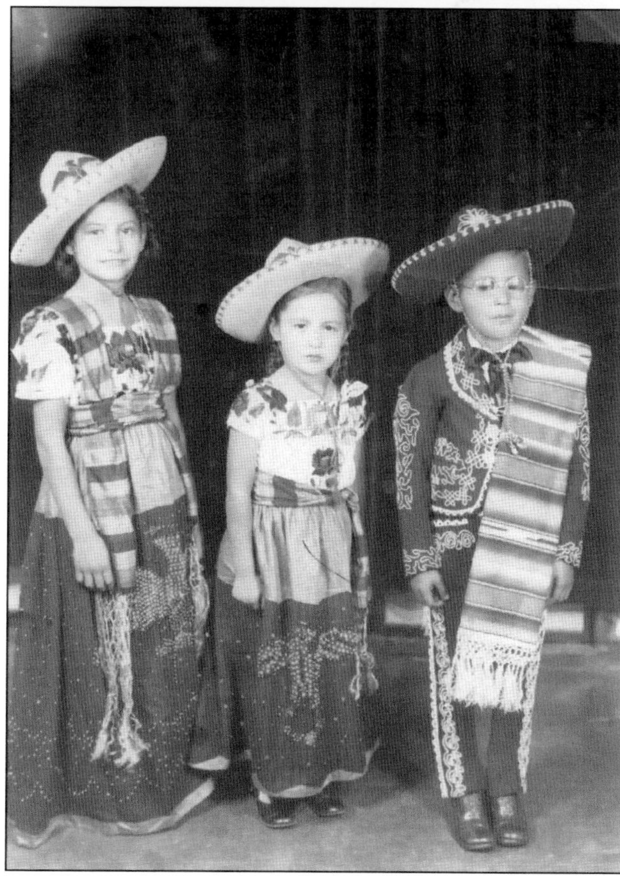

September 16 is the date of the annual celebration of Mexican independence from Spain. In this 1942 picture, from left to right, Nellie, Clara, and Paul Rios are wearing traditional costumes, which many families brought from Mexico. Their grandfather Silverio Rios went to Guadalajara, Jalisco, to buy these costumes for the event. (Clara Rios Gauna.)

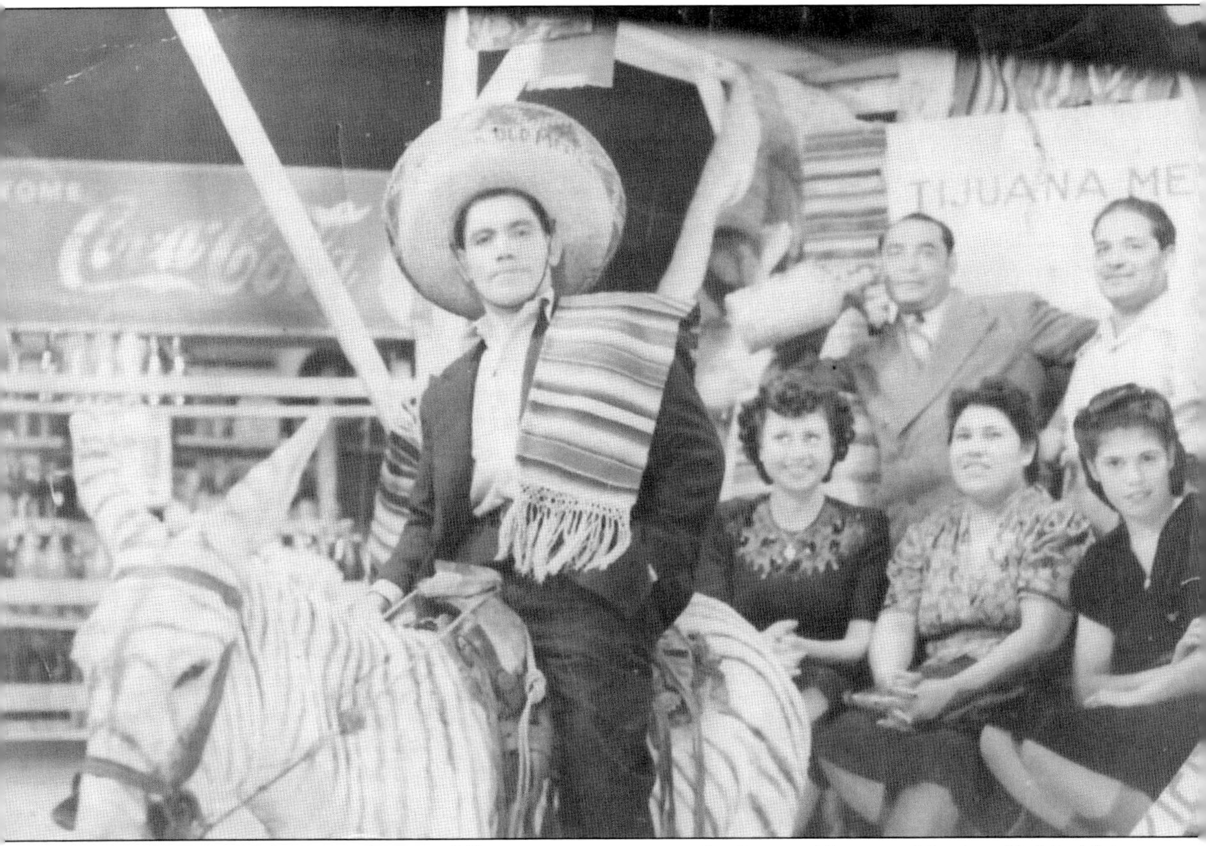

In this 1940s photograph, Jose Olloque is sitting on a donkey in Tijuana, Mexico. Behind him are, from left to right, (first row) Tillie Ordaz, Jenny Olloque, and Pearl Olloque; (second row) Francisco (Pancho) Ordaz and band leader Tony Alverez. This group traveled to Tijuana often to listen to music, watch bullfights, and visit with friends. (Raymond Vidal.)

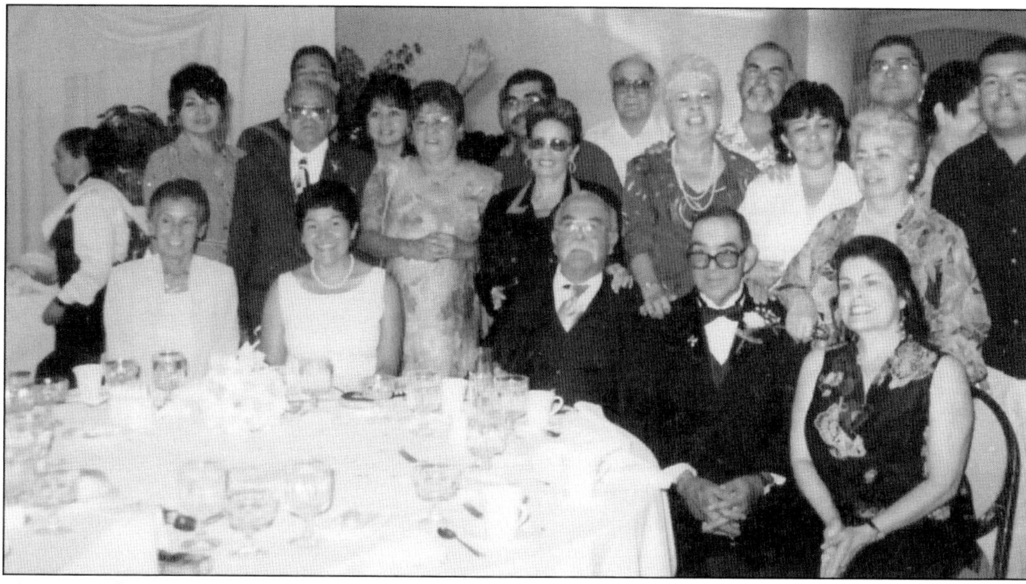

Henry and Carmen Castillo celebrated their 50th wedding anniversary in 2002. Family and friends enjoyed a happy time at the Ports O' Call restaurant in San Pedro. Pictured from left to right are (seated at the table) Carmen Estolano Castillo, Dolores Castillo (Carmen's daughter), Leo Castillo, Henry Castillo, and Joanie Castillo (Leo's daughter). Many other members of the family are in the background. (Beatrice Castillo.)

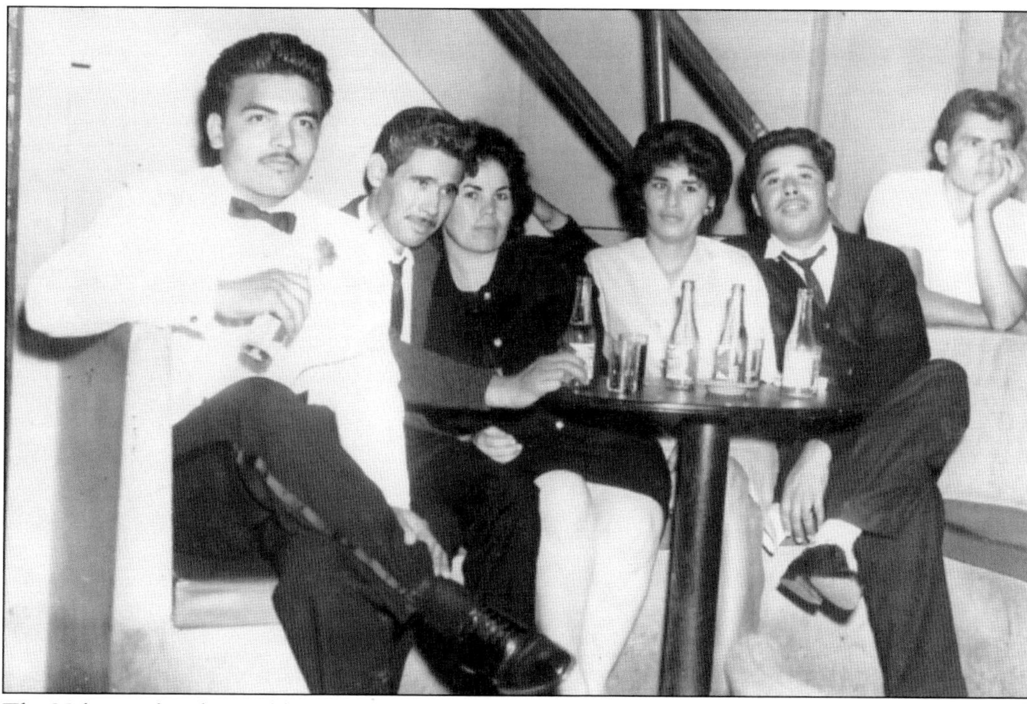

The Valencia family would travel to Tijuana, Mexico, to enjoy the company of family and friends. Pictured seated at a nightclub on Revolution Street in Tijuana in 1955 are, from left to right, Benny (Negro) Flores, Art Valencia, Nellie Padilla Valencia, Beatrice Castillo Valencia, and Alejandro Valencia. (Beatrice Castillo.)

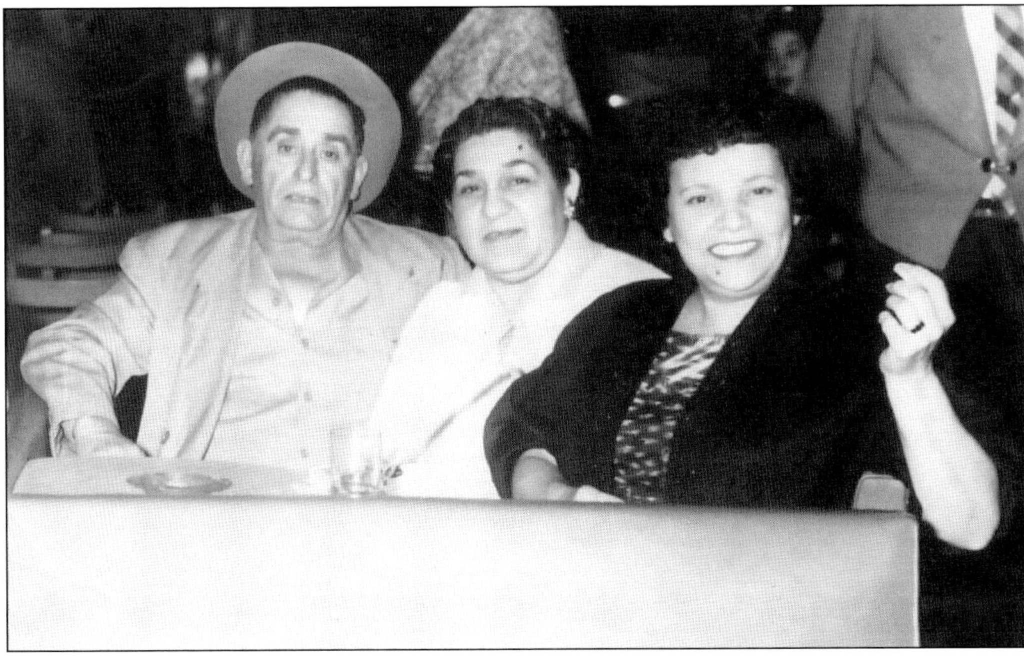

Pictured here are Ramon (Guayaba) Martinez, Eloisa Castillo Olivarez, and Emilia Flores. Martinez came from Purépero, Michoacán, Mexico, in the early 1920s and worked for U.S. Steel and lived in La Rana for most of his life. He later moved to Redondo Beach, California, to be near relatives. (Beatrice Castillo.)

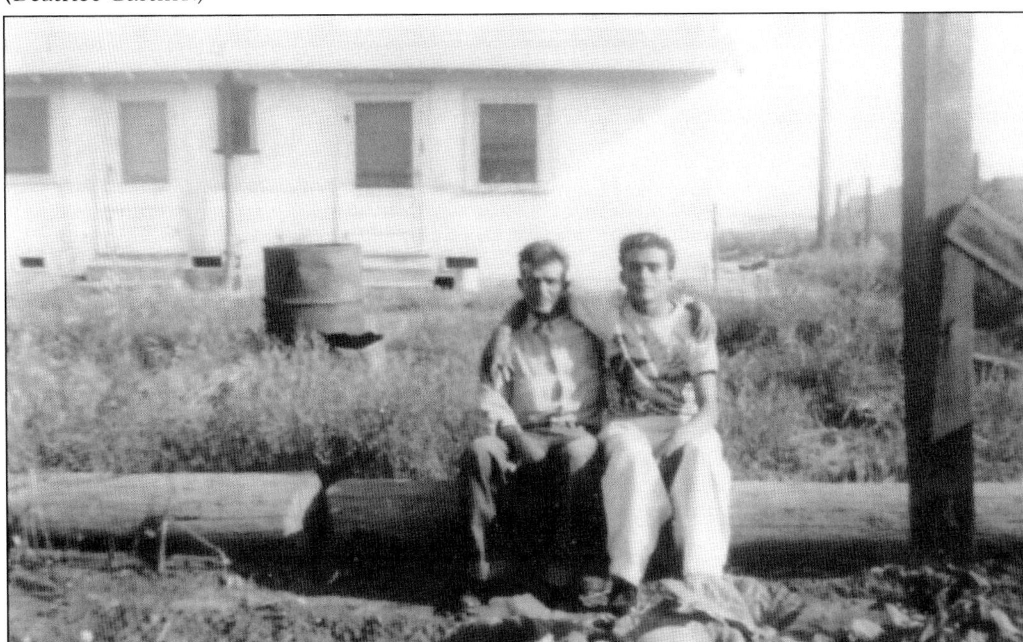

Angel (Jelo) Garnica (left) and Norberto Alcala are pictured here. Garnica lived in La Rana for many years. After retiring, he moved back to his hometown of Purépero, Michoacán, Mexico. Alcala was born in La Rana and returned to Purépero when he was a young boy, then came back to the United States as an adult. (Beatrice Castillo.)

Three

Religion

Families who fled Mexico's religious persecution and revolution of 1910 immigrated to the United States in search of freedom of worship and a better life. They began arriving in 1908, with a large influx during 1916 and 1917. In 1919, T.J. Nestor donated 10,000 square feet of land near the homes on Del Amo Boulevard for the construction of St. Joseph's Mission. The mission was built by area residents in 1920.

The church was initially a simple structure without an altar, seating, or electricity. However, it was enough to celebrate Sunday services. The church was dormant temporarily after the initial building was erected. In approximately 1938, Petra Madrigal and her daughter Josephina Gutierrez began organizing fiestas to raise funds to reopen the church.

Our Lady of Guadalupe Church began to assign priests to conduct masses at St. Joseph's Mission. The first, Father Tolosa, was a Colombian priest who initially reopened the church but was reassigned shortly after. Monsignor Gutierrez was the second priest and served for approximately four years before he returned to Mexico. Father Cyrial Wood was the last priest assigned to St. Joseph's Mission by Our Lady of Guadalupe. Father Wood assisted with the wiring of the church and the plastering of the walls. St. Monica Catholic Church donated benches and kneelers. Father Wood also supervised the construction of the church hall, which became the center of many neighborhood social events.

One of the major traditions celebrated at St. Joseph's Mission was held each year on December 12, the Feast of Our Lady of Guadalupe, which was an all-day celebration. There was food, and men played the guitar and serenaded "our blessed mother." The women would prepare Mexican food to raise funds to help maintain the church. In spring there was the May Crowning of the statue of Mary. This was another all-day celebration with food, music, and entertainment. The church was the place for many other religious celebrations, including baptisms, First Communion ceremonies, and weddings. Sadly, St. Joseph's Mission closed on September 16, 2000.

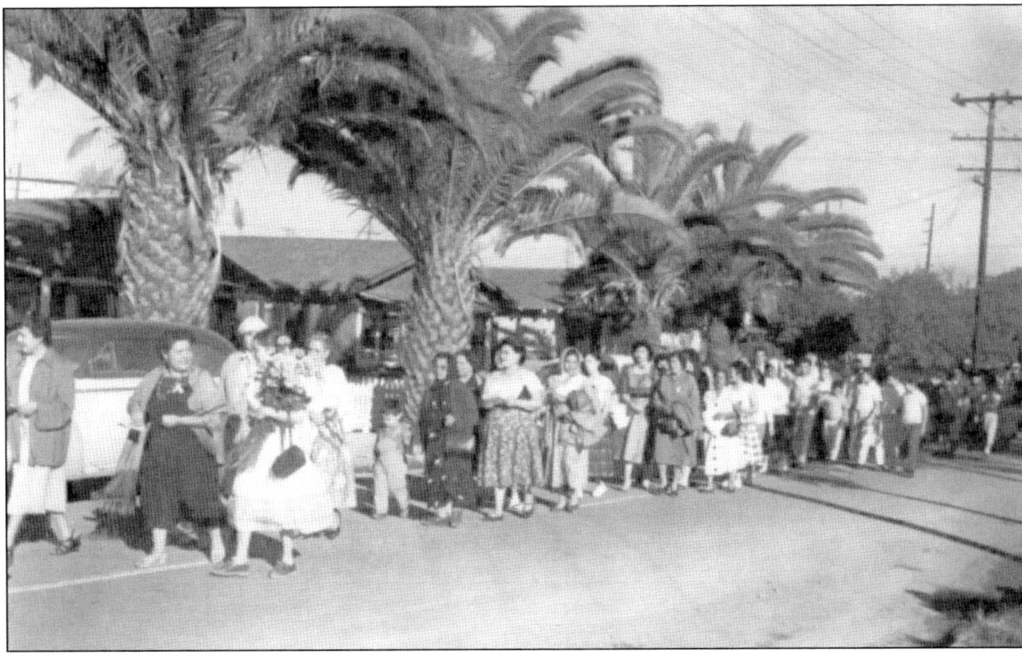

The nuns from St. Joseph's Mission led the procession for Our Lady of Guadalupe in 1955, which is shown in these photographs. The procession began on what is now Van Ness Avenue and traveled to St. Joseph's Mission on Del Amo Boulevard. The children were actively involved in the procession; they would dress in traditional costumes made by their parents. (Virginia Ybarra.)

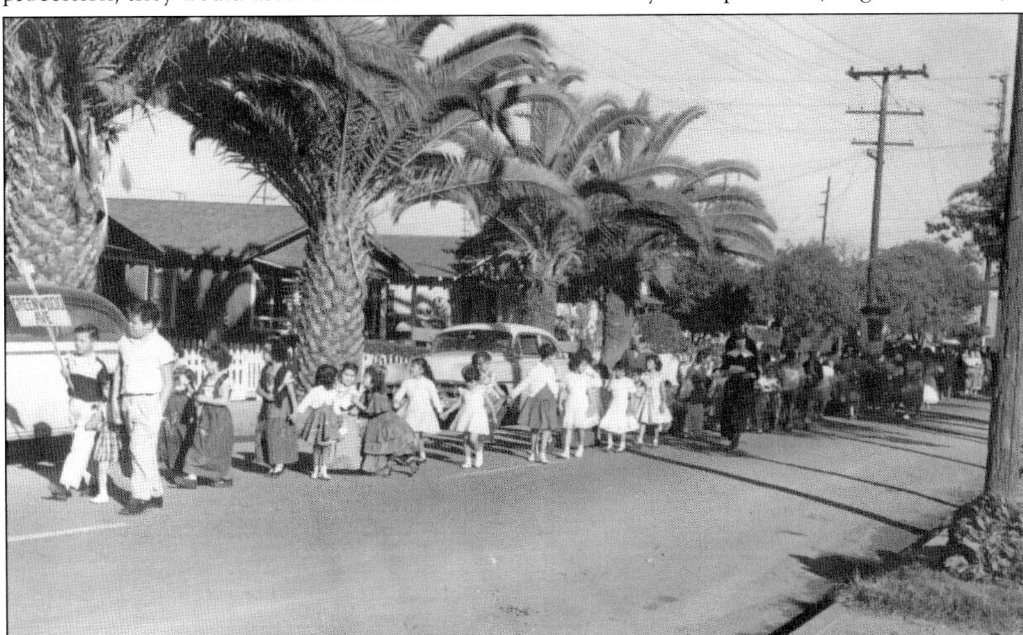

This annual religious event to honor Our Lady of Guadalupe began at 4:00 a.m. with the singing of "Las Mañanitas." Once the procession traveled to St. Joseph's Mission, a Mass was celebrated in honor of the Virgin Mary. The children would place flowers at the feet of the Virgin Mary. (Virginia Ybarra.)

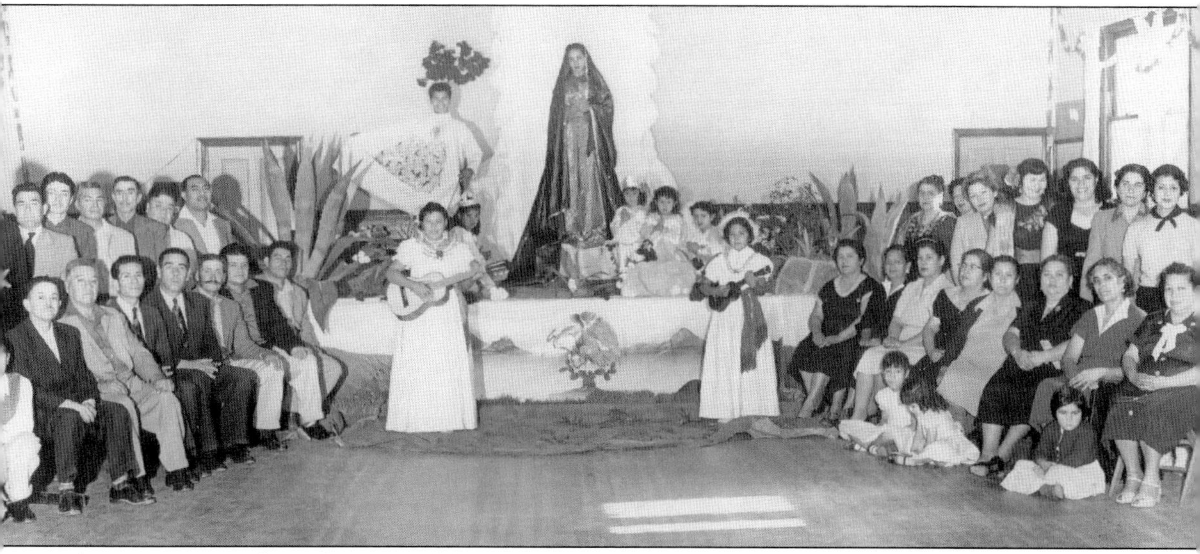

This is a picture of parishioners celebrating the Feast of Virgin de Guadalupe on December 12, 1952. The Feast of Guadalupe is celebrated on the day she appeared to Juan Diego, a Mexican peasant, on the morning of December 12, 1531. She left her imprint on his cloak. This cloak is still on display in the Basilica of the Virgin de Guadalupe in Mexico City. La Rana always celebrated the Feast of Guadalupe. It was one of the most important holidays for the community, because 95 percent of the residents were Catholic; it was—and still is—a means for keeping a proud Mexican heritage alive in the United States. (Virginia Ybarra.)

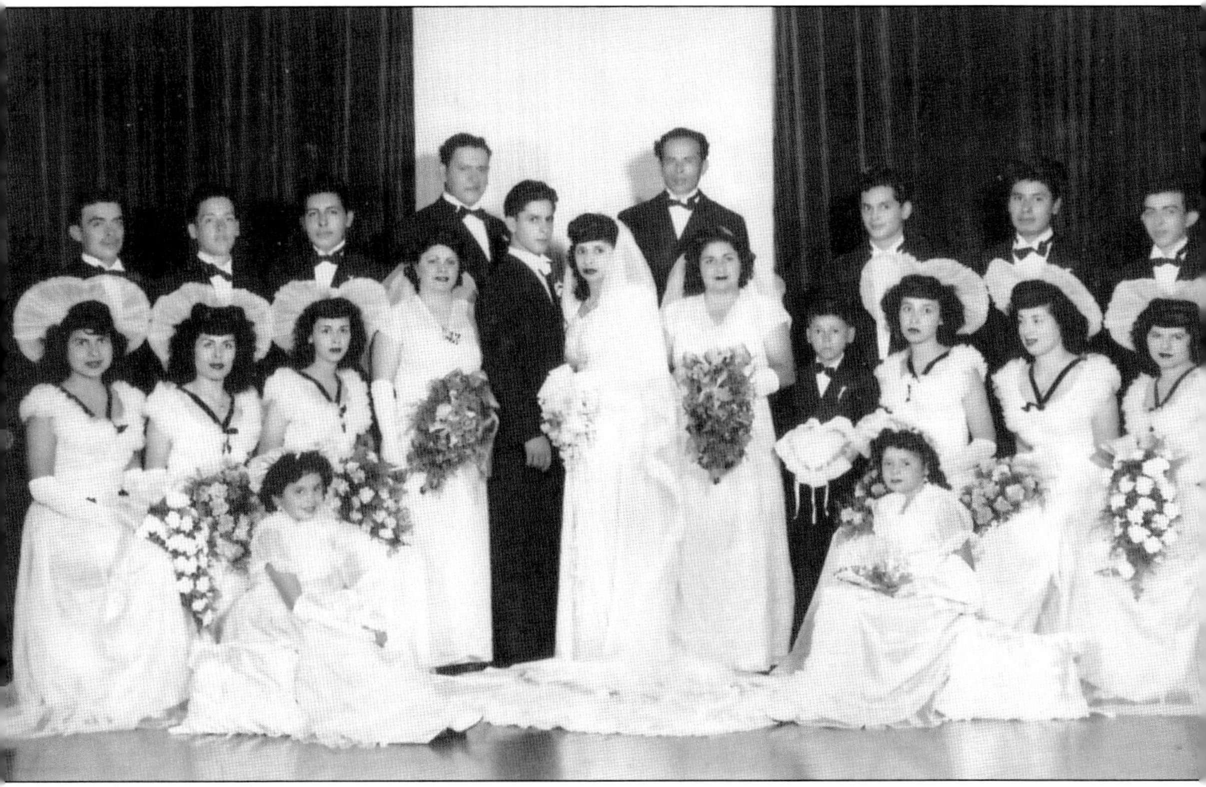

The wedding of Maria Louisa Ordaz and Abelino Gonzales took place on September 19, 1945. Pictured here from left to right are (first row) unidentified, Esther Guzman, unidentified, Lola Lopez, Abelino Gonzales, Maria Louisa Ordaz, Rosa Alvarez, Tony Ordaz, unidentified, Dolores Hernandez, and Mellie Castillo; (second row) Toby Reynaga, Alfonso Ordaz, Ruben Ordaz, Juan (La Baca) Lopez, Leo Alvarez, unidentified, Edmundo Ordaz, and George Camou. The flower girls in front are Carmen (left) and Mellie Grajeda. (Dora Camou.)

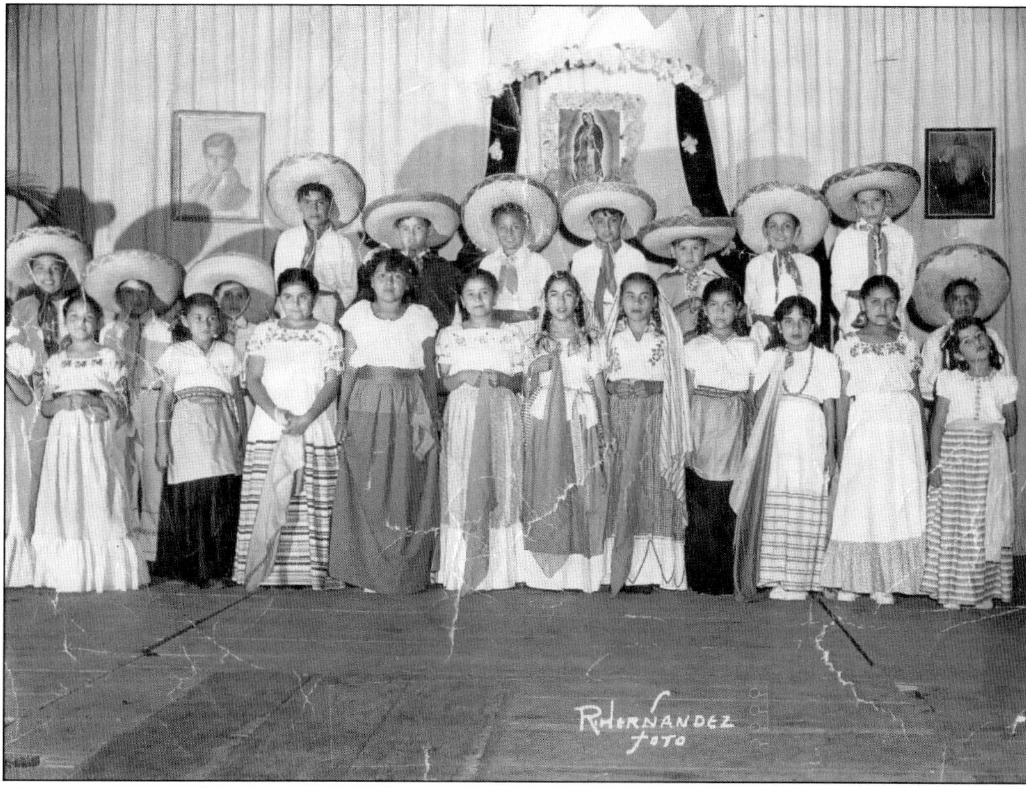

This is a picture of the Feast of the Virgin de Guadalupe celebration in St. Joseph's Mission hall in 1947. The procession of parishioners would start in front of Don Luis and Doña Carmen Ordaz's house. Along with a float, both sides of the street would be decorated with streamers. Mothers would make elaborate native costumes representing the various regions in Mexico where the participants were from. (Connie Molina.)

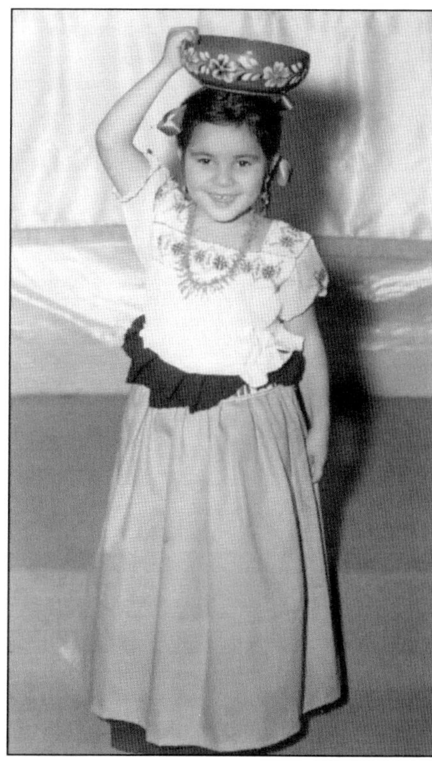

Julia Ybarra was four years old and dressed in traditional costume for the feast day celebration for Guadalupe at St. Joseph's Mission hall in 1955. She is the daughter of Julia and Reyes Ybarra. The costume she is wearing is from the state of Michoacán, Mexico. (Longa Alvarez.)

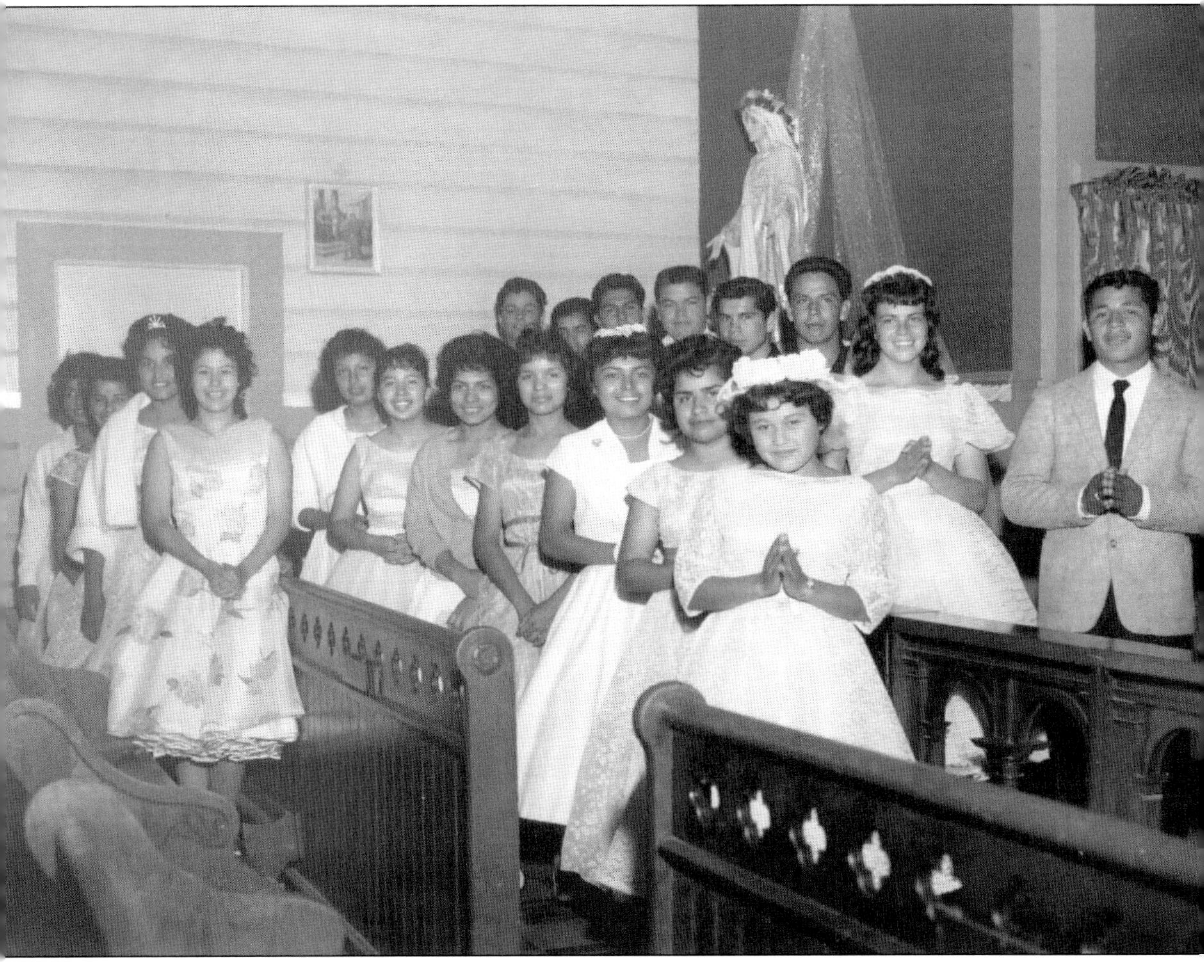

Every year, a group of young women would be selected to participate in the crowning of the Virgin Mary in the church. The nuns would then pick one of the young women to do the actual crowning of the blessed mother during a Mass. Pictured here second from right is Mary Marta Duarte, who was the young woman selected to do the special crowning in 1959. (Maggie Alvera.)

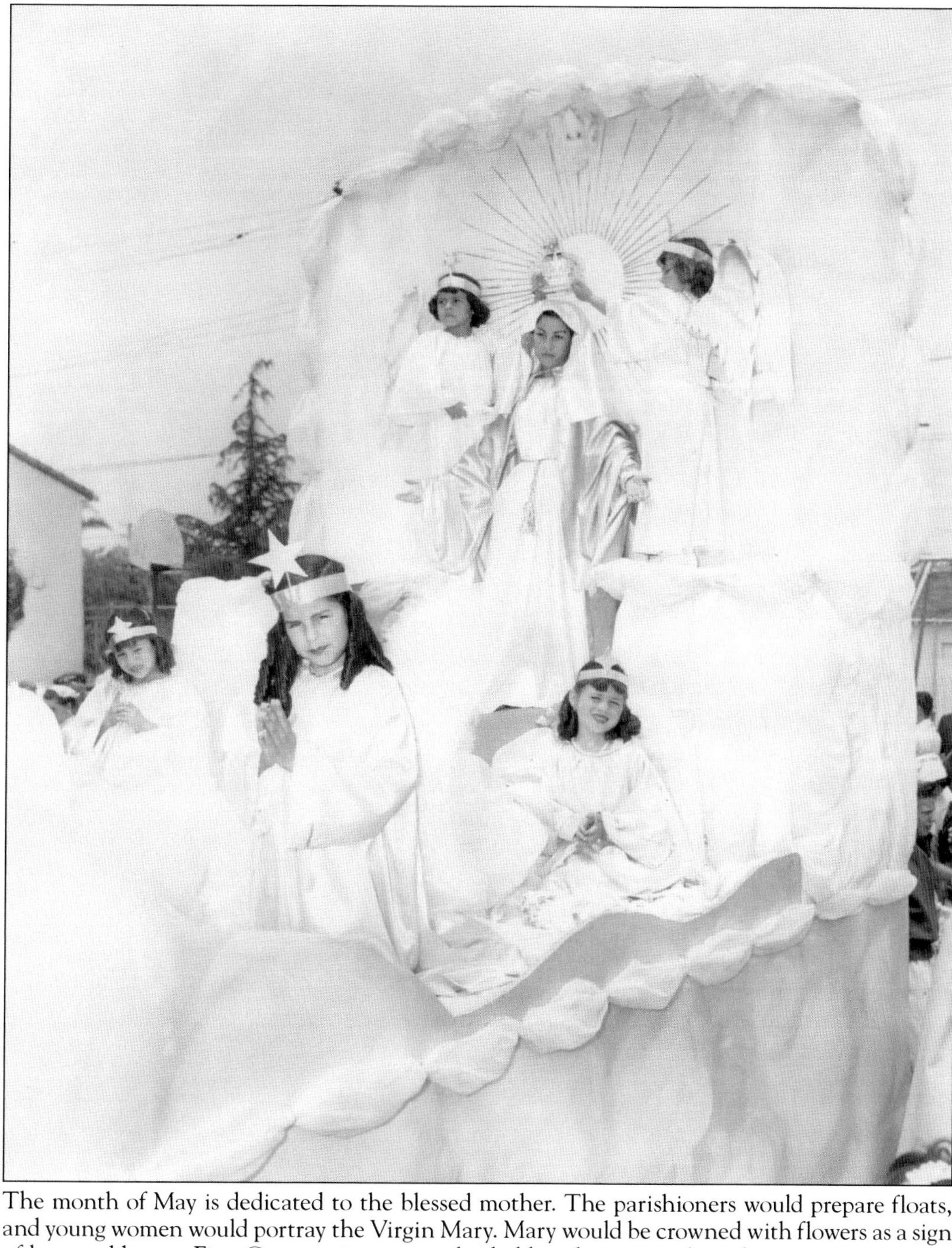

The month of May is dedicated to the blessed mother. The parishioners would prepare floats, and young women would portray the Virgin Mary. Mary would be crowned with flowers as a sign of love and honor. First Communions were also held at this time, when the entire community would come together for various special Masses and celebrations. This is the float that was built in 1954. Mary was portrayed by Connie Solis. The angels on the top are unidentified. The angels on the bottom are, from left to right, unidentified, Alice White, and Laura Jean Solis. (Connie Molina.)

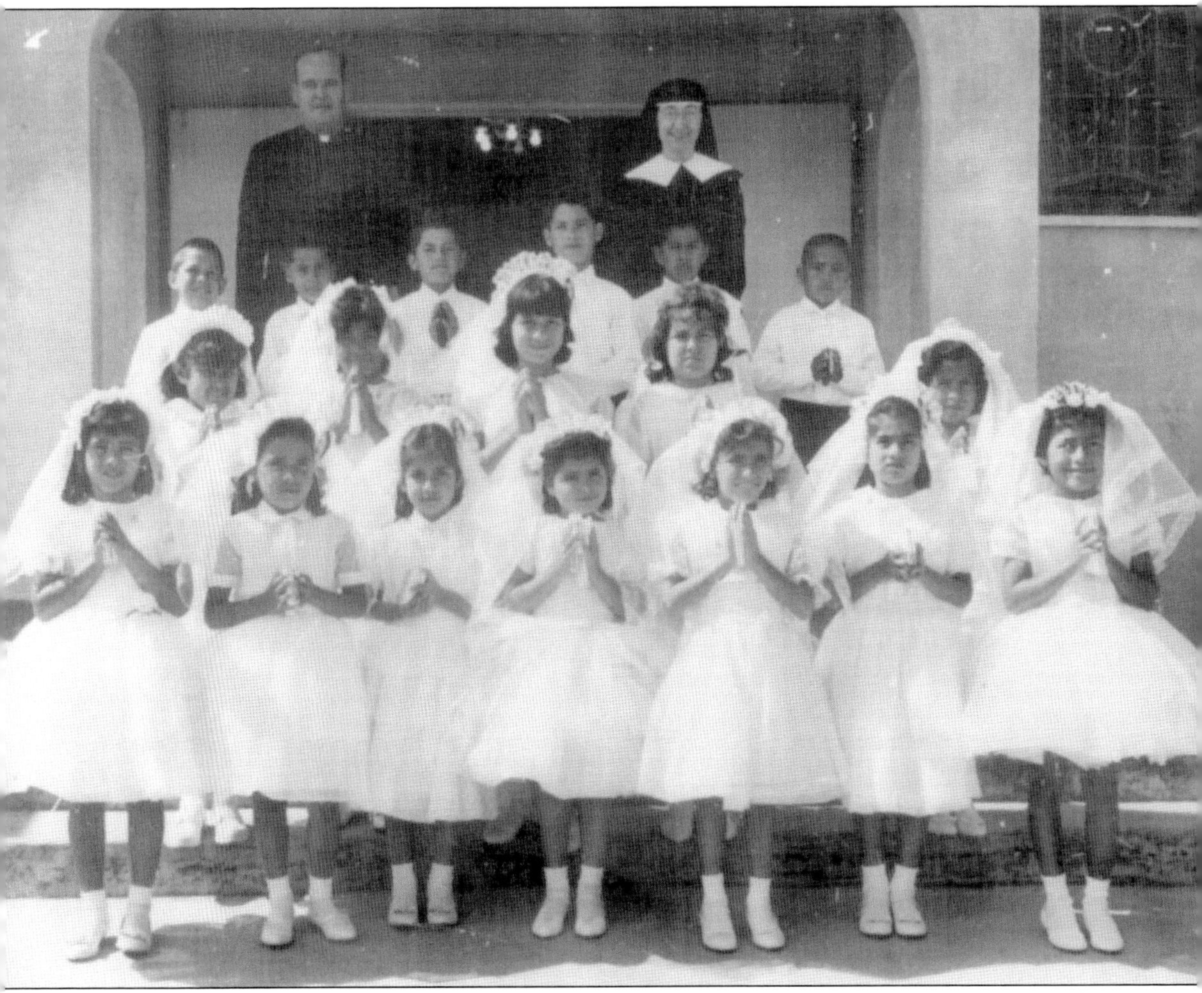

This group of children received their First Communion in 1961. Children learn that the Eucharist is the body of Christ and to gather with family and friends for the celebration of this sacrament. Father Cremins pictured here (top left) was pastor at Nativity Catholic Church in Torrance. By this time, St. Joseph's Mission had become part of Nativity Church. (Alice Duarte Solis.)

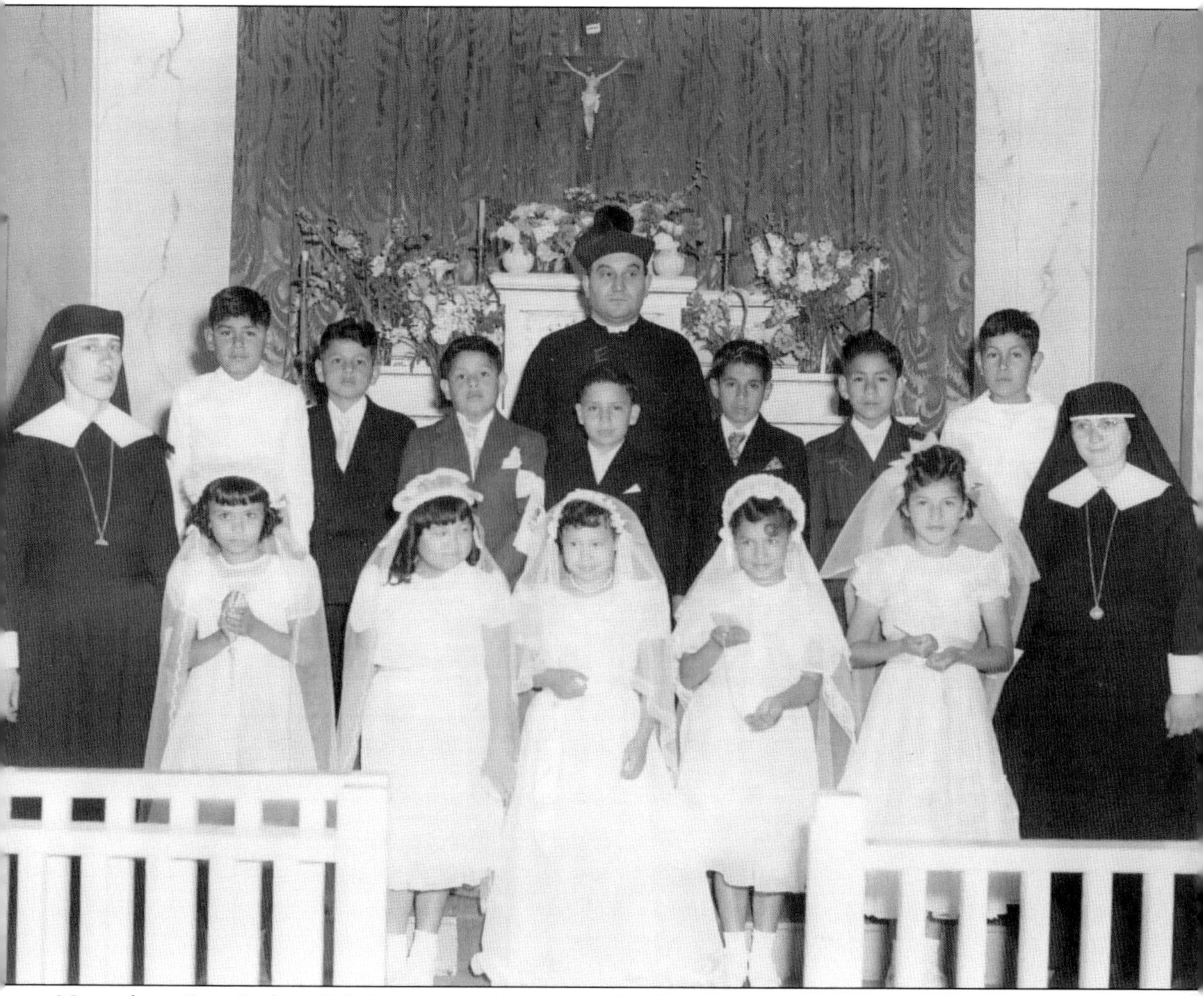

Nuns from San Pedro, California, would come to La Rana to prepare children for their First Communion. On this day in approximately 1947, these children received their First Communion. The names of the nuns and the priest are unknown. The priest was from Our Lady of Guadalupe Church in Hermosa Beach. The children are, from left to right, (first row) all unidentified; (second row) Frances Avila, Esperanza (Peli) Sezate, Lupe Acevedo, unidentified, and Armida Molinar; (third row) unidentified, Manuel Torrez, Elizar Ybarra, Manuel Alvarez, Ralph Solis, and unidentified. (Armida Grajeda.)

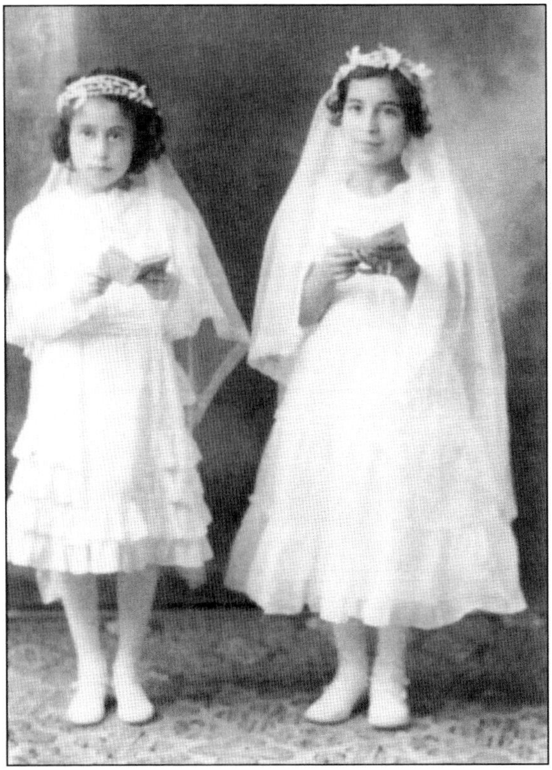

Aurora Torres (left) and Virginia Arellano are dressed for their First Communion ceremony in this c. 1935 photograph. They were part of a group of children receiving their first holy Eucharist during a Mass at St. Joseph's Mission. St. Joseph's had recently reopened after being closed for a time. (Aurora Camou.)

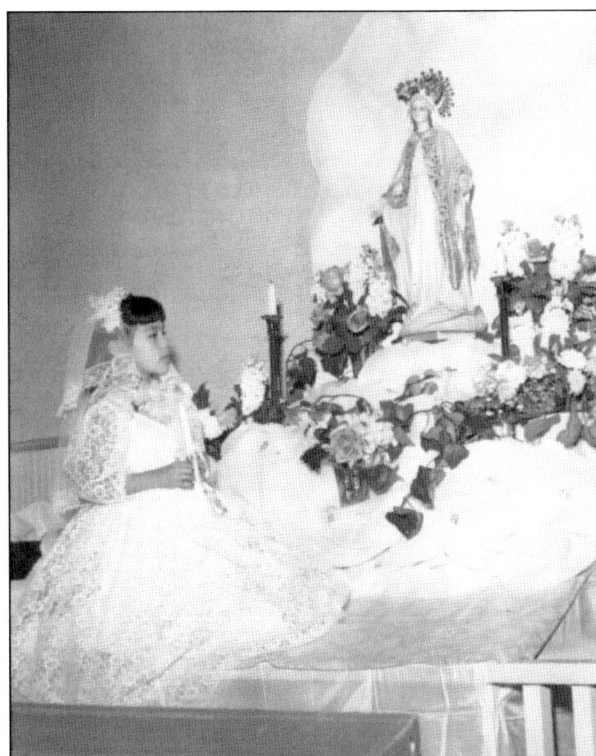

Virginia Solis is offering flowers to the blessed mother during the Mass held on the day she made her First Communion in 1951. After the Mass, when children received their First Communion, the communicants and their families would all gather for a celebratory breakfast in the church hall. (Virginia Ybarra.)

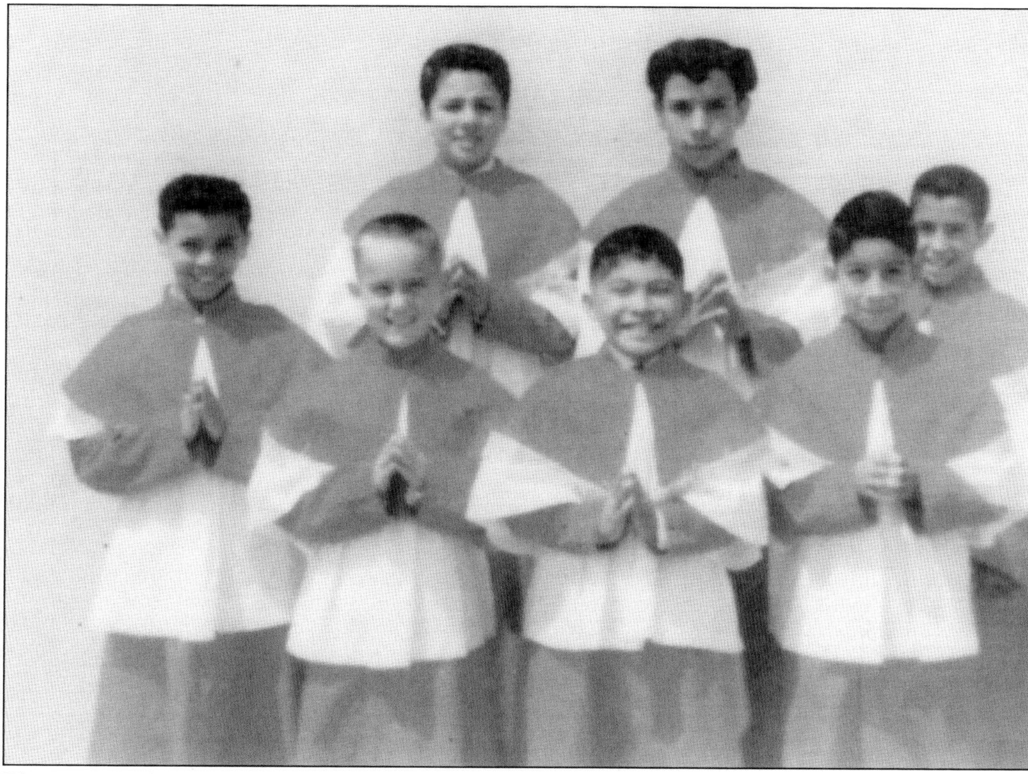

These young boys were commissioned to be altar servers for St. Joseph's Mission in 1954. From left to right are (first row) Gilbert Griego, unidentified, Raymond Vidal, and Peter Hernandez; (second row) Joe Torres, Elizar Ybarra, and unidentified. (Raymond Vidal.)

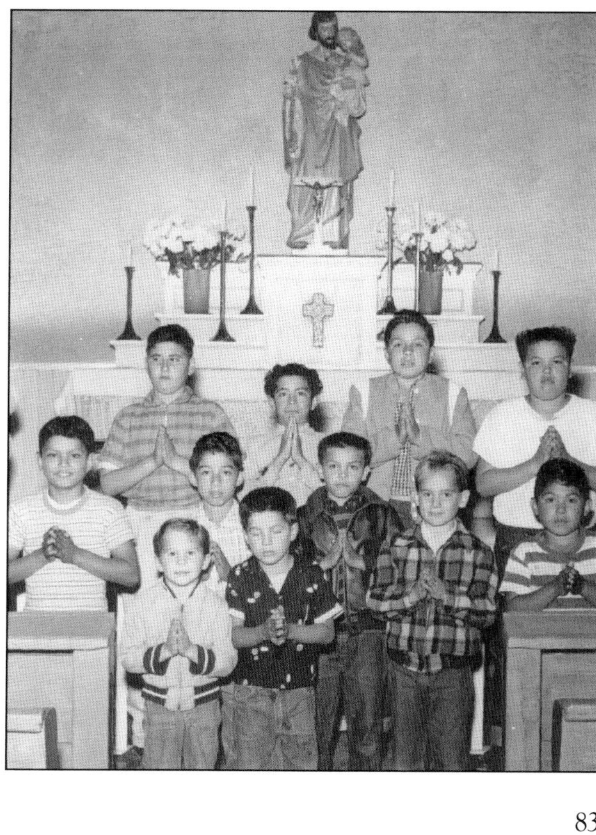

These young boys are either preparing to be altar servers or are already altar boys. From left to right are (first row) Steve Manzanares and David White; (second row) unidentified, Peter Hernandez, Gilbert Griego, Danny Manzanares, and Raymond Vidal; (third row) Manuel Montoya, Rene Ponce, Joe Torres, and Joe Solis. (Raymond Vidal.).

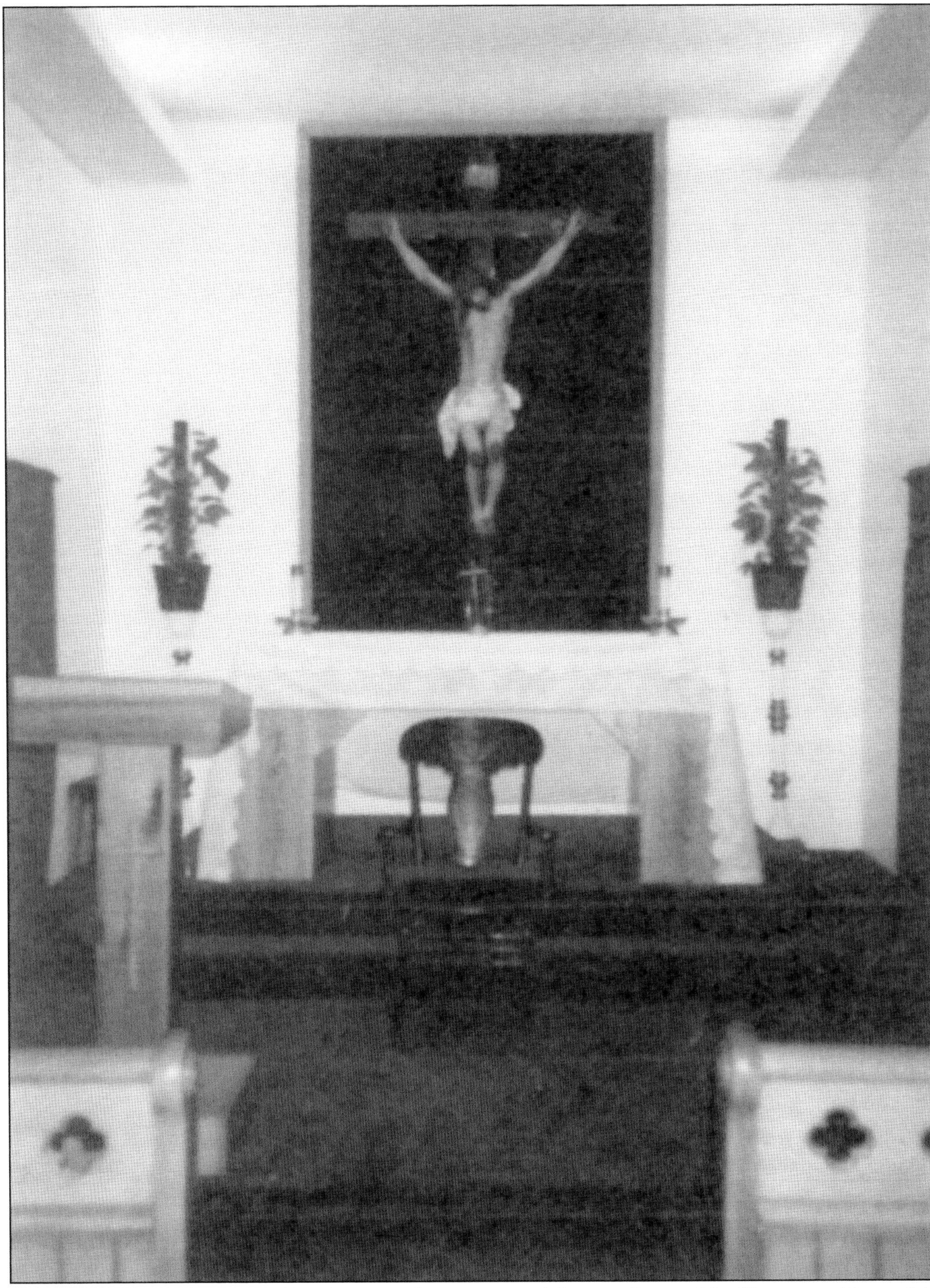

This is the altar of St. Joseph's Mission, where many of the residents of La Rana would worship on Sundays. Many baptisms, First Communions, weddings, funerals, and religious holidays were celebrated in this church. The tabernacle had already been removed in this photograph. The church closed in September 2000. (Dora Camou.)

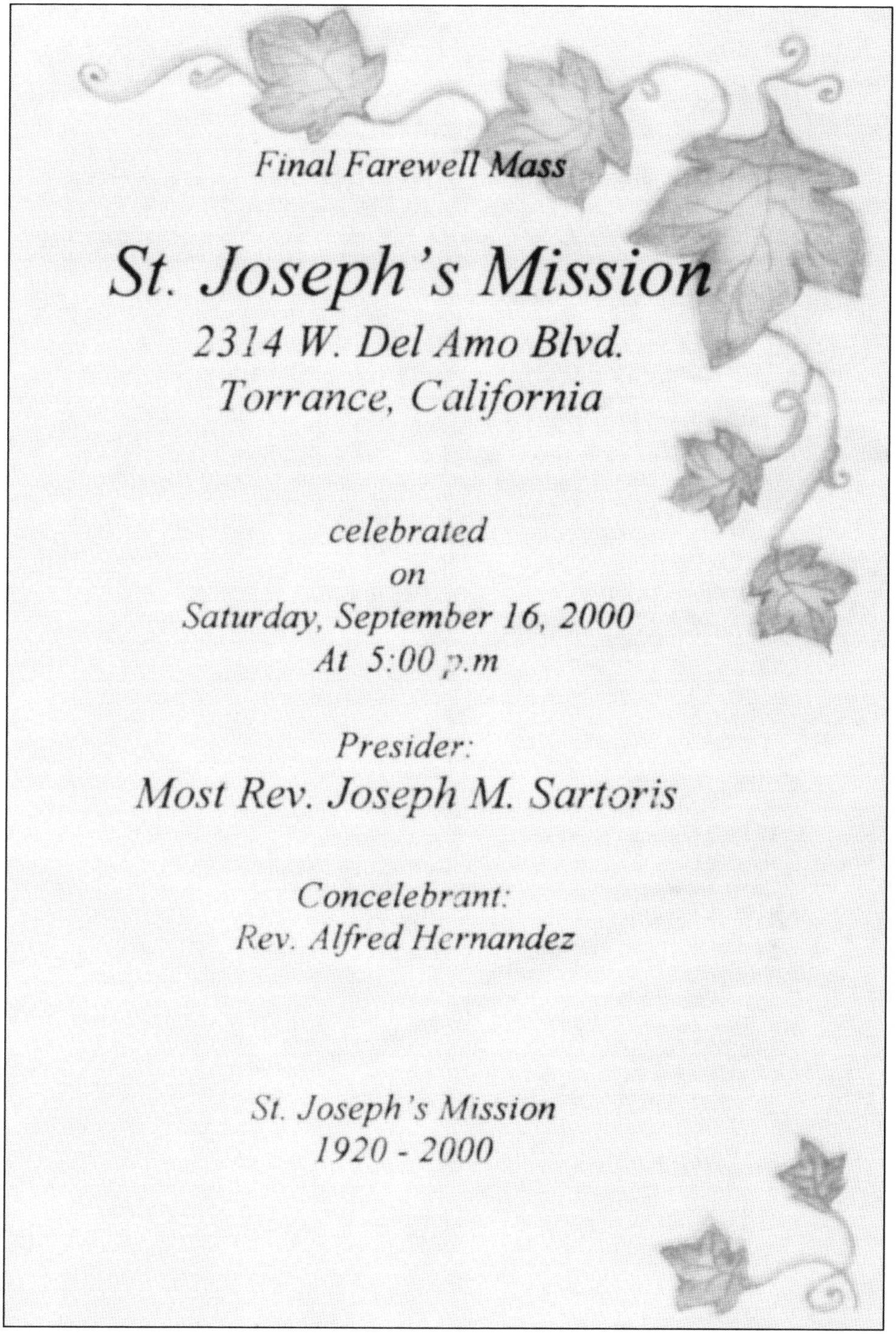
Final Farewell Mass

St. Joseph's Mission
2314 W. Del Amo Blvd.
Torrance, California

celebrated
on
Saturday, September 16, 2000
At 5:00 p.m

Presider:
Most Rev. Joseph M. Sartoris

Concelebrant:
Rev. Alfred Hernandez

St. Joseph's Mission
1920 - 2000

This is the flyer that was circulated for the final farewell Mass for St. Joseph's Mission. St. Joseph's was the foundation for keeping family faith strong and uniting the community. There are many memories of sacraments and celebrations, but one memory that stands out is December 7, 1941. The church bells rang at 2:00 p.m., calling all parishioners to come to the church and pray, since the country was at war. (Dora Camou.)

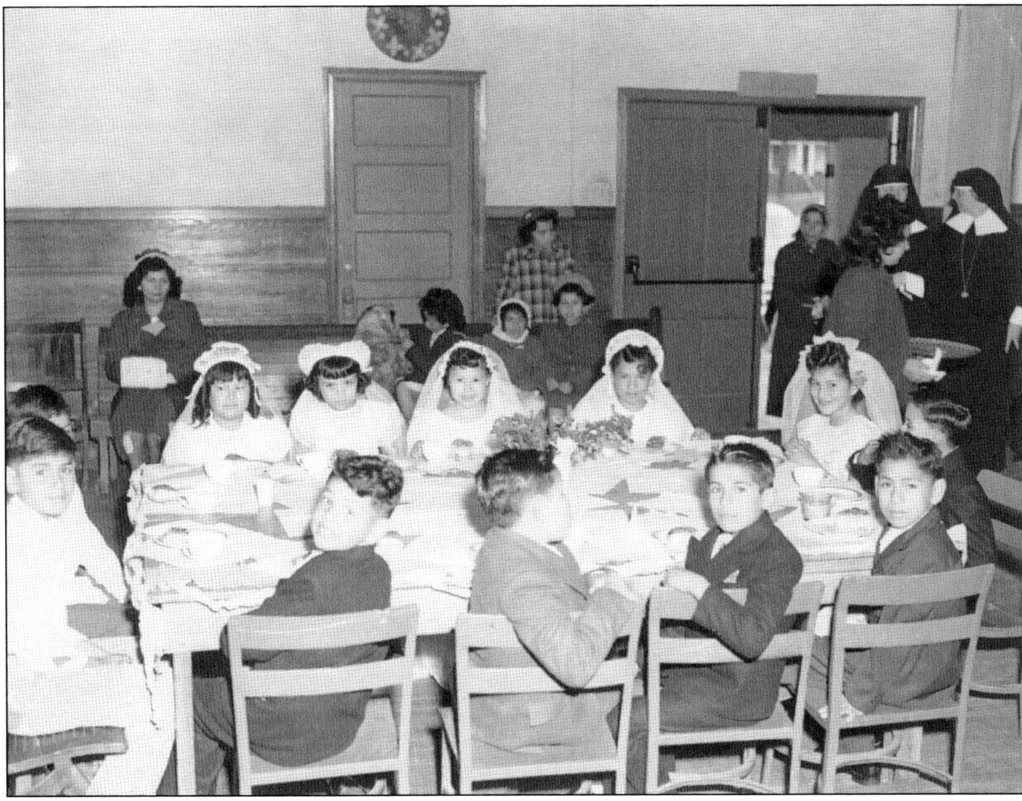

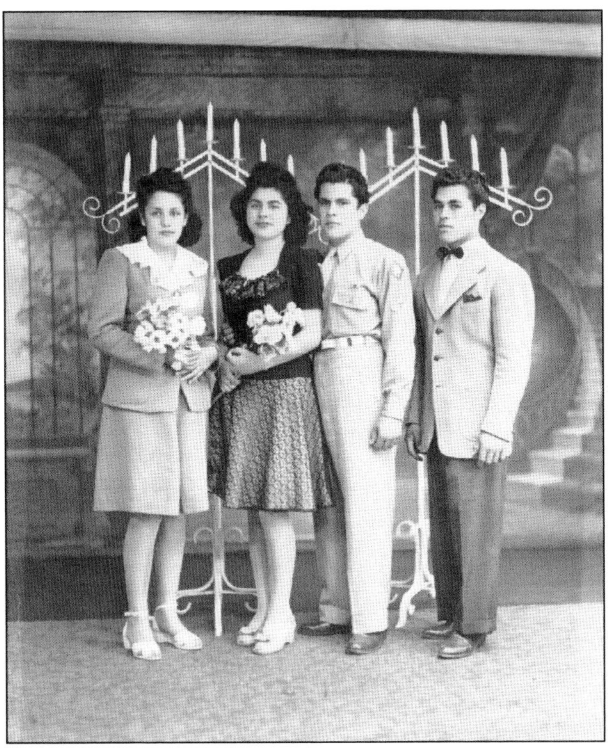

These children are celebrating their First Communion at St. Joseph's Mission in 1949. Pictured at the table are, from left to right, (girls in the back) Esperaza Sezate, Francis Avila, Lupe Acevedo, Judy Torres, and Armida Molinar. The boy on the right is Eleazar Ybarra. The boys at the front are three unidentified, Manuel Alvarez, Ralph Solis Jr., and Eleazar Ybarra. (Armida Grajeda.)

Andy Alvarez and Kate Castillo were married in Los Angeles in 1944. Pictured here are, from left to right, Angie Contreras, Kate Castillo, Andy Alvarez, and Joe Solis. Alvarez was home on leave after serving in Europe during World War II. Kate is the daughter of Eloisa Castillo. (Beatrice Castillo.)

Helen Castillo and Tony Armeda were married in Los Angeles in 1944. Armeda was born in Douglas, Arizona. Helen is the daughter of Eloisa Castillo and sister to Kate, Henry, Leo, Beatrice, Phillip, and Boni Castillo. Helen attended Torrance schools and currently lives with family in Oregon. (Beatrice Castillo.)

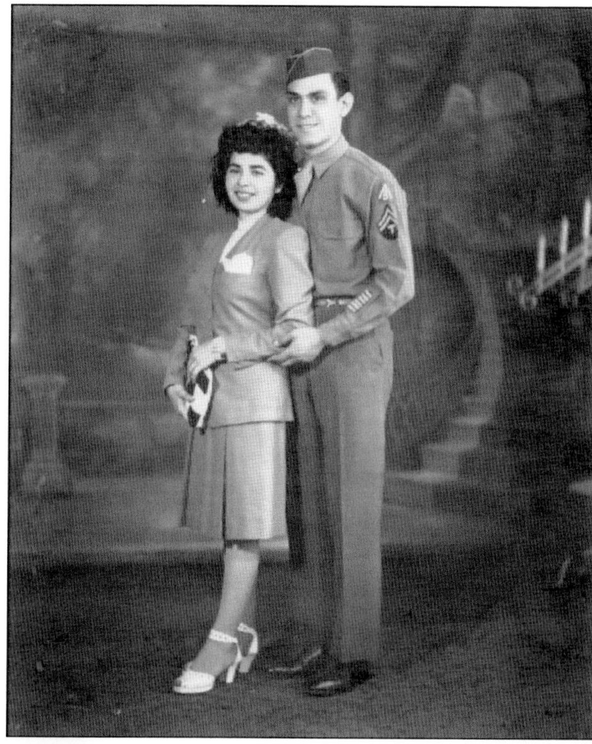

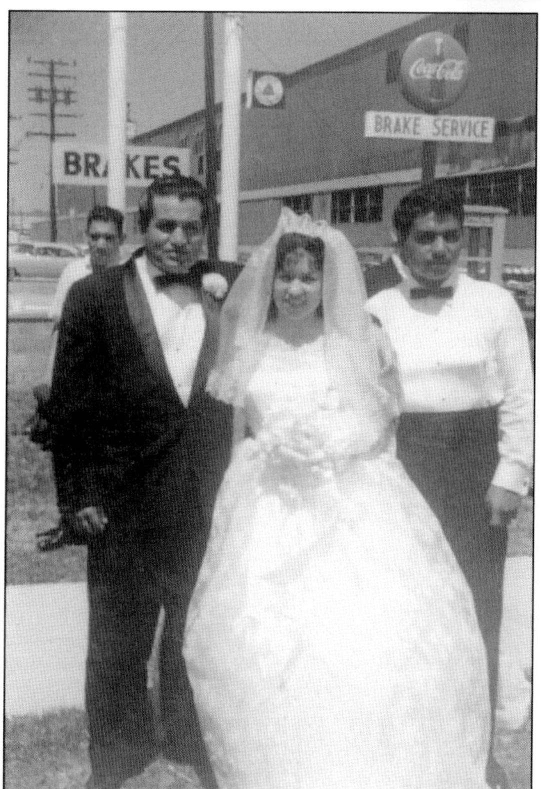

Judy Torres celebrated her wedding to Ignacio Ybarra in July 1961. They were married at Nativity Catholic Church in Torrance. John Reyes (left) gave her away at her wedding, and her younger brother Tony is at right. This picture shows them entering the Moose lodge for the wedding reception. (Judy Ybarra.)

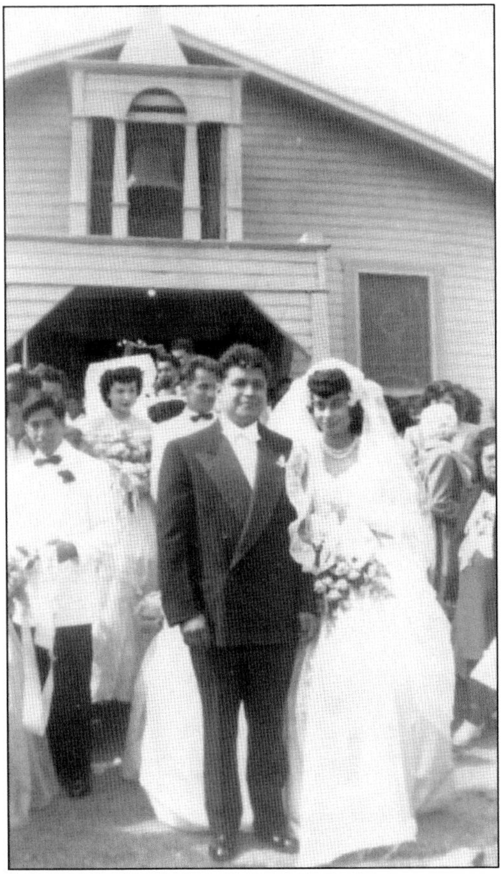

Margaret and Tony Razo are pictured on their wedding day in front of St. Joseph's Mission in 1949. Among those in the background are Tony Valdez, Olga Camou, and Ralph Eredia. St. Joseph's was later replaced by a public park. (Virginia Camou.)

This float honored Our Lady of Guadalupe in the 1950s. Children from La Rana would portray the apparition. Here, the Virgin Mary is portrayed by Carmen Valdivia. The man at her feet is Ignacio Ybarra. One man at the front of the float is Mario Torres, and the other is unidentified. (Virginia Ybarra.)

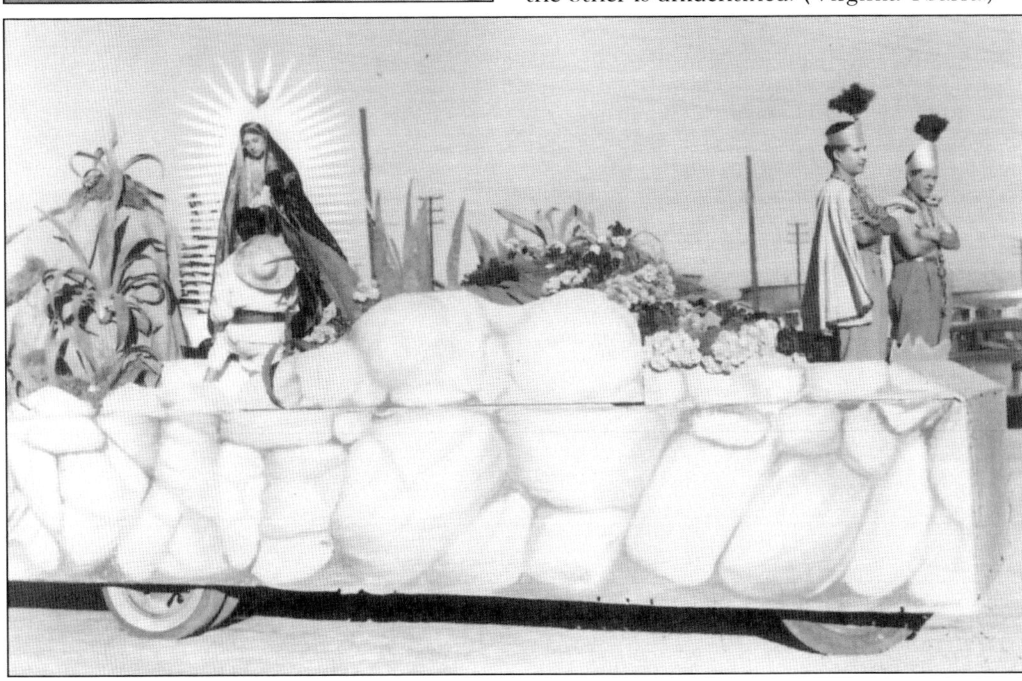

Four

Military

In the late 1930s and early 1940s, most of the families in La Rana were large, with many children. In the evening, mothers and fathers would sit outside on their porches and watch their children playing in the street. The Castillo and Alvarez boys would sit outside at night and play guitars and sing, entertaining the entire neighborhood. La Rana men who fought in the Mexican Revolution would sit and reminisce about their experiences in the war. They thanked God that they found a safe place in the United States for their families. Radio was another means of entertainment. Music and news about other cities could be heard across the community of La Rana. On December 7, 1941, the music was interrupted and Pres. Franklin D. Roosevelt announced that the country was at war. The street became very quiet that night.

Many of the young men were happy to take the call when they were asked to serve their country. Over time, La Rana's young men were called to fight in World War II, the Korean War, and the Vietnam War. Boys who were 18 and older were drafted. Even men as old as 30 were taken from the neighborhood to fight in World War II. When the war ended, many men happily came home. Sadly, several men lost their lives and did not get the chance to return home. The fallen soldiers include Louis Alvarez, Dario Chavez, Nestor Flores, and Renaldo Verdugo in World War II and Miguel Duarte and George Escobar in Korea.

In the 1960s, many young men of La Rana fought valiantly in the Vietnam War; some were honored with Purple Hearts, and others received recognition—thankfully, they were all able to return home to their families.

Below, we honor those who valiantly served this country in the US military. Unfortunately, there were no pictures or detailed information available about these men.

Manuel Alvarez Sr.
Angel Arellano
Gilbert Atensio
Joe Ayalla
Peter Ayalla
Joe Baca
Jason Castillo
Leo Castillo
Gilbert Cisneros
Joe Escobar
Tony Escobar
Abelino Gonzales
Salvador Gonzales
Tommy Grande
James Griego
Joe Griego
Manuel Gutierrez
Arthur Lucero
Louie Martinez
Francisco Ordaz
Ralph Ornelas
Victor Quiñones
Gilbert Rojas
Joe Solis
Robert Solis
Joe Torres
Manuel Torres
Tommy Torres
Charlie Villegas
Albert White
Charlie White
Henry White
Mike Zamora

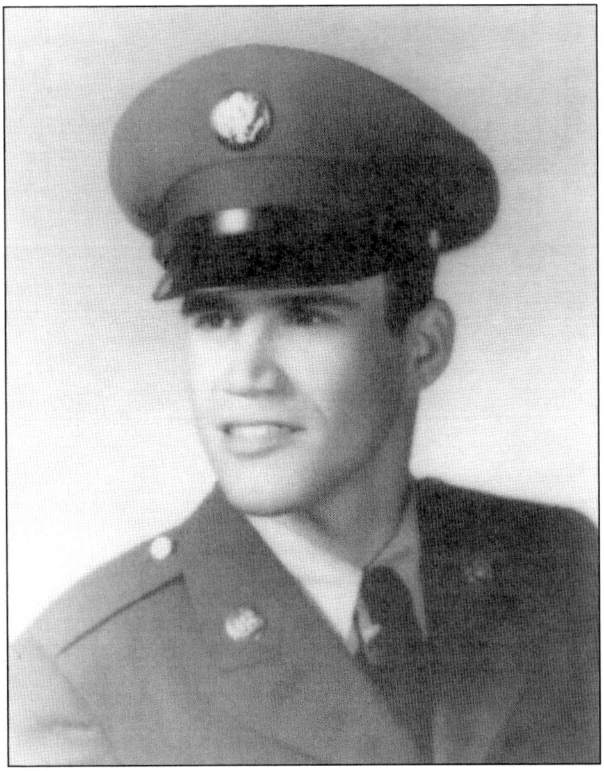

Five Acosta brothers from La Rana served in the military. Angel Acosta was born in Anaheim, California, in 1933. He attended Torrance schools. Angel and his family moved to La Rana in 1943, and he served in the US Army from 1958 to 1960. Angel and his wife have five children. He retired from L.A. Harbor General Hospital after 28 years. He is the son of Eloisa and Paulo Acosta. (Angel Acosta.)

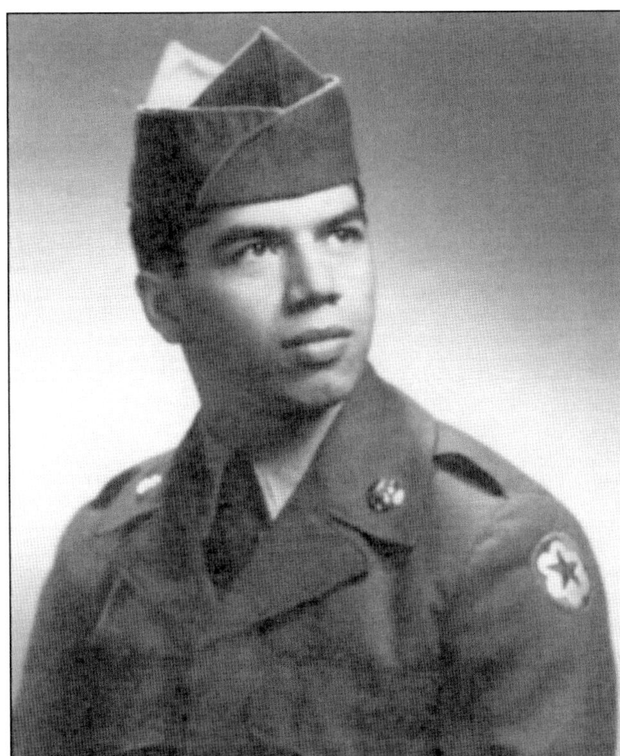

Aurelio Acosta was born in Anaheim in 1935. He and his family came to La Rana in 1943. Aurelio attended Torrance schools. Unfortunately, no information on his military service was available. He is the son of Eloisa and Paulo Acosta. (Angel Acosta.)

Carlos Acosta was born in Anaheim in 1939. He graduated from Torrance High School in 1958 and joined the US Navy, serving in the Vietnam War. He was employed by the Department of Water and Power for 34 years and is the father of three sons. He is the son of Eloisa and Paulo Acosta. (Carlos Acosta.)

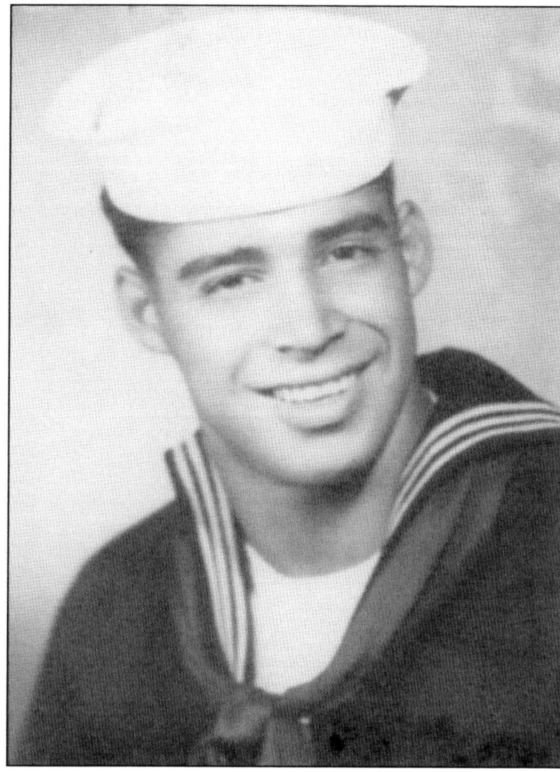

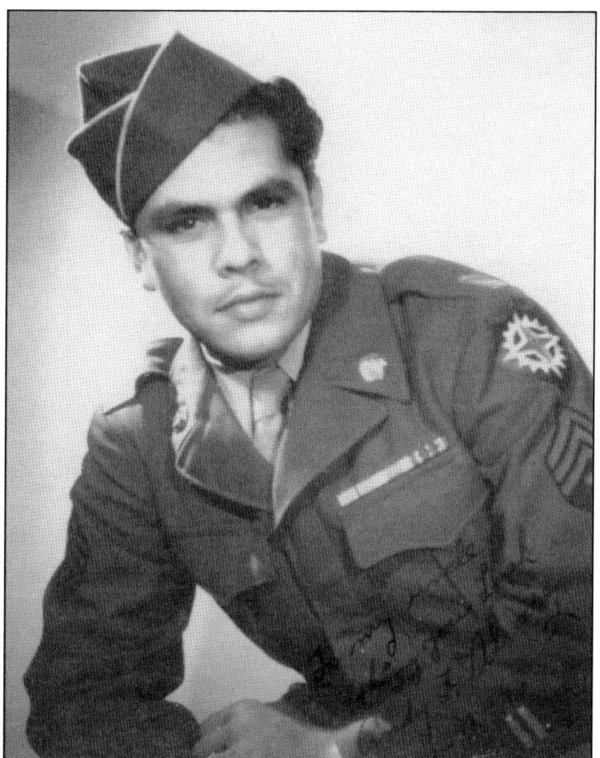

Andres (Andy) Fernandez Alvarez was born in Huntington Beach in 1921. He was the son of Andres and Agapita Alvarez. He served in the US Army during World War II in England, France, Belgium, Holland, and Germany. He was hospitalized with frostbite for a period of time. Andy was involved in the recovery of Nuremberg's Palace of Justice. He was awarded the Purple Heart and the Bronze Star. (Longa Alvarez.)

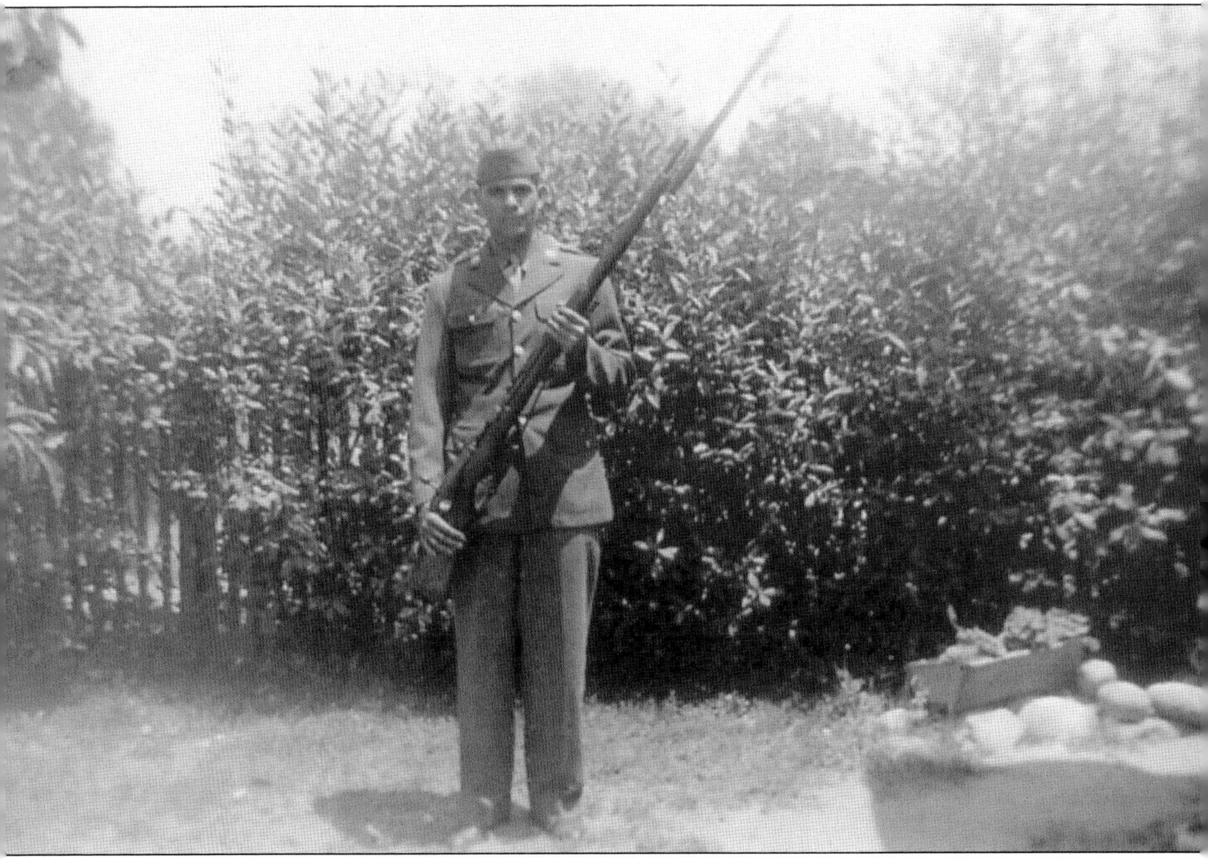

Jesus Alvarez was born in Purépero, Michoacán, Mexico, in 1918. He came to the United States in 1919 with his family, and attended Torrance schools. In 1943, he was drafted into the US Army and served in Greece. He became a US citizen while serving in the military. Jesus is the son of Agapita and Andres Alvarez. (Longa Alvarez.)

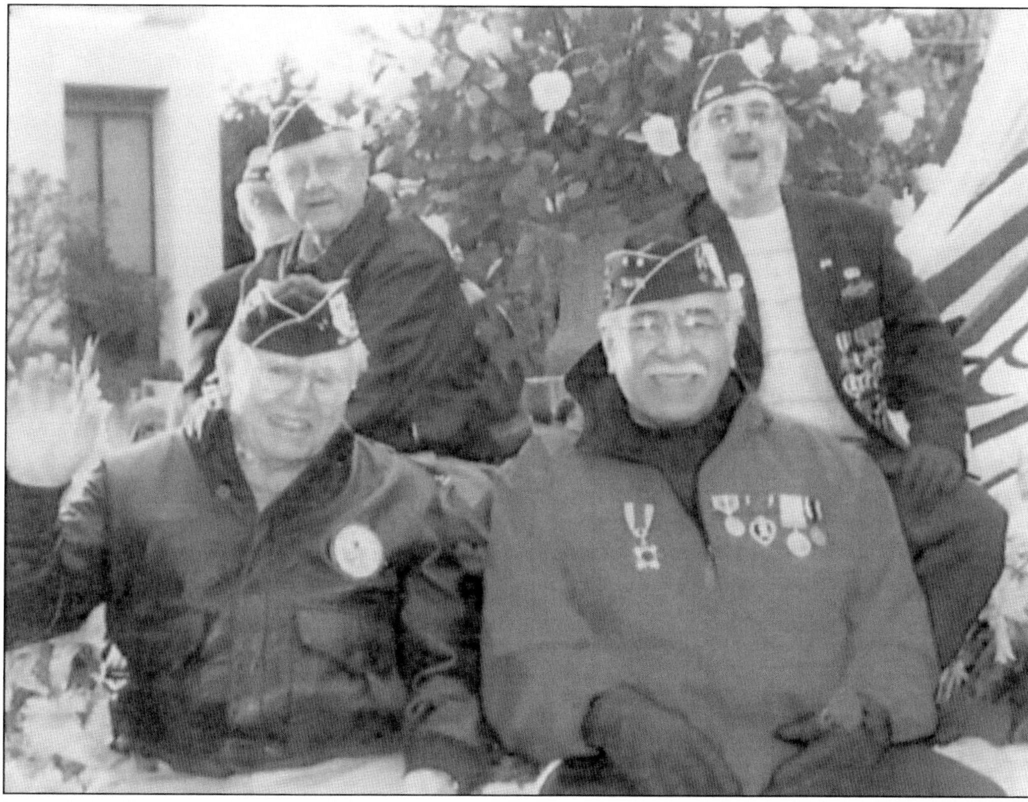

Daniel Arellano was born on July 19, 1931. A private first class in the US Army, Arellano was held as a prisoner of war during the Korean War. He was captured on December 2, 1950, and held until August 17, 1953. After his return from the war, the *Torrance Herald* interviewed him: "We were 20 miles behind communist lines trying to get back to our outfit when we were captured. I had it my mind that I would get back, I never doubted for a moment. A lot of guys gave up hope." This and the grace of God is the explanation Daniel gave for his survival. He was given the Prisoner of War Medal for action during the Korean War. Arellano is pictured above (bottom right) years later with other veterans on a float at a local community parade. He was the son of Josephina and Angel Arellano. (Both, Dora Camou.)

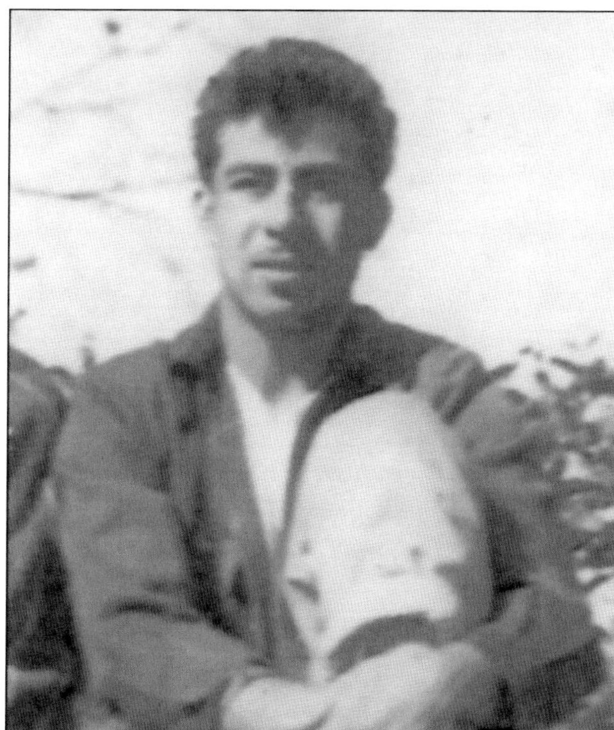

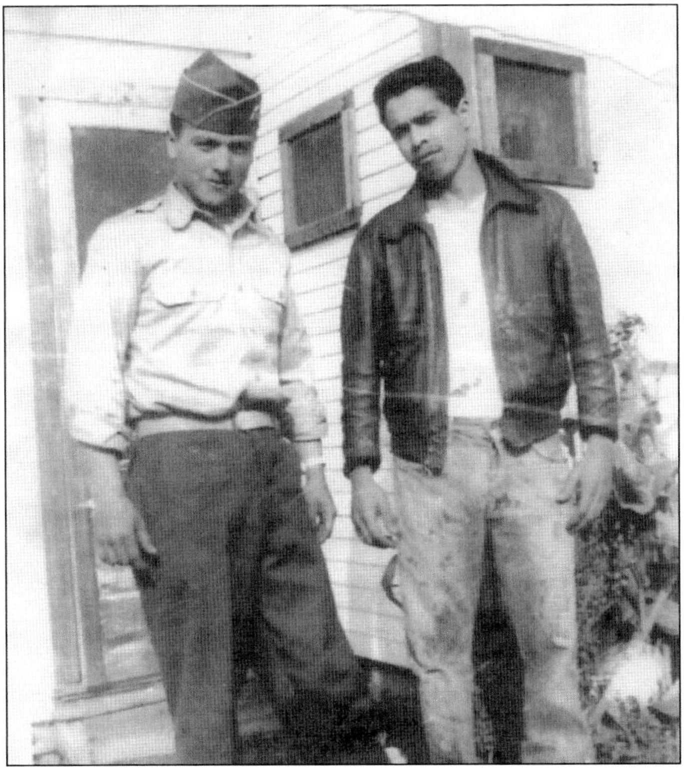

Arnulfo Vernon Banda was born in 1935. He attended Torrance schools. He joined the US Army in October 1953 and served in the Korean War. When Banda returned from service, he was employed by the City of Torrance. He was the son of Santiago and Petra Banda. (Debra Banda.)

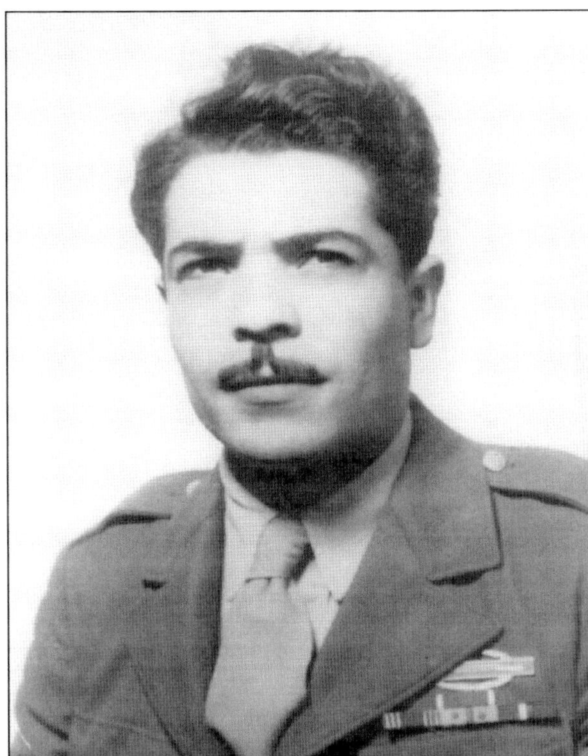

Gabino Banda was born in Zacatecas, Mexico, and came to La Rana in the early 1920s. He attended Torrance schools and served in the US Army during World War II in the Philippines and the Marianas Islands from 1942 to 1945. While in the Philippines, he was missing in action for a time and was later awarded the Purple Heart. He was the son of Santiago and Petra Banda. (Banda Family.)

Gilbert (Beto) Bernal was born in Torrance and graduated from Torrance High School. He was an Eagle Scout, which is the highest rank of the Boy Scouts of America. He began his military career in the US Army in 2003 and is currently a master sergeant. Bernal has served in Turkey, Greece, South Korea, and Japan. He is the son of Edward and Sally Bernal. (Sally Bernal.)

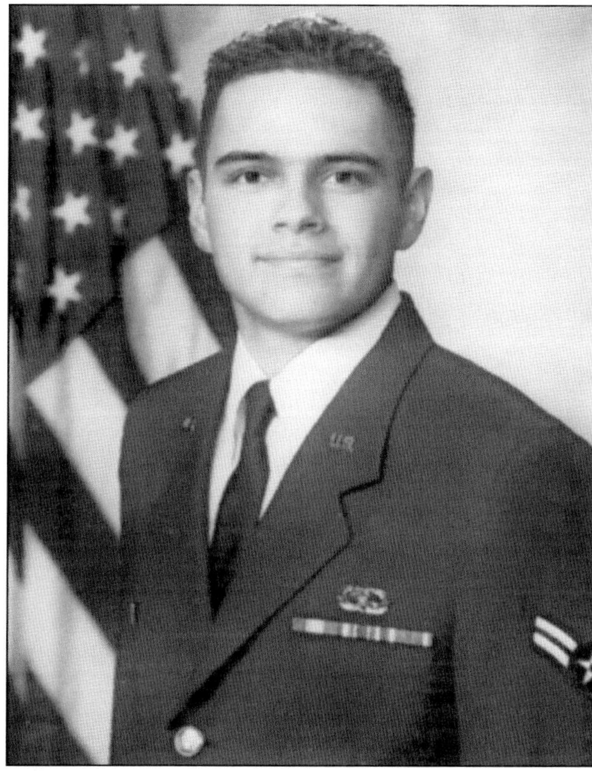

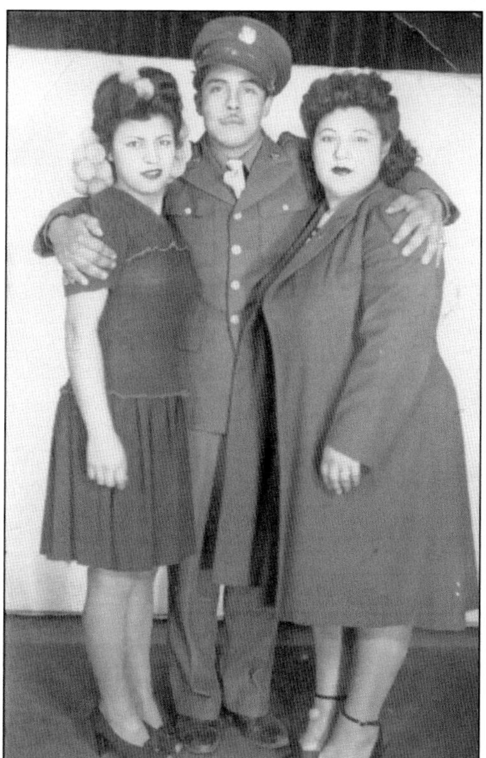

Trino Banda was born in Zacatecas, Mexico, in 1923 and came to La Rana shortly after his birth. He served in the US Army during World War II in Saipan and the Marianas Islands from 1942 to 1945. He served on bombers and took part in air strikes in Japan. He received the Purple Heart. He was the son of Santiago and Petra Banda. He is pictured here with Porfiria Banda (left), and Jenny Ortega. (Albert Banda.)

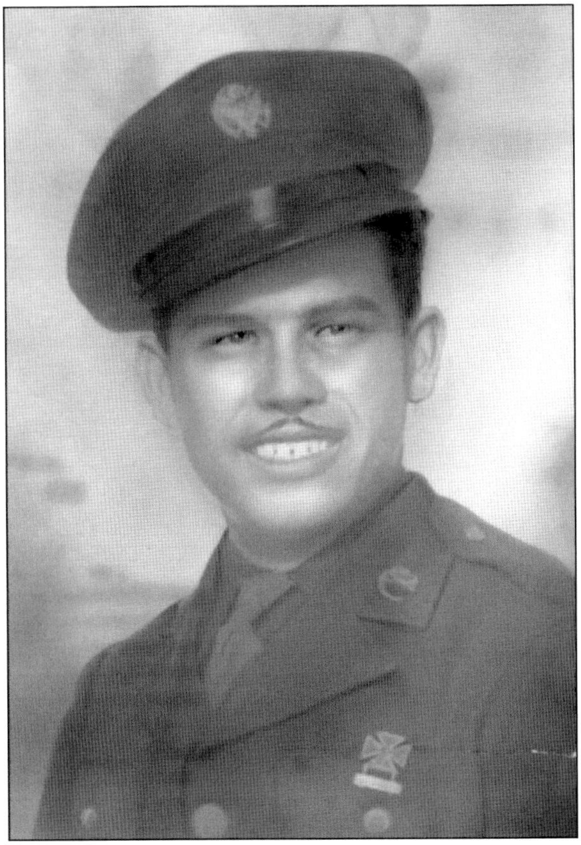

Clemente Camou was born in Torrance in 1926. He was drafted from Torrance High School in 1944. He became a staff sergeant in the US Army and served in the Philippines. After the military, Clemente worked for Torrance Laundry as a truck driver. He married Dora Arellano, and they had three children. He is the son of Cuca and Enrique Camou. (Dora Camou.)

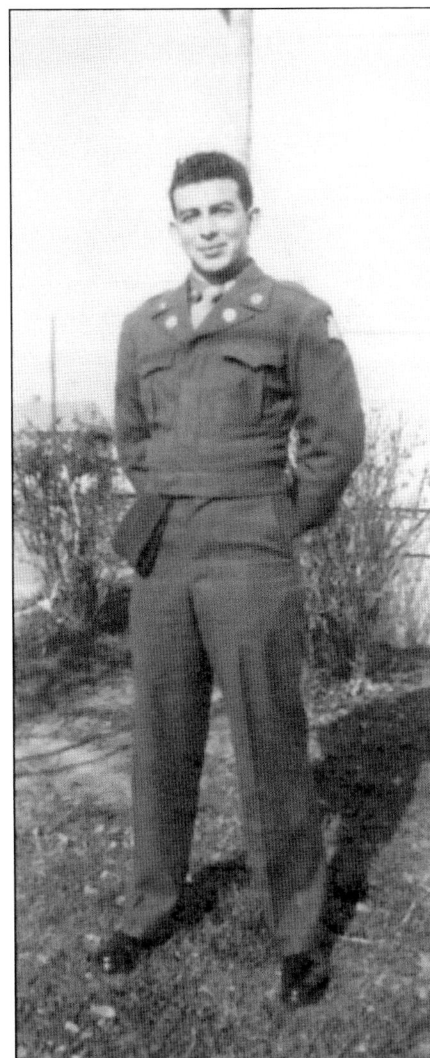

George Camou was born on November 17, 1928. He attended Torrance schools. He joined the US Army in 1947 and was sent to Fort Worth in Livington, Kansas. He joined the service with his friend Armando Guzman thinking they would not be accepted; to their surprise, they were. Camou went to Kansas, and Guzman went to Germany. He is the son of Cuca and Enrique Camou. (George Camou.)

Hank Camou was born in 1921 and graduated from Torrance High School in 1942. He was one of the first groups of men from Torrance to be drafted into the US Army at the beginning of World War II. He was a staff sergeant and was assigned to chemical warfare, serving in Belgium and France. He was the son of Cuca and Enrique Camou. (Virginia Camou.)

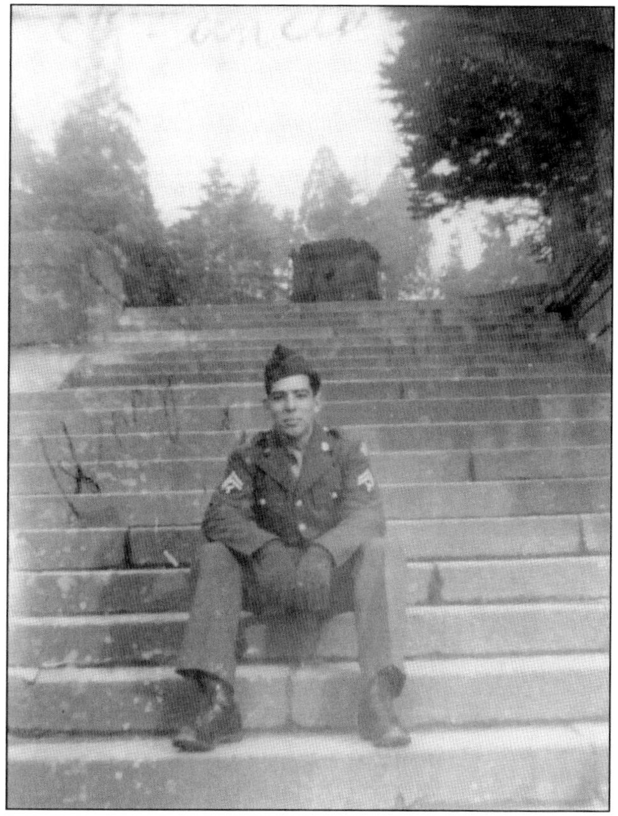

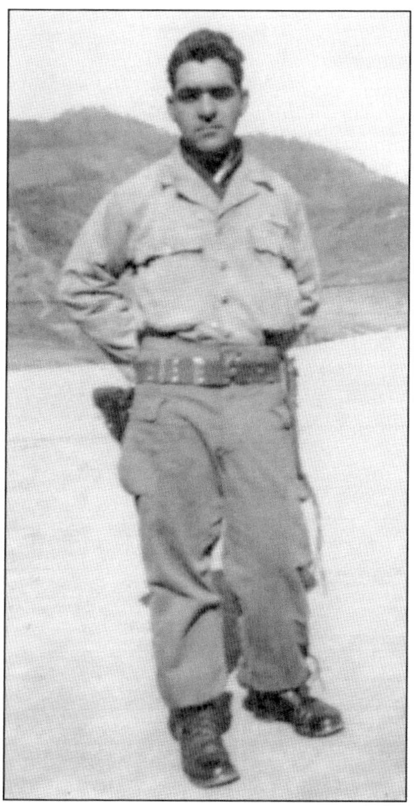

Henry (Chato) Castillo was born in Richmond, California, in 1927. He served in the US Army from 1952 to 1953. His brother Leo also served in Korea. After serving in the military, Henry was employed at U.S. Steel. He was the son of Eloisa Castillo. (Carmen Estolano Castillo.)

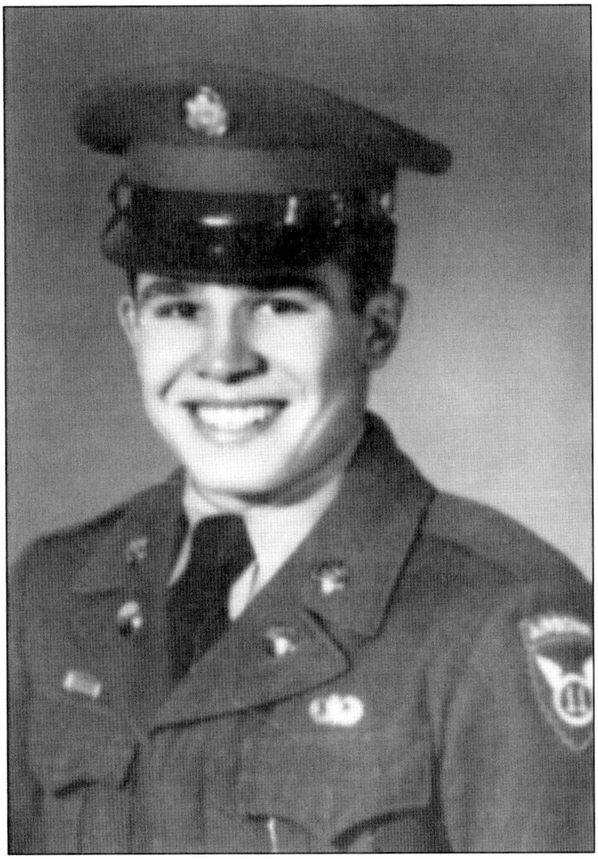

Henry (Carrots) Escobar and his family came to La Rana from Arizona in 1929. He attended Torrance schools and later moved to Redondo Beach. He served in Korea from 1948 to 1952 and is the son of Lupe and Herman Escobar. (Henry Escobar.)

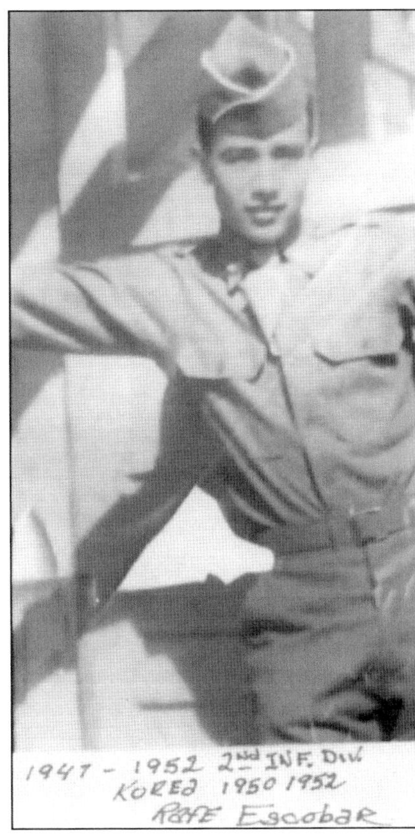

Rafael "Ralf" Escobar served in the US Army 2nd Infantry Division. He entered the military in 1947 and served in Korea from 1950 to 1952. He was the son of Sebastiana and Jesus Escobar. (Lucy Villegas.)

Apolinar Espinosa was born in Colton, California, in 1926. He and his family came to La Rana in the early 1930s. He attended Torrance High School. He served in the US Army from 1944 to 1945 as a gunner. He was later employed at U.S. Steel. He was the son of Chavela and Apolinar Espinosa. (Diana Espinosa.)

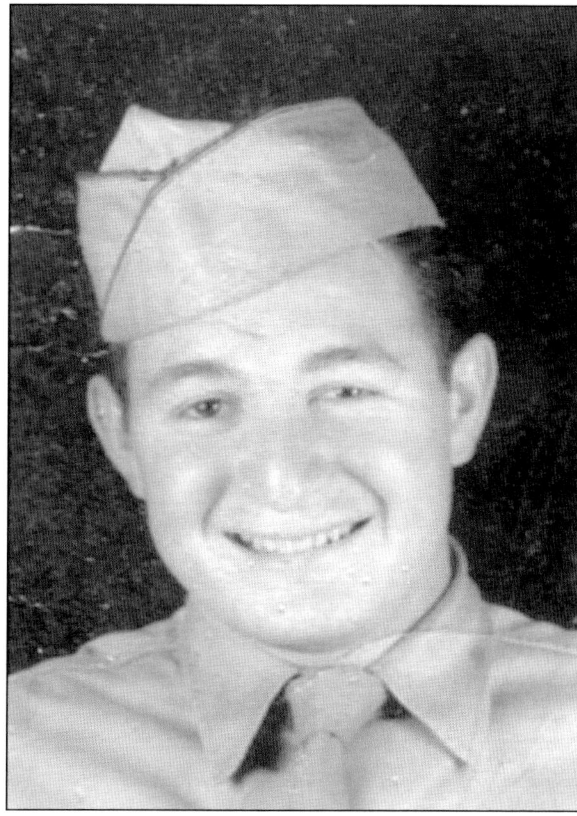

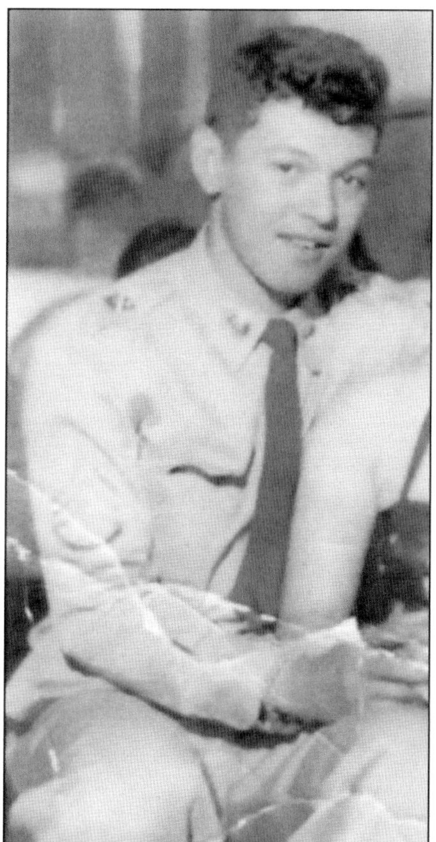

Rafael Estelano was born in Los Angeles in 1931. He and his family came to La Rana in 1942. He graduated from Torrance High School in 1949. He served in the US Army during the Korean War from 1952 to 1953. He had five children. (Carmen Castillo.)

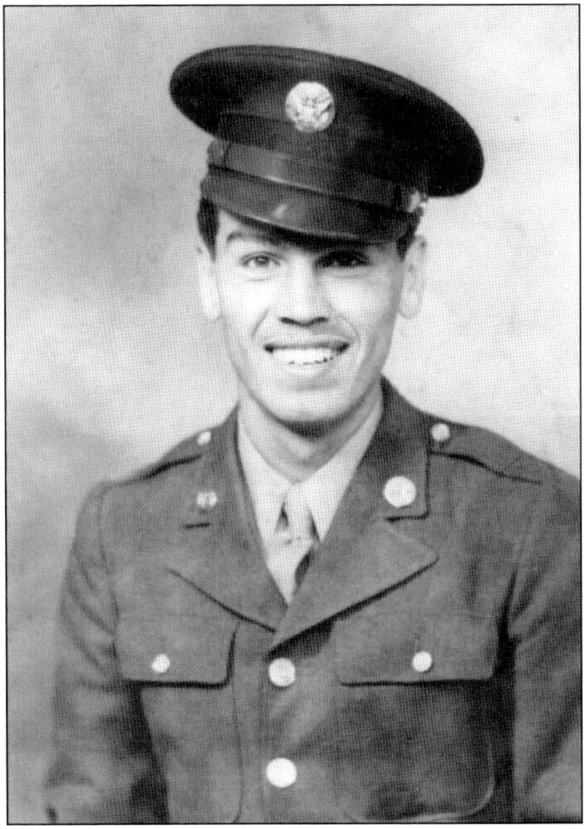

Joe Flores enlisted in the US Army in 1943. He did his basic training in Fort Knox, Kentucky, and was later promoted to staff sergeant. He served in France under Gen. George Patton, and his unit participated in the invasion of Normandy, and later, the Battle of the Bulge. He is the son of Victoria and Nestor Flores. (Gloria Flores Castañeda.)

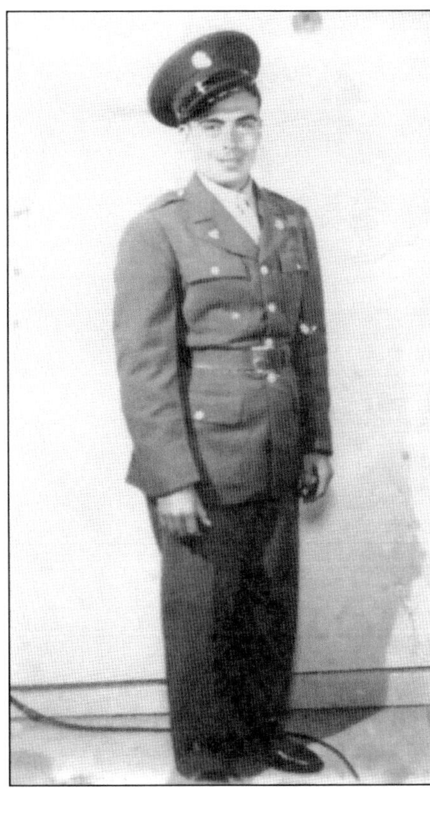

Five Flores brothers from La Rana served in the military. Tony Flores is pictured here. He was born in La Rana on June 10, 1921, and attended Torrance schools. He served in the military during World War II. When he returned from the service, he was employed by U.S. Steel. He later moved to Northern California, where he opened an upholstery business. He was the son of Victoria and Nestor Flores. (Gloria Castañeda.)

Benny Flores was born in Torrance in 1934. He attended Torrance schools. He joined the National Guard and later joined the US Army with his brother Rudy. Benny served from 1952 to 1953 with his brother in Korea. He is the son of Victoria and Nestor Flores. (Gloria Casteñeda.)

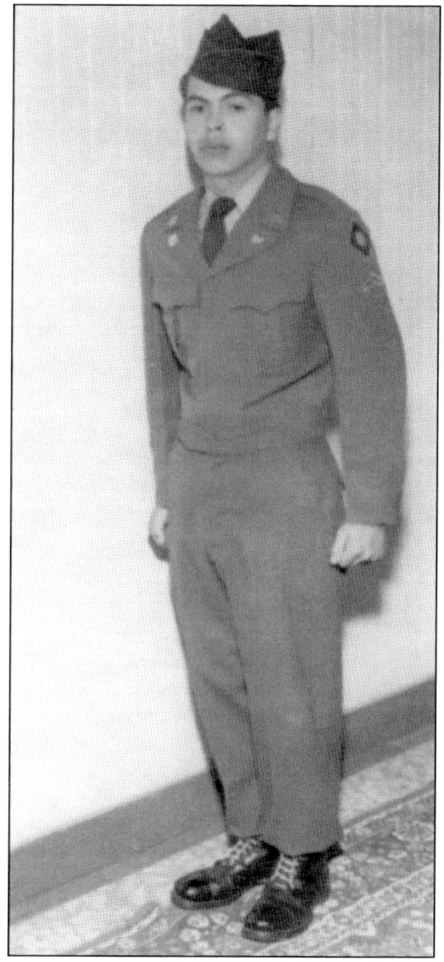

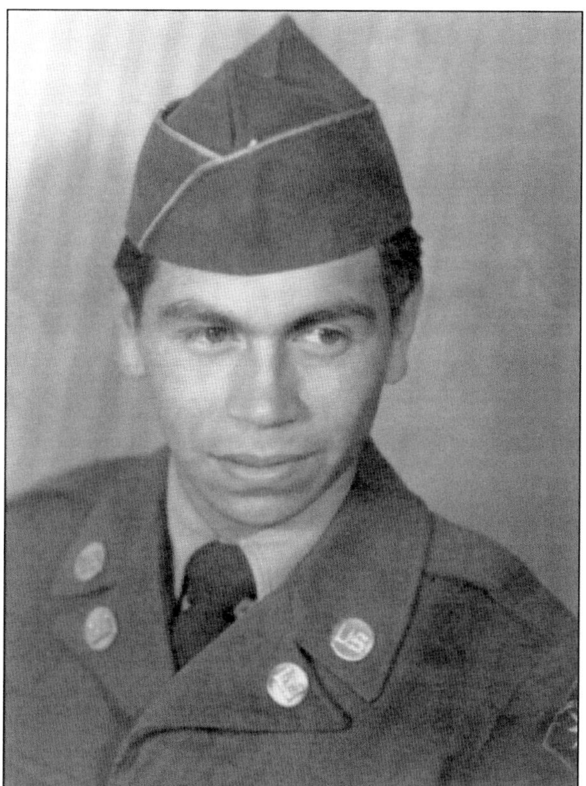

Rudy Flores was born in Torrance in 1931 and graduated from Torrance High School in 1951. He joined the National Guard and later joined the US Army, serving in Korea from 1952 to 1953. He is the son of Victoria and Nestor Flores. (Gloria Casteñeda.)

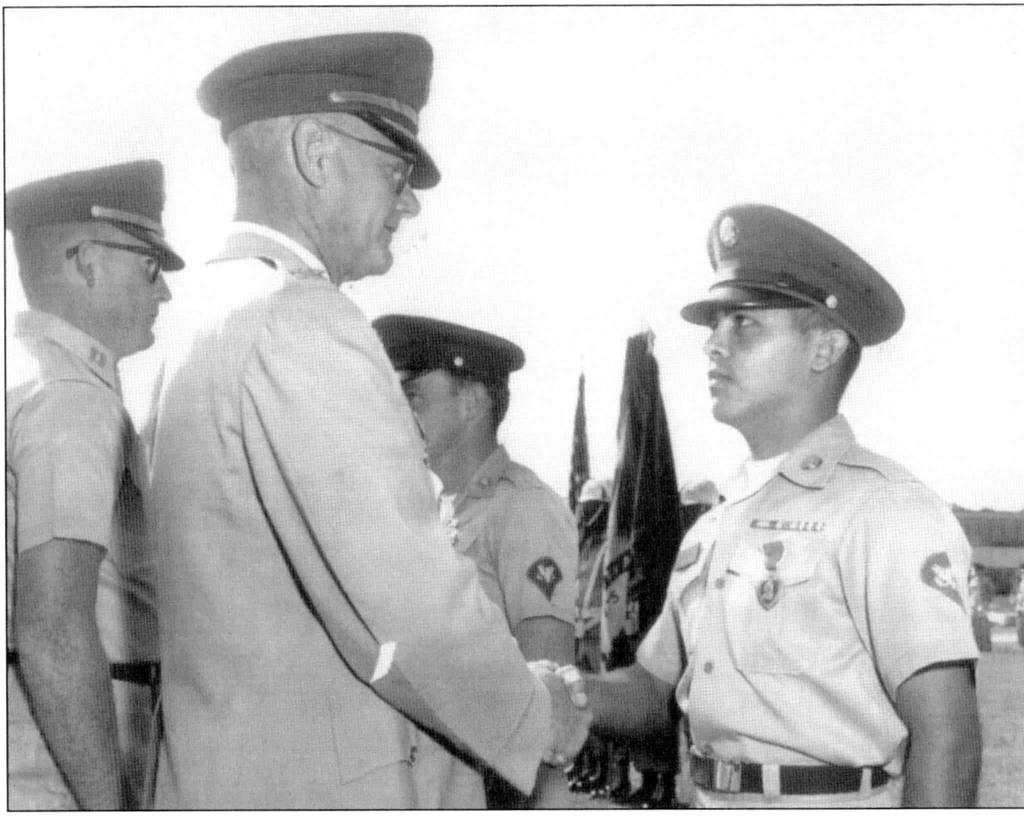

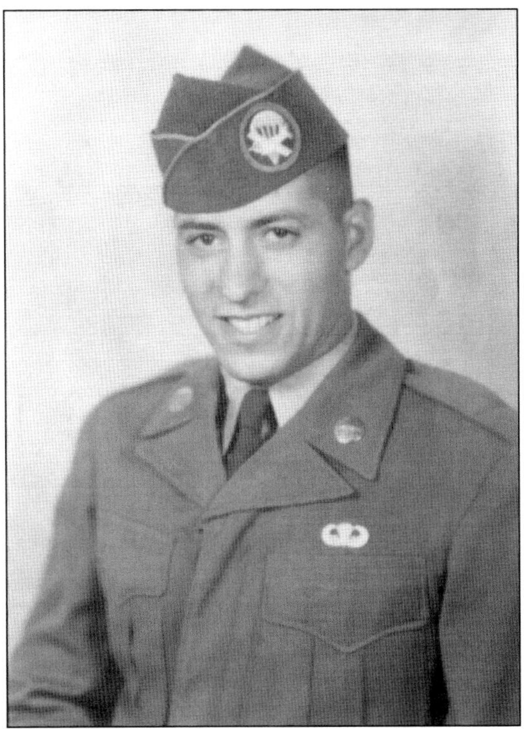

Gilbert Griego (right) was born in Alamogordo, New Mexico, in 1944. He and his family came to La Rana in 1949. He graduated from Torrance High School in 1962 and entered the US Army, serving in the Vietnam War from 1966 to 1967. Griego was awarded the Purple Heart in 1969. Two other Griego brothers served in the military. They were the sons of Ralph and Lugardita Greigo. (Gilbert Greigo.)

Freddy Guerra was born in Torrance in 1934 and attended Torrance schools. He was a corporal in the US Army Airborne and was in the 187th Regiment. He served in Japan from 1953 to 1956. He is the son of Virginia and Cruz Guerra. (Freddy Guerra.)

Robert Guerra was born in Gardena, California, and attended Torrance schools. He was drafted into the US Army and served in Korea from 1960 to 1962. After his return, he was employed by the City of Torrance. He has three children. He is the son of Virginia and Cruz Guerra. (Robert Guerra.)

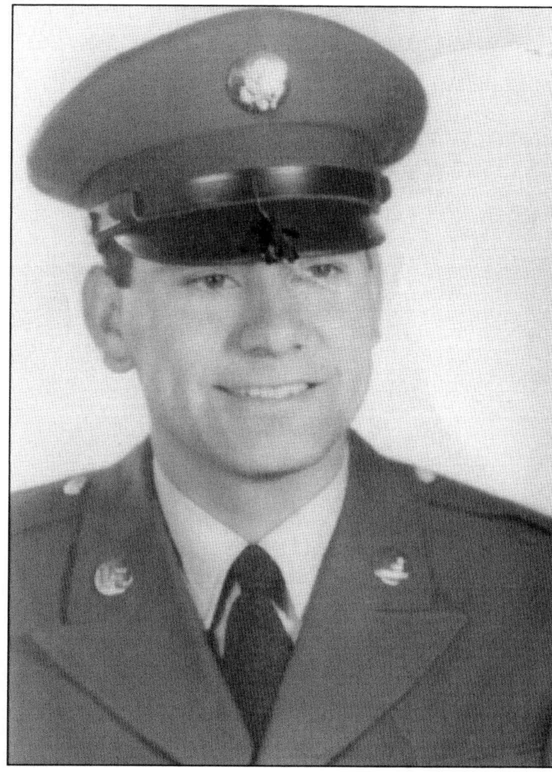

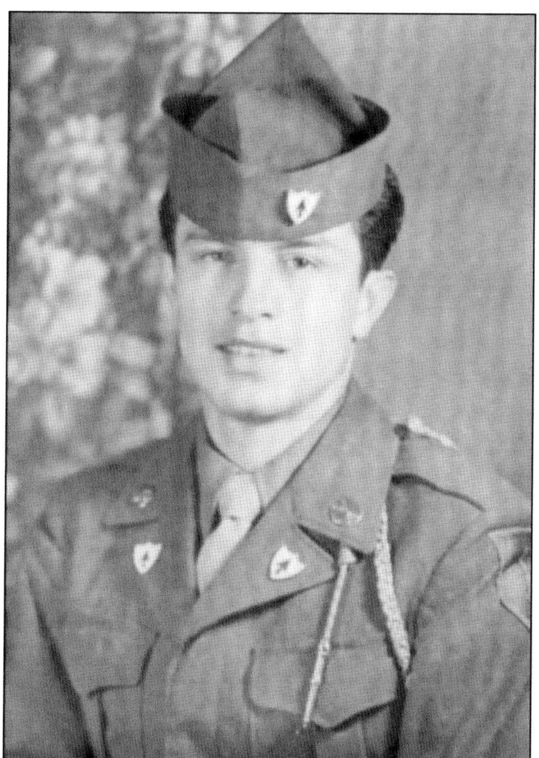

Armando Guzman was born in Torrance on July 22, 1928, and attended Torrance schools. He tried to join the Merchant Marines but was too young to be accepted. He later joined the US Army and served from 1947 to 1948. He is the son of Dona Ester Guzman. (Rudy Vega.)

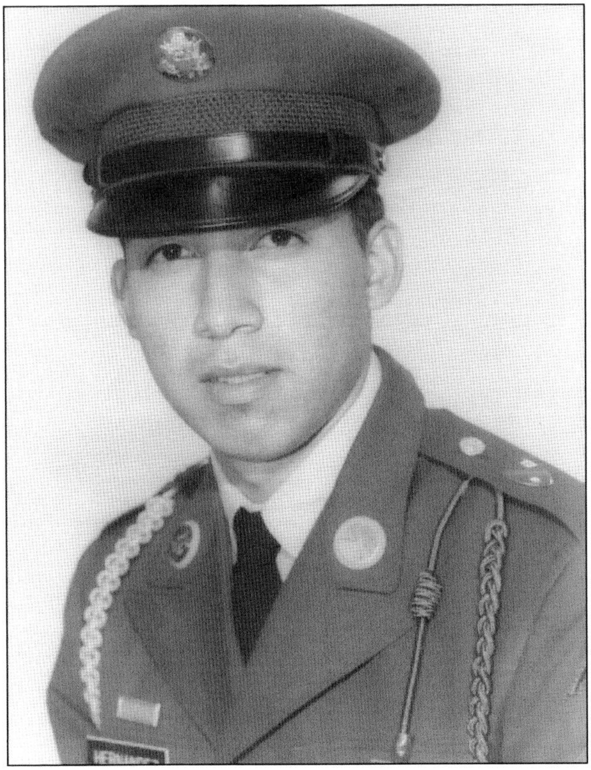

Peter Hernandez was born in Torrance and graduated from Torrance High School in 1964. He joined the US Army and served from 1966 to 1968. He retired after 32 years working for Los Angeles city schools. He is one of five sons of Eloisa Acosta and Pedro Hernandez who grew up in La Rana and served in the military. (Peter Hernandez.)

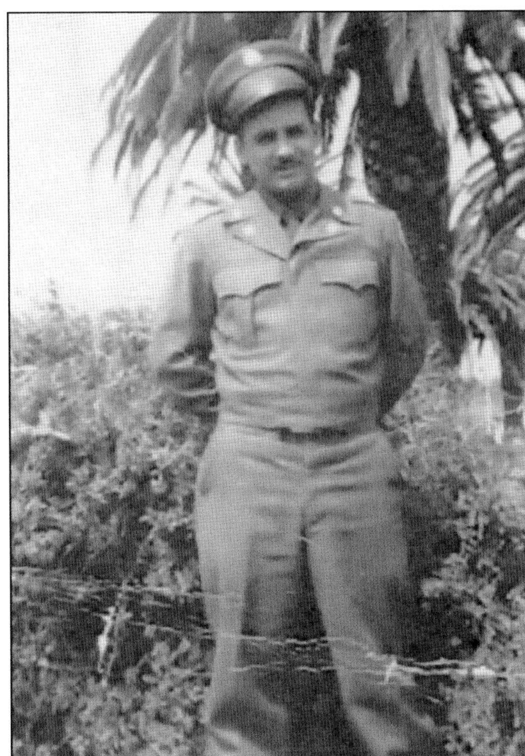

Felix (Chino) Herrera came to La Rana from Colorado with his family in 1944. He was drafted into the US Army and served in Korea from 1951 to 1952. He was employed at U.S. Steel. He is the son of Aleja Herrera. (Felix Herrera.)

Gerald Laird and his wife, Dorothy, moved to La Rana in 1950. He was a sergeant first class in the 45th Infantry Division of the US Army. He served in Korea from 1952 to 1954. He is the grandfather of professional baseball players Gerald and Brandon Laird. (Gerald Laird.)

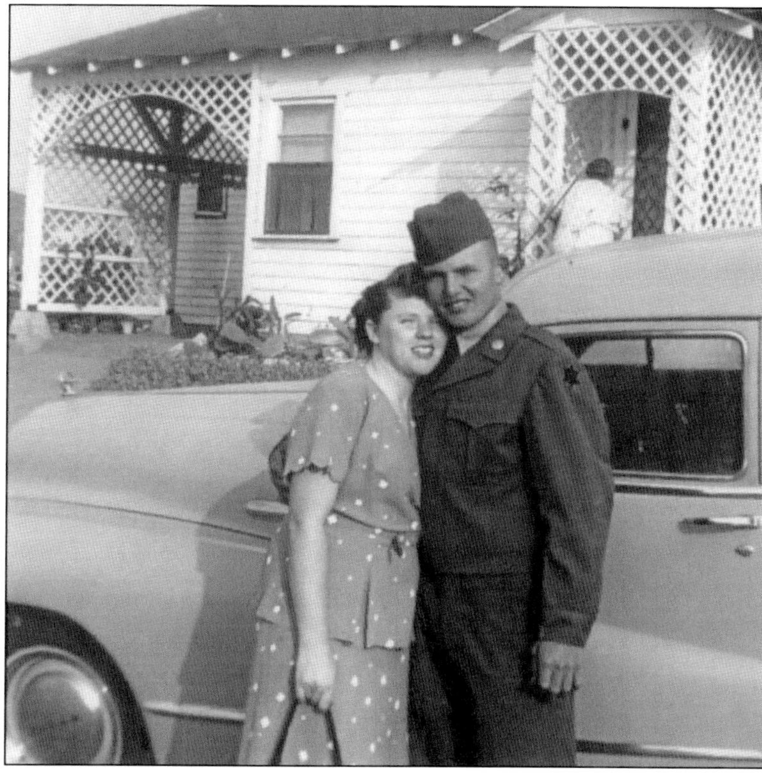

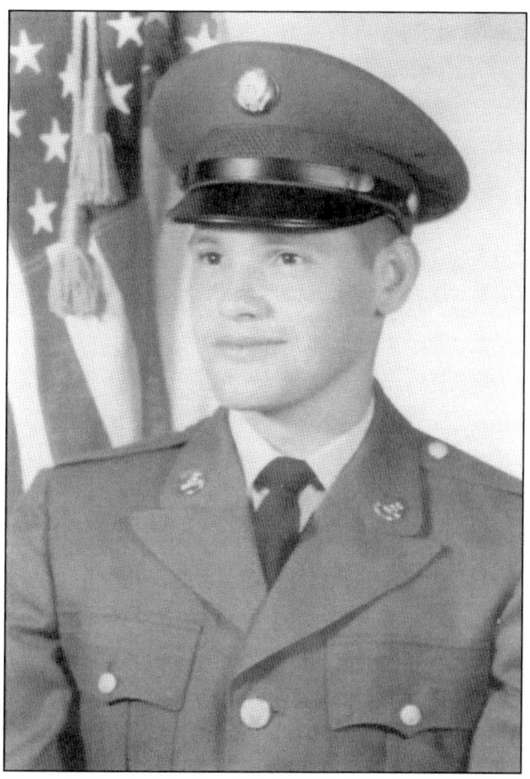

Billy Moreno was born in Torrance in 1949. His parents came from Purépero, Michoacán, Mexico, in the 1920s. He graduated from Torrance High School in 1967 and was drafted into the US Army in 1969. He served in Korea from 1969 to 1971. He was the son of Maria and Antonio Moreno. (Longa Alvarez.)

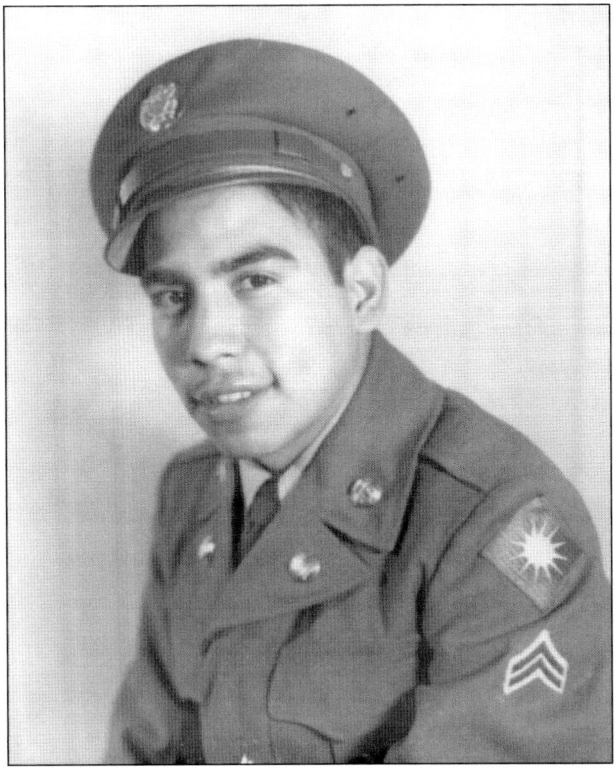

Mike Martinez's family came to La Rana in 1920, and he was born in Torrance in 1931. He attended Torrance schools. He served in the US Army in Korea from 1952 to 1953. He worked at Douglas Aircraft and Reynolds Metals and was the son of Gabriela and Antonio Martinez. (Louie Martinez.)

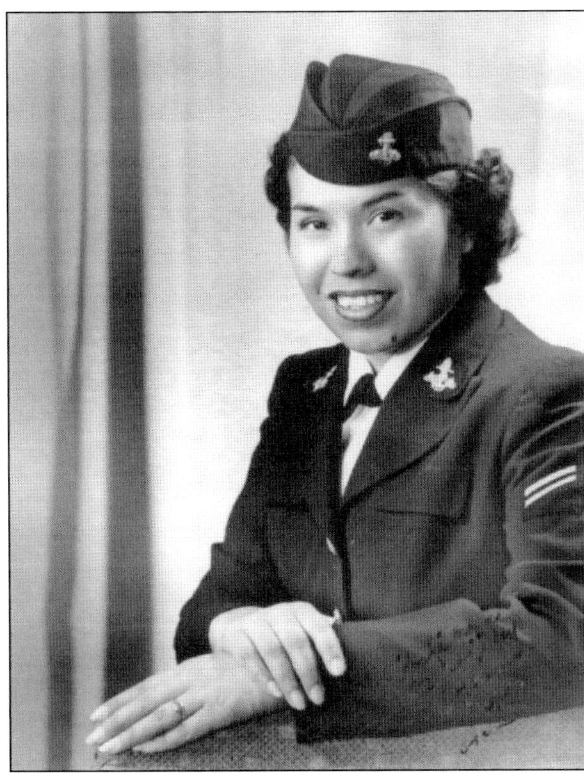

Dorothy Mora Medina attended Torrance schools. She entered the US Naval Women's reserves (known as the WAVES) in 1954 at age 21. She received her basic training at the US Naval Training Center in Great Lakes, Illinois. She was the daughter of Florencio Mora. (Dorothy Mora Medina.)

Hector Molina and his family came to La Rana in 1949. At 17 years of age, he joined the Marine Corps and served in Korea from 1954 to 1955. After his military service, he worked for Douglas Aircraft and the City of Torrance. He is the son of Juanita Irarte. (Hector Molina.)

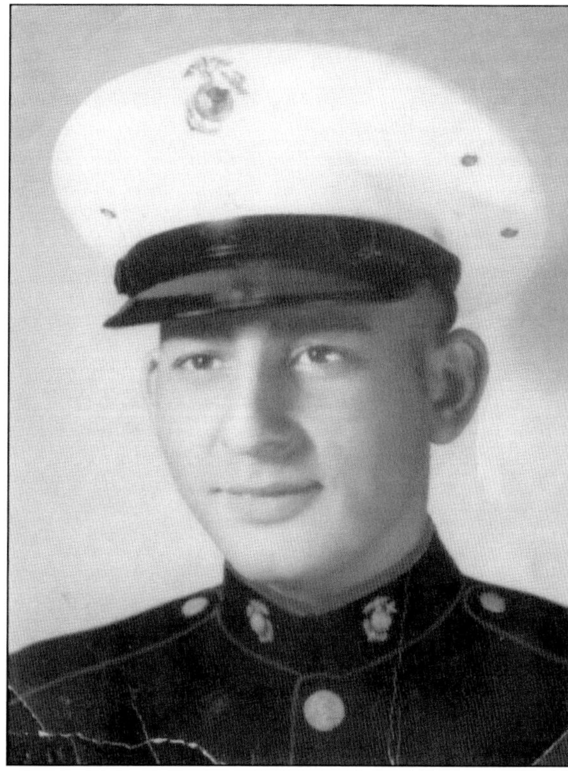

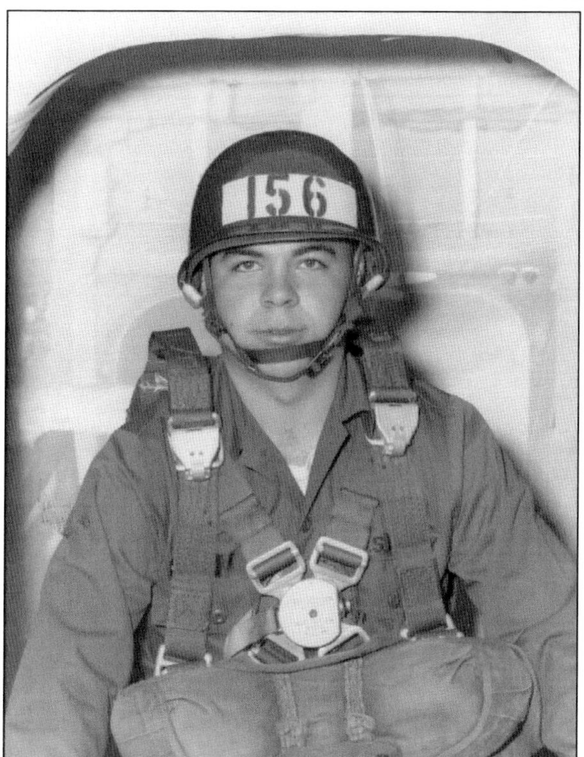

Arthur Molina was born in Torrance in 1960 and attended Torrance schools. When he graduated from West High School in 1978, he joined the US Army Airborne and trained at Fort Bragg, North Carolina. He served from 1978 to 1980. He is the son of Connie and Hector Molina. (Arturo Molina.)

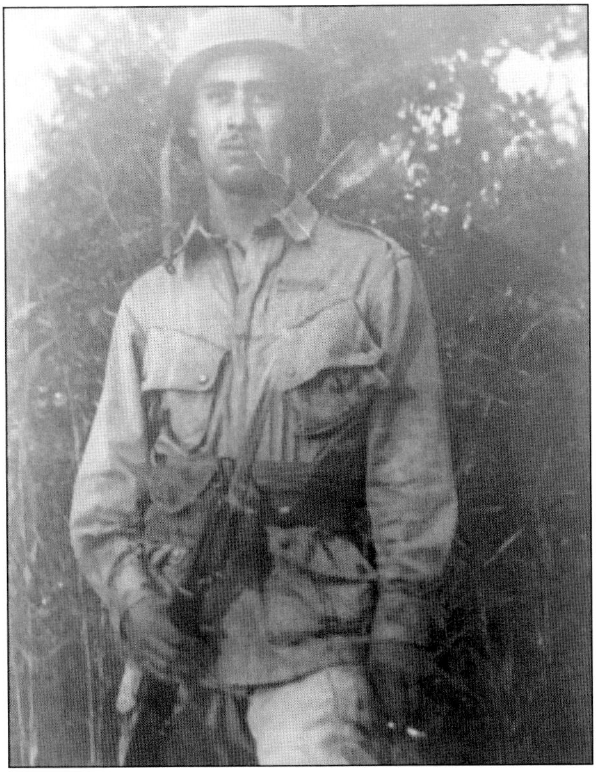

Lauro Torres was born in Torrance in 1925 and attended Torrance schools. He was drafted into the US Army in 1942. Torres served in US Army Airborne and made the jump during the Normandy invasion. He was injured during the invasion and received a Purple Heart. He was the son of Maria and Lauro Torres. (Laura Anaya.)

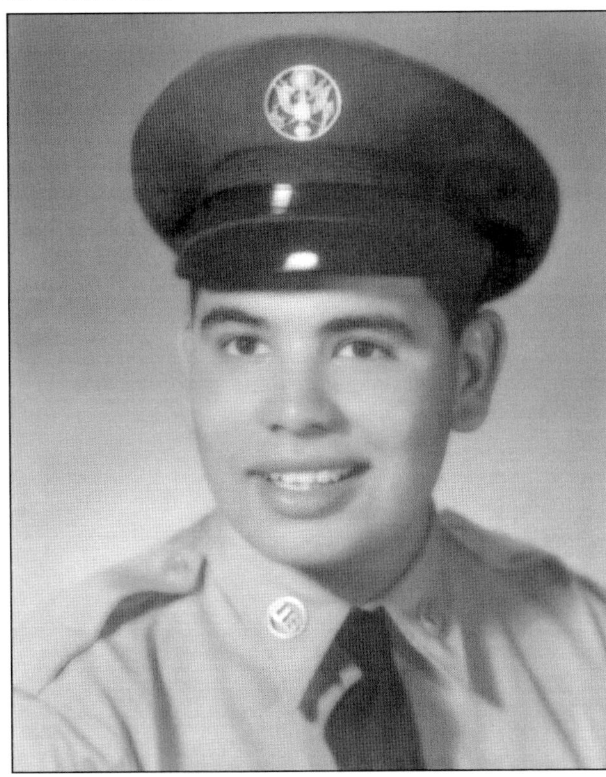

Manuel Olloque was born in Torrance in 1936 and attended Torrance schools. He joined the US Air Force in 1952 and served until 1956. Olloque served in Korea and French Morocco. He was an airman second class. He was the son of Juanita and Jose Olloque. (Manuel Olloque.)

Rudolph (Rudy) Rivera was born in Colton, California, in 1922. He and his family came to La Rana in 1929. He served during World War II from 1942 to 1945. He participated in the Normandy invasion and went on to serve in the Rhineland Battle and the Battle of the Bulge, serving under Gen. George Patton. He received the Purple Heart, Oak Leaf Cluster, and three Bronze Stars. He was also awarded the World War II Victory Medal. He was the son of Juana and Faustino Rivera. (Rudy Rivera Jr.)

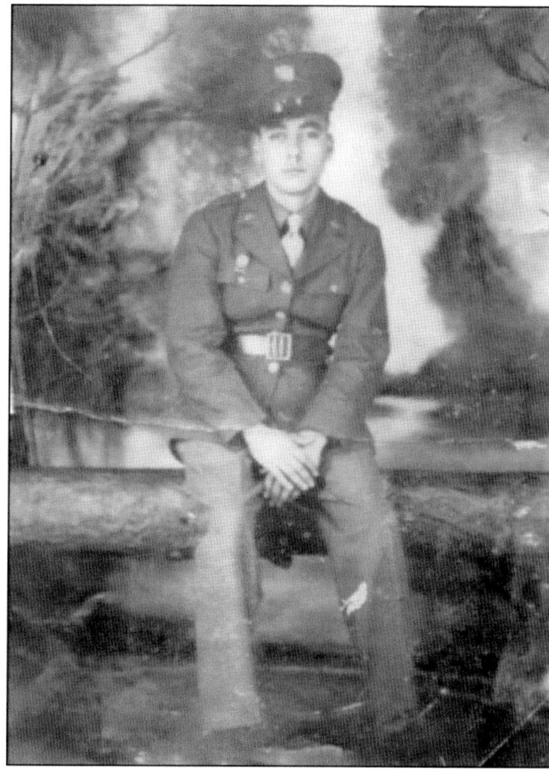

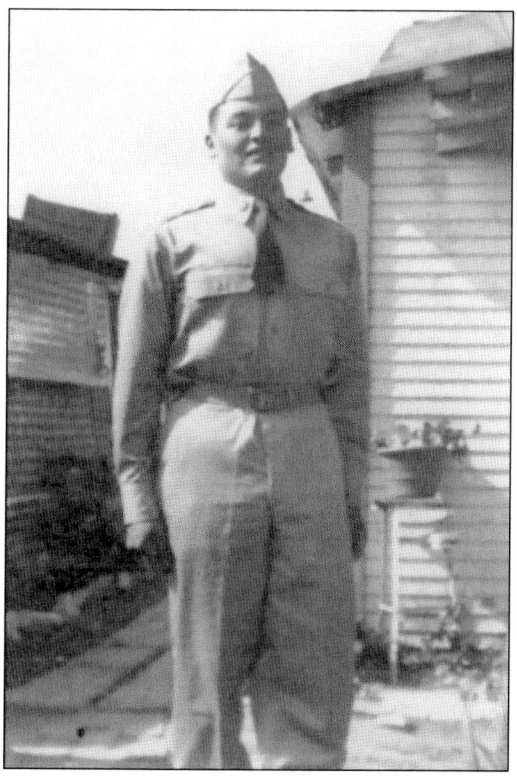

Alfonso (Ponchi) Ordaz was born in Torrance in 1929. His family came to La Rana in 1920. He was drafted into the Army while attending El Camino College in 1951. Ordaz served in Okinawa during the Korean War as a medic and is the son of Tula and Ruben Ordaz. (Alfonso Ordaz.)

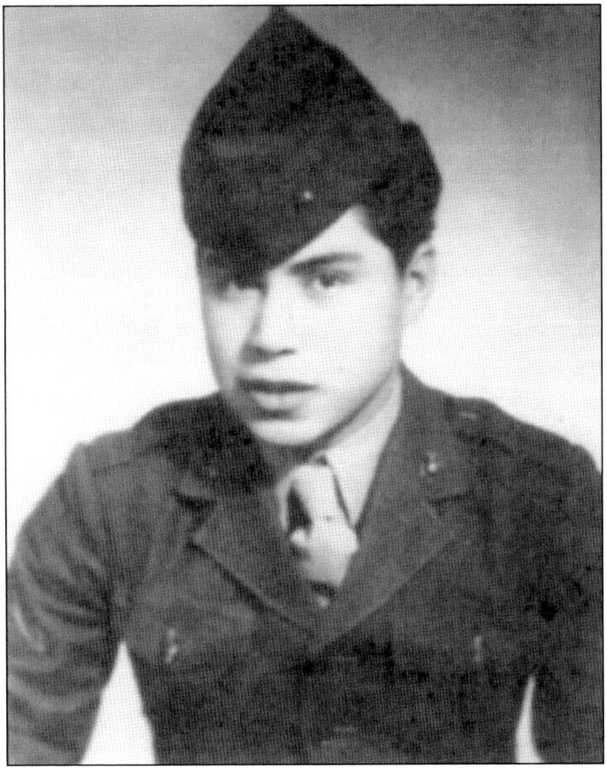

Ramiro (Rum) Ordaz was born in Torrance. He was drafted into the service while attending Torrance High School. He served in the US Marine Corps from 1945 to 1947. He was on a ship in the Pacific Ocean when the announcement was made that World War II had ended, and he was sent to China. He is the son of Dona Carmen and Don Luis Ordaz. (Ramiro Ordaz.)

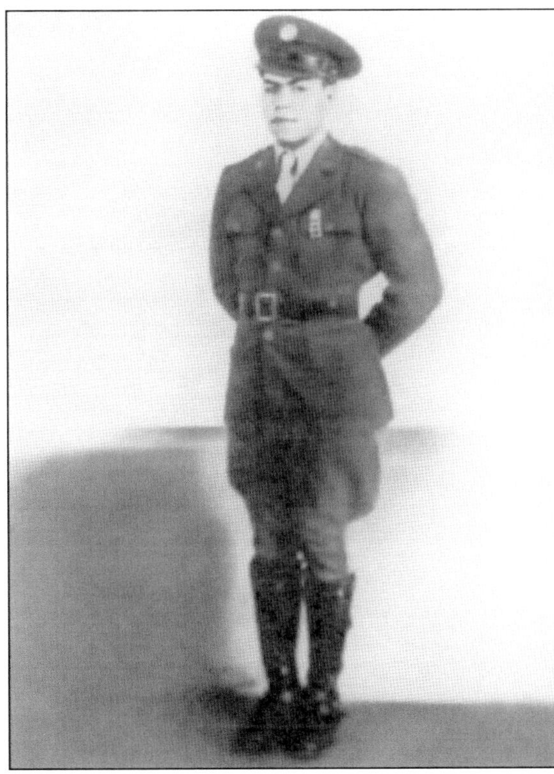

Felix Phillip Ortega was born in Granada, Colorado, in 1923. He and his family moved to La Rana in 1943. He was drafted into the US Army in 1945 and served until 1950. He was deployed to the Philippines and was awarded the Purple Heart. He is the son of Eustolia and Augustine Ortega. (Melinda Ortega.)

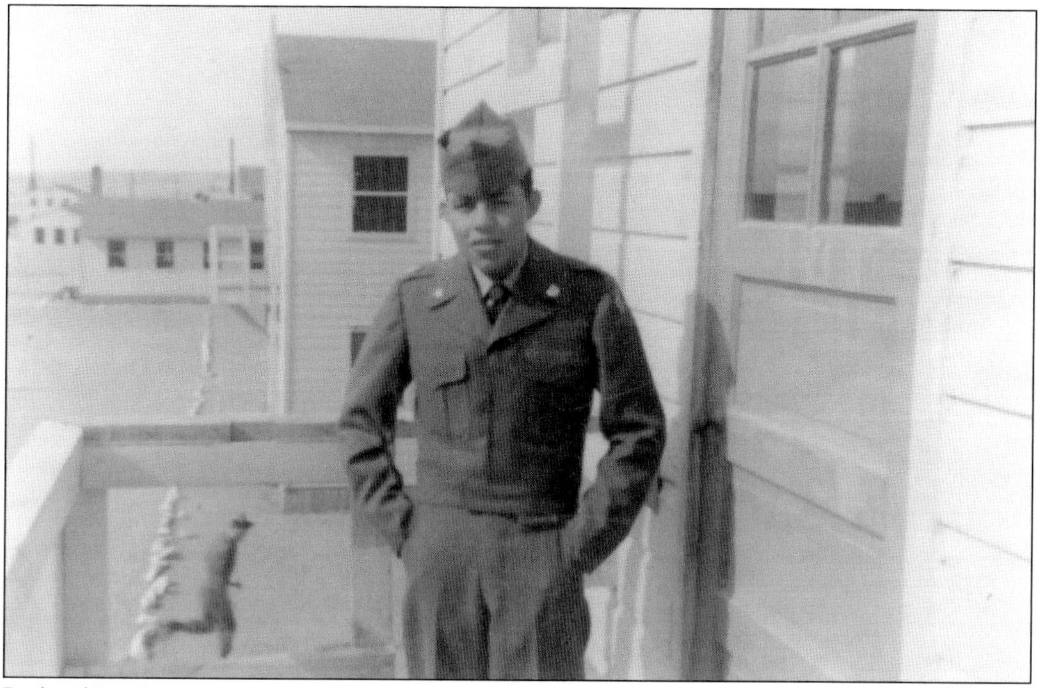

Richard Joe Ortega was born in Granada, Colorado, on July 29, 1935. He was the youngest child born to Augustine and Eustolia Ortega. The family moved to La Rana in 1943. He went to Torrance High School, graduating in 1953. He was drafted into the Army in January 1955 and stationed at Fort Benning, Georgia. He was a specialist/light weapons infantryman and was awarded the Good Conduct Medal and given an honorable discharge in January 1957. He returned to Torrance and served in the Army Reserves until December 1962. Although he moved away from Torrance in 1967, he had a lifelong love for La Rana and often told stories of his childhood to his children and grandchildren. He even had a collection of frogs! He started working at McDonnell Douglas in 1966 and took classes at Long Beach City College in order to advance his career, and retired from McDonnell Douglas/Boeing in 1999. During his retirement, he became an avid golfer. His three big loves were God, golf, and family. He passed away on April 12, 2012. He is survived by his wife of 53 years, Nina (Asencio); two sons and three daughters; six grandchildren; and eight great-grandchildren. Nina still has his Army uniform hanging in her closet. (Melinda Ortega.)

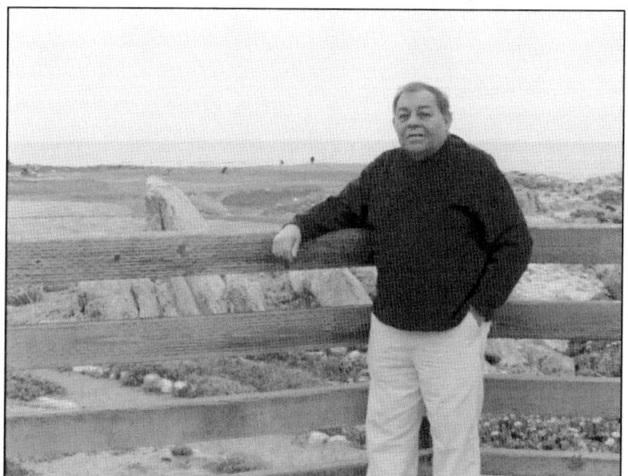

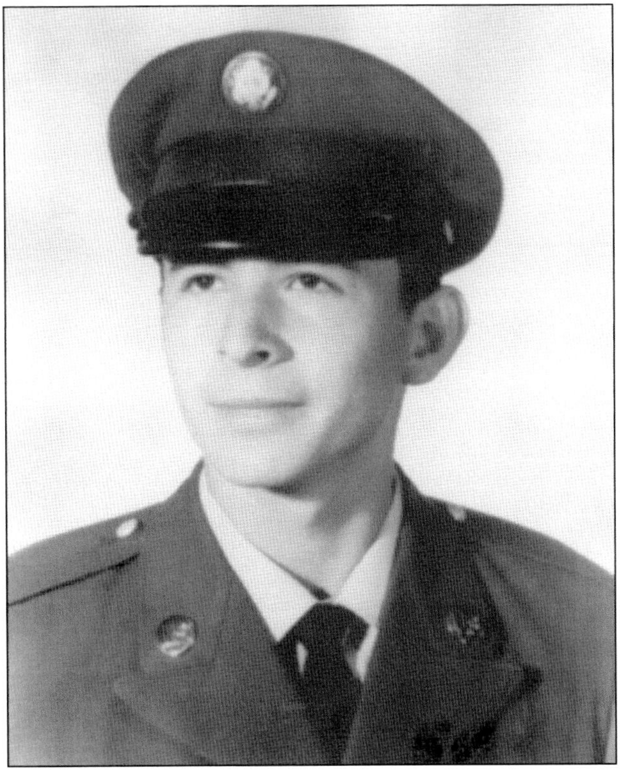

Edward (Eddie) Solis was born in Torrance in 1949 and graduated from Torrance High School in 1967. He served in the US Army in Vietnam from 1968 to 1969 and received the Purple Heart and Bronze Star. He is the son of Nellie and Alfredo Solis. (Yolanda Camou.)

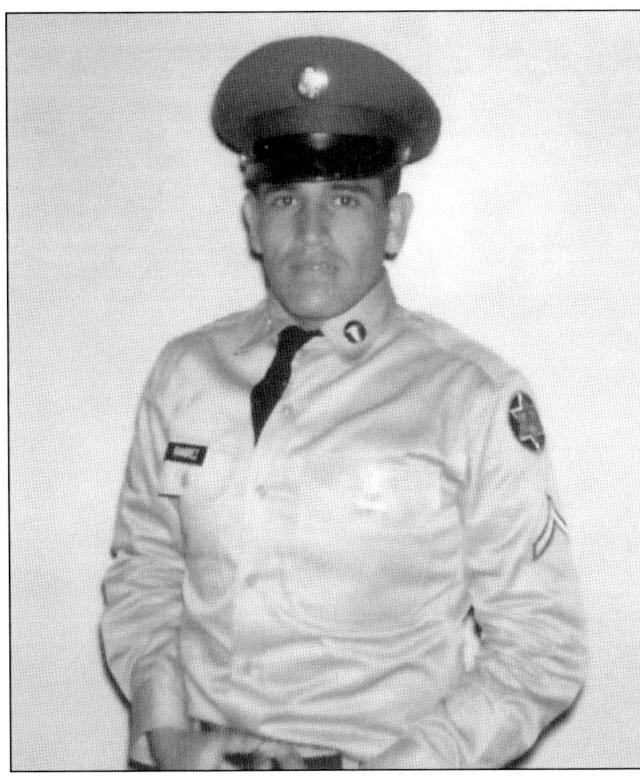

Victor Ramirez was born in Chihuahua, Mexico, in 1940 and came to La Rana with his family in 1950. He graduated from Torrance High School in 1959. Ramirez served in the US Army in Vietnam from 1965 to 1966. He worked for Harbor-UCLA Medical Center in the Radiology Department for 40 years. He is the son of Rosario Ramirez. (Victor Ramirez.)

Manuel Valencia was born in Hermosa Beach. He came to La Rana with his family in 1940 and attended Torrance schools. Manuel served in the US Army in the Korean War from 1947 to 1950 and his brother Avelino served in Italy during World War II. He is the son of Fermina Valencia. (Jessie Valencia.)

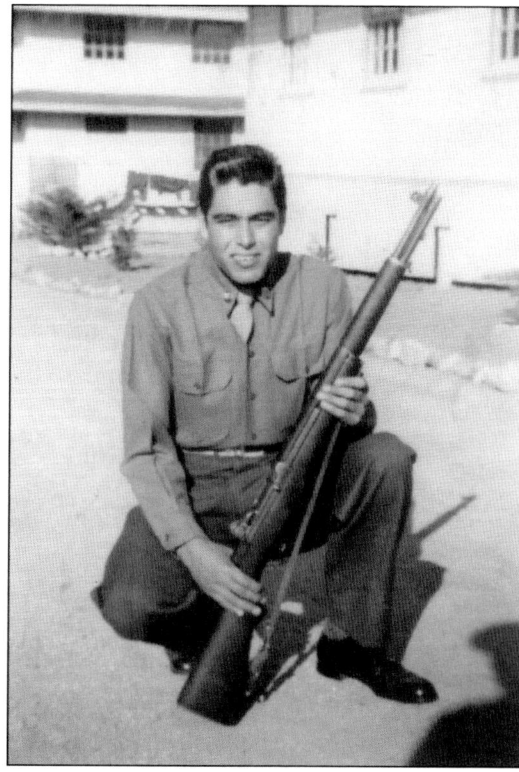

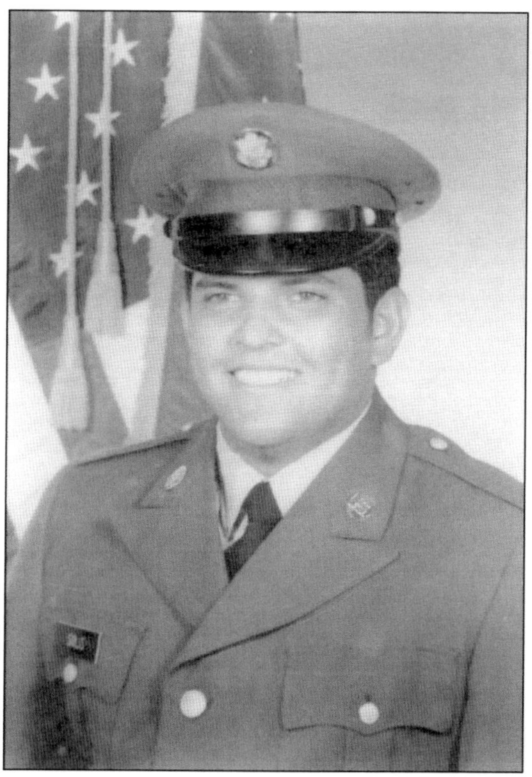

Raymond Solis was born in Torrance in 1953 and graduated from Torrance High School in 1971. He then joined the US Army and served in Korea from 1972 to 1973. His rank was corporal specialist 4. He is the son of Nellie and Alfredo Solis. (Raymond Solis.)

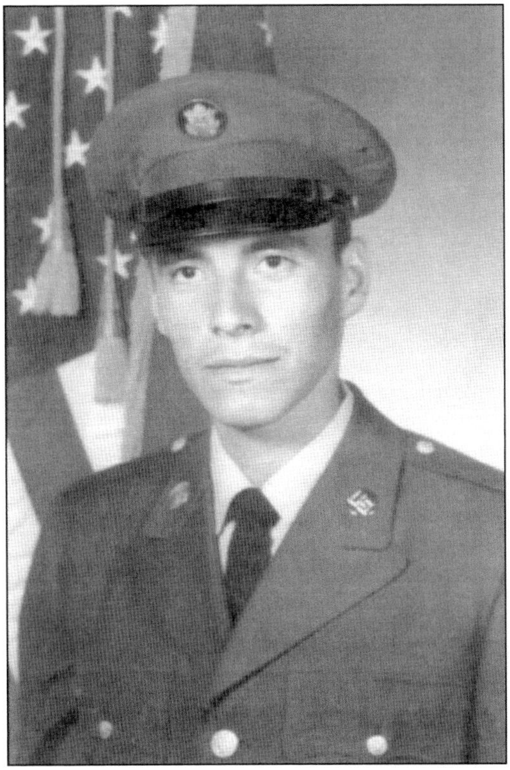

Carlos Villalobos was born in San Pedro, California, in 1952 and raised in La Rana. As a teenager, he moved to Sacramento, where he graduated from Elk Grove High School in 1970. He enlisted in the US Army in 1972 and served in Germany. He was the son of Ermalinda and Alfred Villalobos. (Longa Alvarez.)

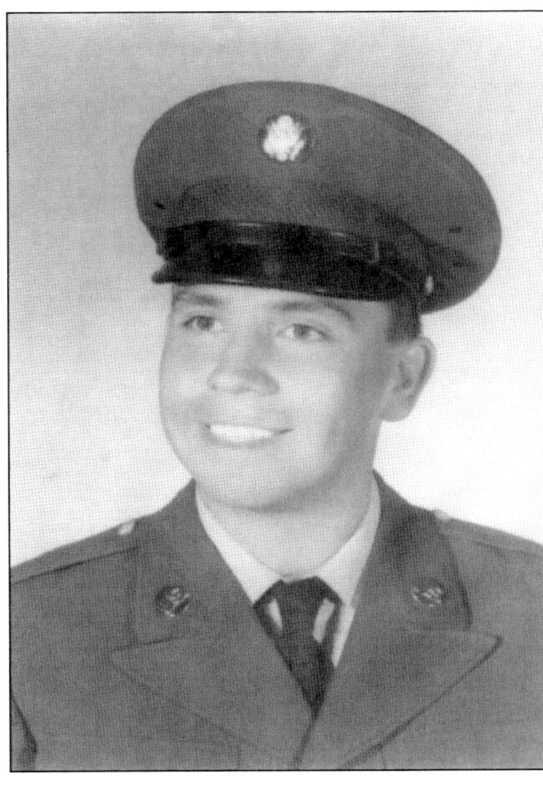

Eleazar Ybarra was born in Agua Prieta, Sonora, Mexico, in 1943. He and his family came to La Rana in 1945 and he graduated from Torrance High School in 1961. He served in the US Army from 1966 to 1968 as a member of the 101st Airborne Division. He is the son of Elena and Reyes Ybarra. (Eleazar Ybarra.)

Benny Montejano was born in Calexico, California, in 1910. He was married to Cuca Alvarez. He served in the US Army Airborne from 1943 to 1945 in Germany, Italy, and France. Montejano was awarded a Purple Heart. (Gloria Montejano.)

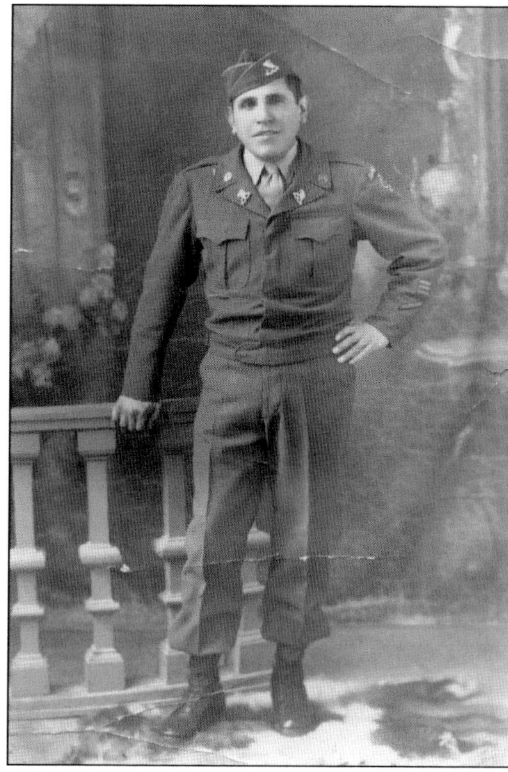

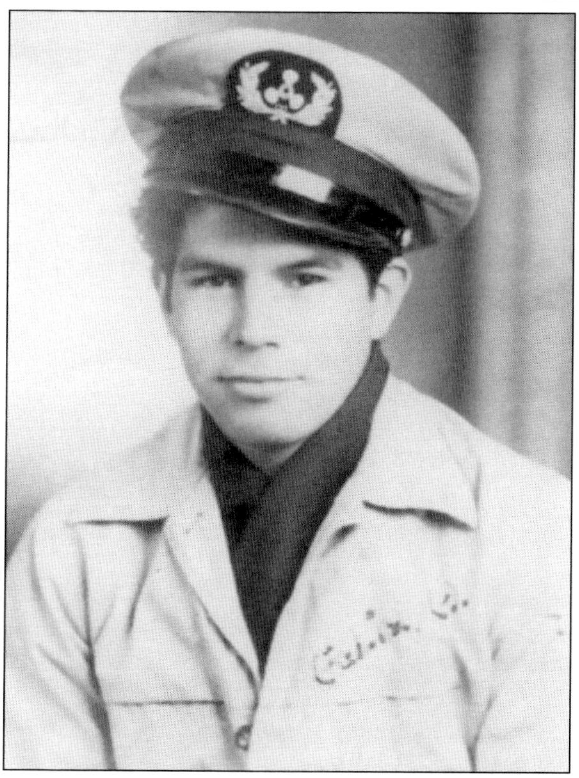

Felix Hernandez was the brother of Jesse, Nellie, and Fuzzy Hernandez. They lived in La Rana in the 1940s. He joined the Merchant Marines along with other young men from La Rana. (Judy Ybarra.)

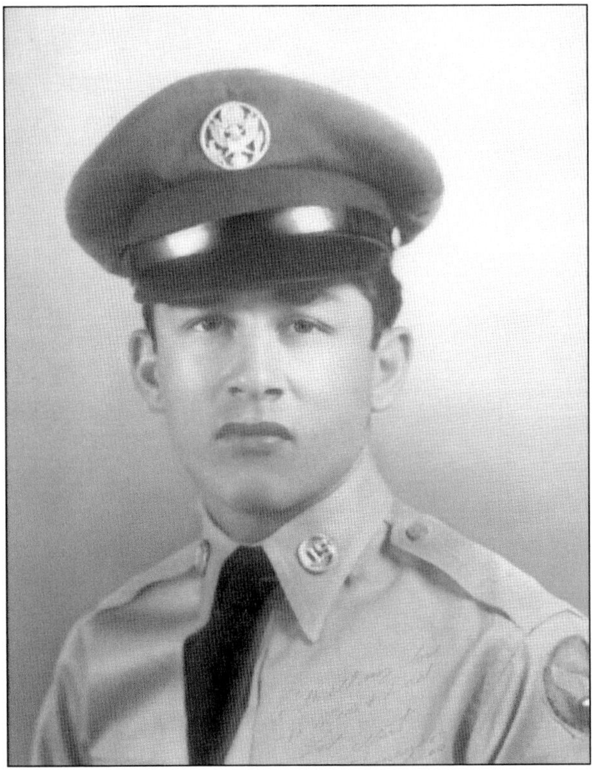

Albert Hernandez served in the US Air Force from 1949 to 1953. He was stationed in Texas. Miguel Duarte and Hernandez joined the military on the same day. Hernandez chose the Air Force, while Duarte chose the Army. Hernandez has four children and is a steamfitter by trade. He is the son of Alfonsa and Beatrice Hernandez. (Albert Hernandez.)

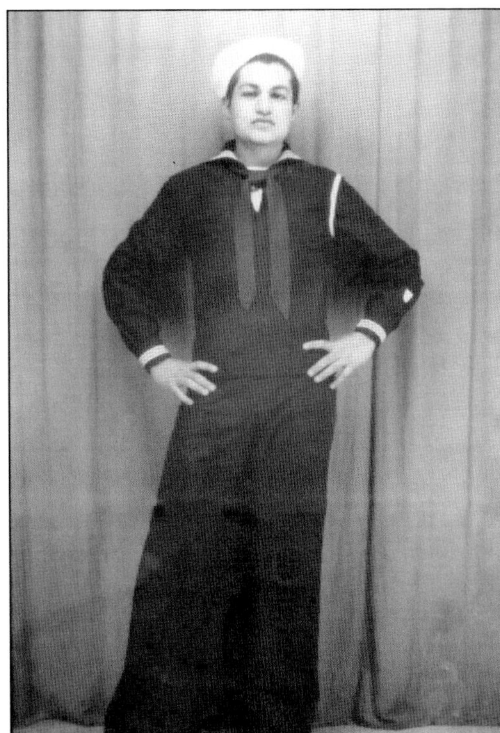

John Cendejas Reyes came to La Rana in the early 1930s. He attended Torrance schools and served in the US Coast Guard from 1944 to 1947. After his military service, he got married and lived in San Pedro. He is the father of five children and worked as a teamster at the Port of Los Angeles. He was the son of Jenny Reyes and brother of Dora, Nellie, Josie, Judy, and Tony. (Judy Ybarra.)

Reyes Ybarra Jr. was born in Douglas, Arizona, in January 1926. He is the son of Reyes Sr. and Rosa Ybarra. He served in the US Army from 1945 to 1947 and took part in the Normandy invasion. He also fought in Italy and North Africa. He has been employed by local steel and aircraft companies and continues to work to this day. He still lives in La Rana with his wife and family. (Longa Alvarez.)

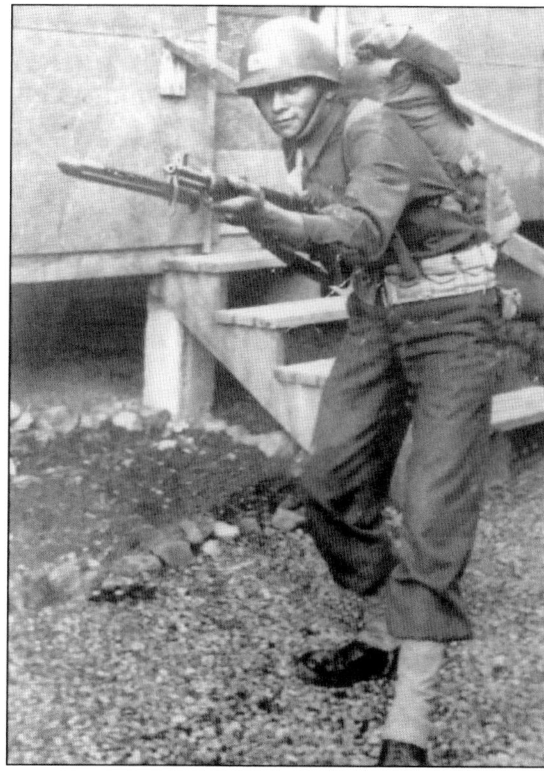

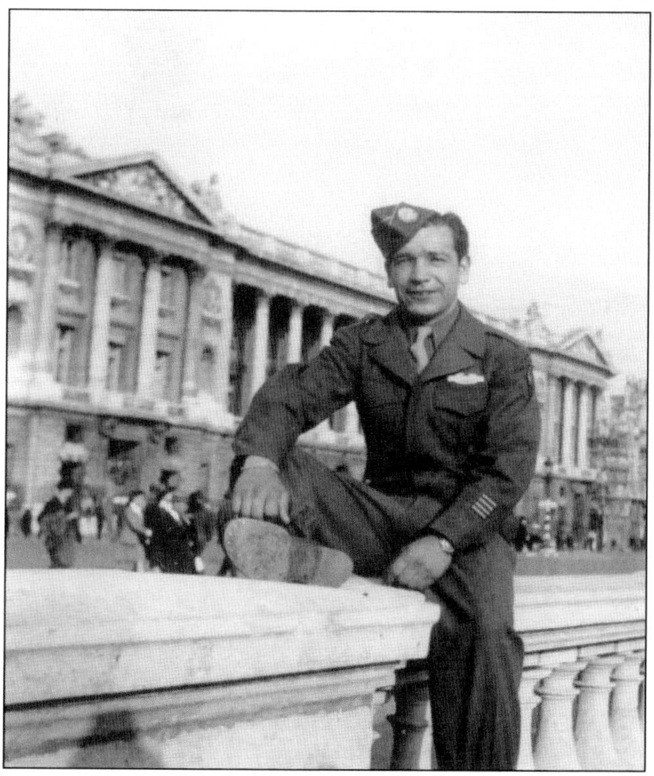

Jason Castillo was drafted and served in the US Army 101st Airborne from November 1942 to July 1945. He performed his basic training in Little Rock, Arkansas, and at Fort Benning, Georgia, before he was shipped to England and served in the Normandy invasion. He sailed across the English Channel on V-Day in a glider. Castillo received the Purple Heart for wounds he received in the invasion and a second Purple Heart in Amsterdam. (Jason Castillo.)

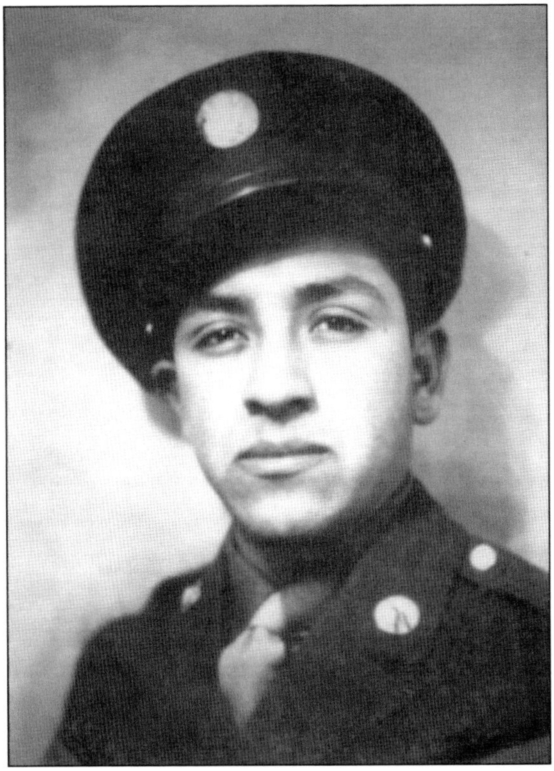

Dario Chavez was born in Chihuahua, Mexico, in 1920. He and his family came to La Rana in the early 1920s. He attended Torrance schools and then entered the military in 1942. He was killed during military maneuvers in Wyoming in 1943. He was the son of Don Augustine and Dona Jesus Chavez. (Ernie Castillo.)

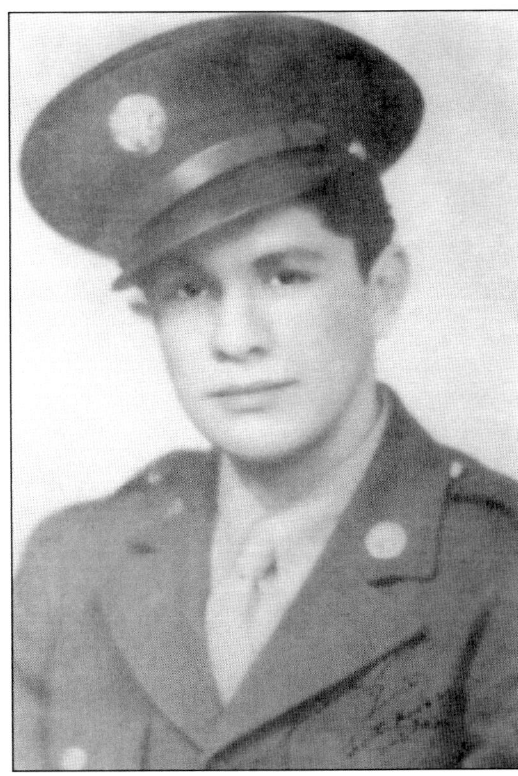

Louis Alvarez was born in Huntington Beach in 1924. He was a private first class in the 145th Infantry in the US Army. He was killed in action on April 22, 1945, at Mt. Pacawagan in Luzon, Philippines, and was posthumously awarded the Purple Heart. He was the son of Agapita and Andres Alvarez. (Long Alveraz.)

Nestor Flores's family came to La Rana in 1919. He was born in Torrance in 1922. He served in the US Army and was stationed in Germany, where he was a technician 5th grade. He was killed in Germany on April 1, 1945. He was the son of Victoria and Nestor Flores (Gloria Cateneda.)

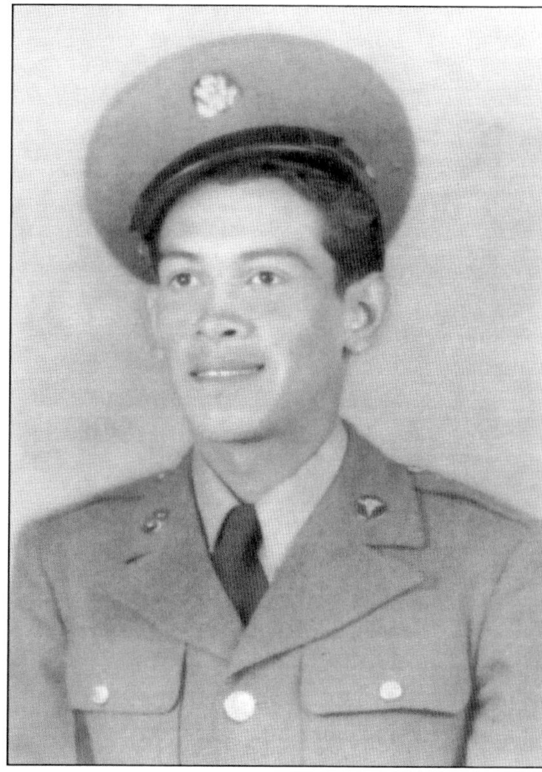

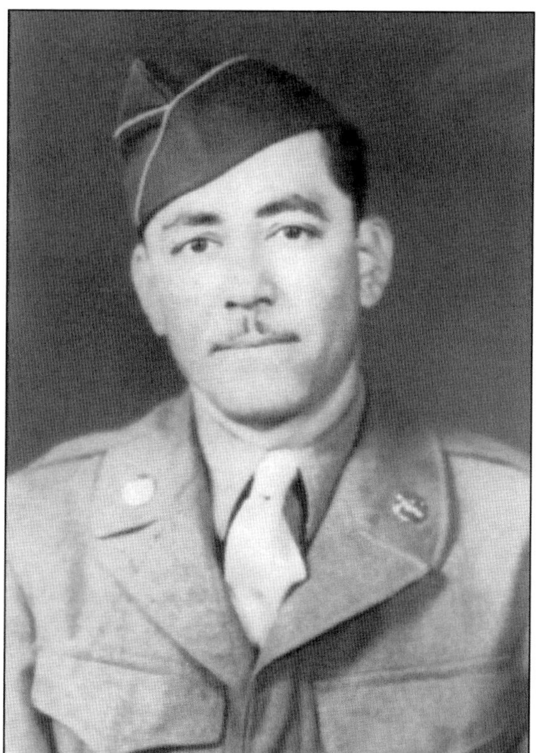

Reynaldo Verdugo came from Douglas, Arizona, to La Rana with his sister Chena Grande in 1930. His friends called him "Blackie," and he worked at U.S. Steel. Verdugo joined the Army and was killed in 1946 in the Philippines by Japanese solders unaware the war had ended. (Ernie Castillo.)

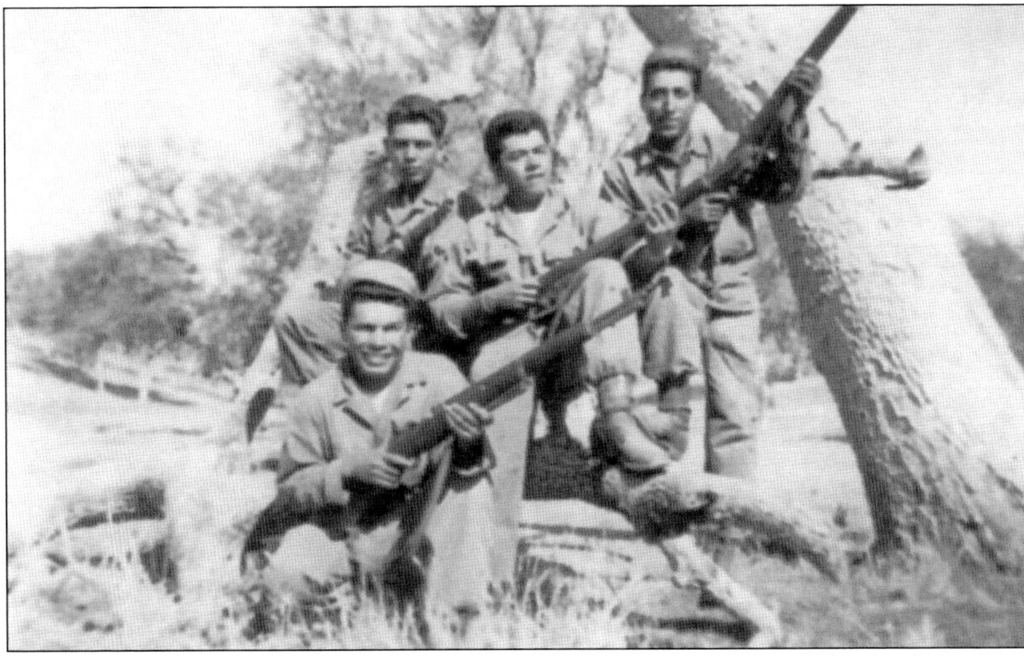

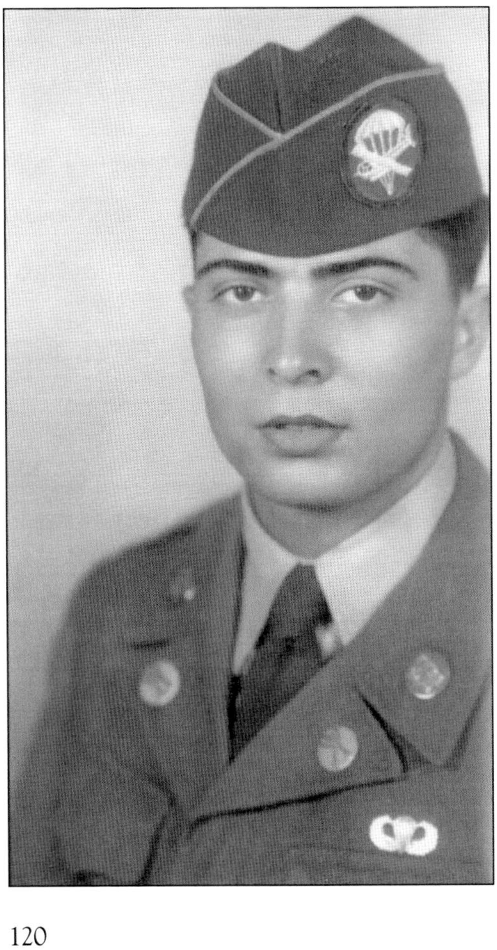

George Escobar (front) and his family came to La Rana in the early 1920s. He graduated from Torrance High School in 1947. He was drafted into the US Army in 1950 and killed in September 1951. On the day he died, he was in a foxhole with other members of his company and heard a cry for help from another serviceman. When Escobar attempted to respond to this person, he was killed. He received the Purple Heart and Silver Star. He was son of Lupe and Herman Escobar. (Henry Escobar.)

Miguel Duarte was born in Torrance in 1931 and attended Torrance schools. He was a private first class as a member of the 187th Airborne Infantry Regiment Combat Team. Duarte was awarded the Purple Heart, the Combat Infantryman's Badge, the Korean Service Medal, the United Nations Service Medal, the National Defense Service Medal, the Korean Presidential Unit Citation, and the Republic of War Service Medal. He made his first jump in December 1950 and was killed fighting in South Korea on February 15, 1951. He was the son of Dolores and Artemio Duarte. (Alice Duarte Solis.)

Five

ACHIEVEMENTS

Life was often a struggle for the young people of La Rana. Many students were unable to finish high school because they had to help support their large families. Families, including youngsters, would leave in the summer to work in the fields in the central valley and other areas of California. They would work along with adults in the fields during the hot summer months and return to La Rana in October. Unfortunately, they would miss the beginning of the semester and quickly fall behind in their schoolwork, resulting in poor grades. This contributed to high dropout rates.

In time, lifestyles became enhanced for the families of La Rana. Their lives improved as they began to acquire better jobs and gain some financial stability, allowing many to buy homes or leave the area for other local communities. This financial stability allowed children to stay in school and benefit from a good education. Today, a large number of the past and present residents of La Rana have pursued a higher education.

La Rana boasts many highly educated professionals who started out in the little community, including educators Marta Alicia Alonzo, Gloria Casteneda, Mary Martha Duarte, Julia Rosalia Olloque, and David White; nurses Maria Dolores Duarte White and Antonio Gassett; attorney Michael Duarte; police officers Larry and Michael Grajeda; sheriff Nick Acosta; doctor James Yanes; accountant Mark Solis; fire department captain Anthony Moreno; graphic designer Melinda Ortega; professional baseball players Manuel Jose Olloque, Jerry Laird, and Brandon Laird; anesthesiologist Eddie Solis Jr.; fashion designer Henry Duarte; sociologists Kristina Rosalia Pulido and Andrew Pulido; communications expert Daniella Gassett; psychology major Amanda Ybarra; and many business owners, among others.

Those who grew up in La Rana feel very proud of the accomplishments of current and past residents of the neighborhood—so much success and good has come from the little two-block neighborhood known as La Rana.

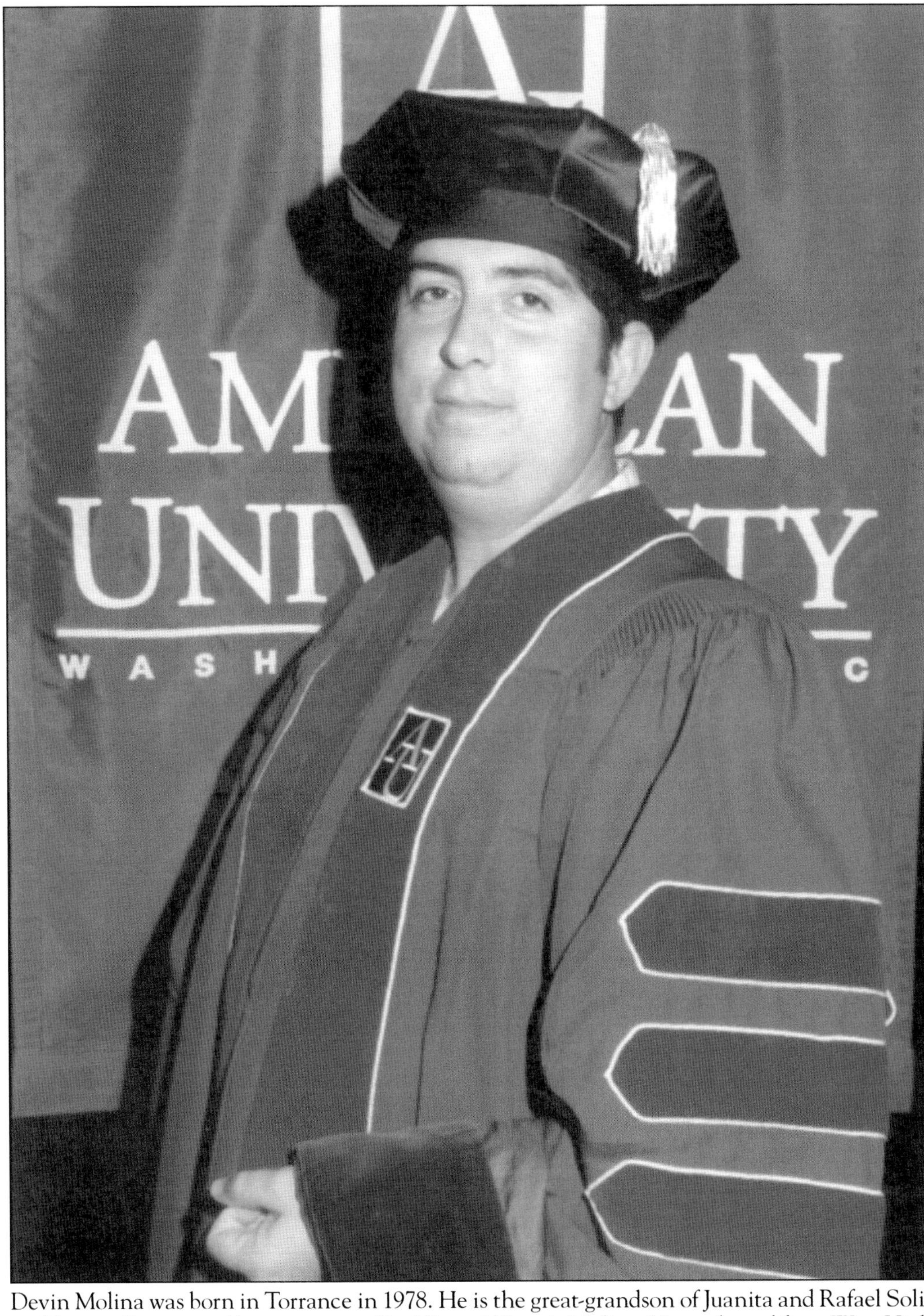

Devin Molina was born in Torrance in 1978. He is the great-grandson of Juanita and Rafael Solis and Juanita Yriarte, and his parents are Freddie and Sherrie Molina. He graduated from West High School and earned his PhD in anthropology from American University in Washington, DC, in 2012. He is employed by the Brooklyn College in Brooklyn, New York. (Sherrie Molina.)

Mark Solis, the son of Augie and Alice Solis, was born in Torrance in 1961. He attended Torrance High School and El Camino College and graduated with a bachelor's degree in accounting from Loyola Marymount University. He started his career with PricewaterhouseCoopers, spent 13 years with Chase Bank as vice president of finance and eight years at BakerCorp as director managing the finance, treasury, and operations, and recently joined UnitedHealthcare in the value-based contracting consulting group. (Mark Solis.)

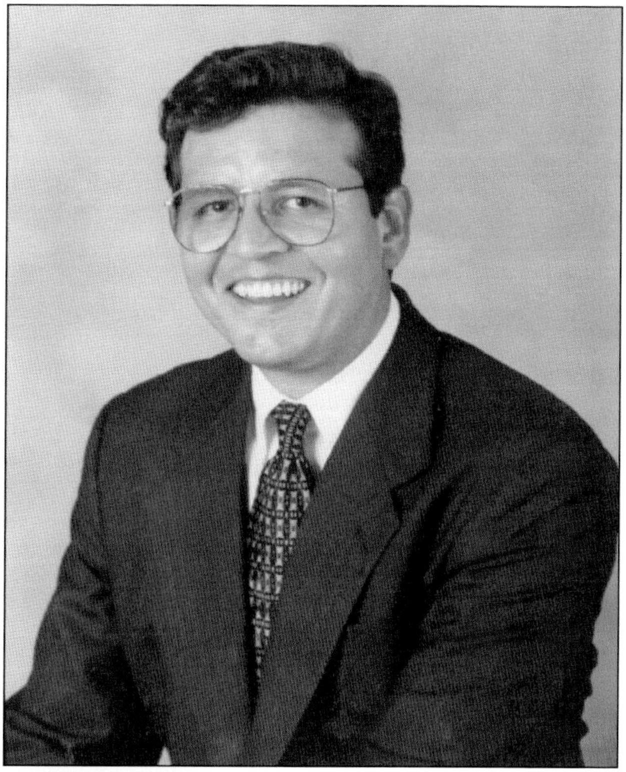

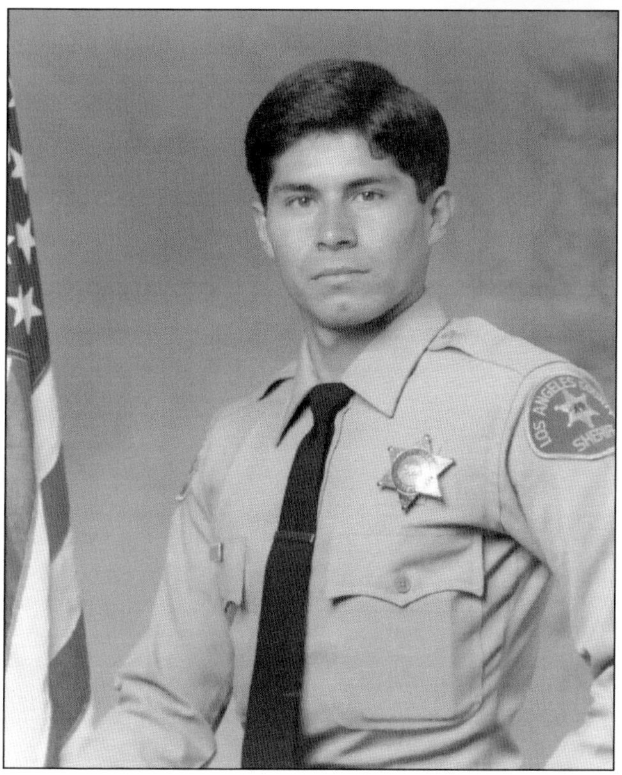

Nick Acosta was born in 1966 to Rachel and Angel Acosta. He attended Nativity Catholic School, Bishop Montgomery High School, El Camino College, and Cal State Long Beach. He worked for the Los Angeles County Sheriff's Department for over 30 years. His son Braden Acosta followed in his footsteps as a Los Angeles County sheriff. (Acosta family.)

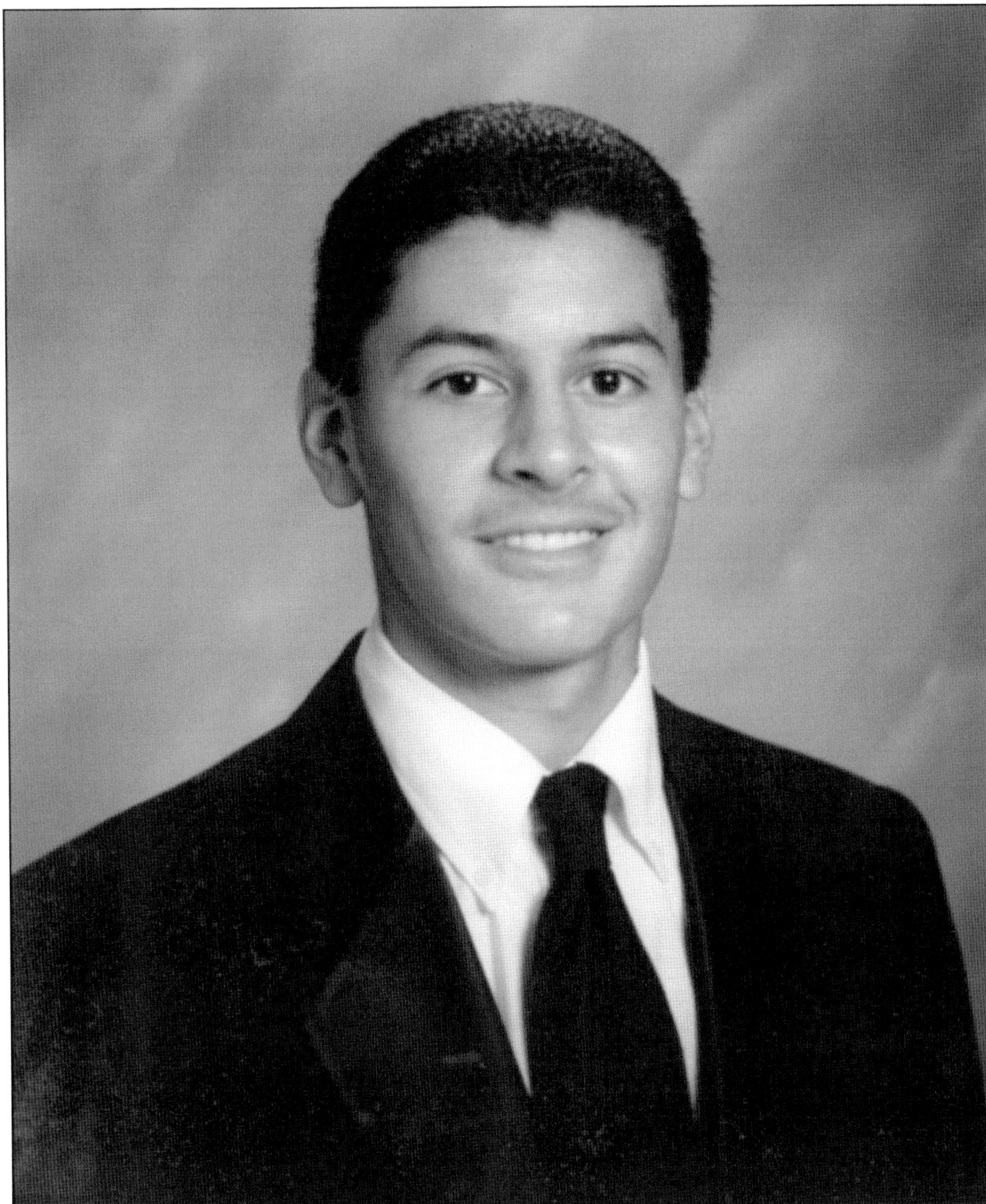

Edward Rios Solis Jr. is the son of Eddie and Carol Solis and the great-grandson of Silverio Rios. He was born on May 17, 1974, and attended North Torrance High School, UC Irvine, and Western University of Health Services in Pomona, California. In 2008, he did his residency at Baystate Medical Center in Springfield, Massachusetts. Today, he is chief of anesthesiology at Southern Hills Hospital in Las Vegas, Nevada. (Carol Solis.)

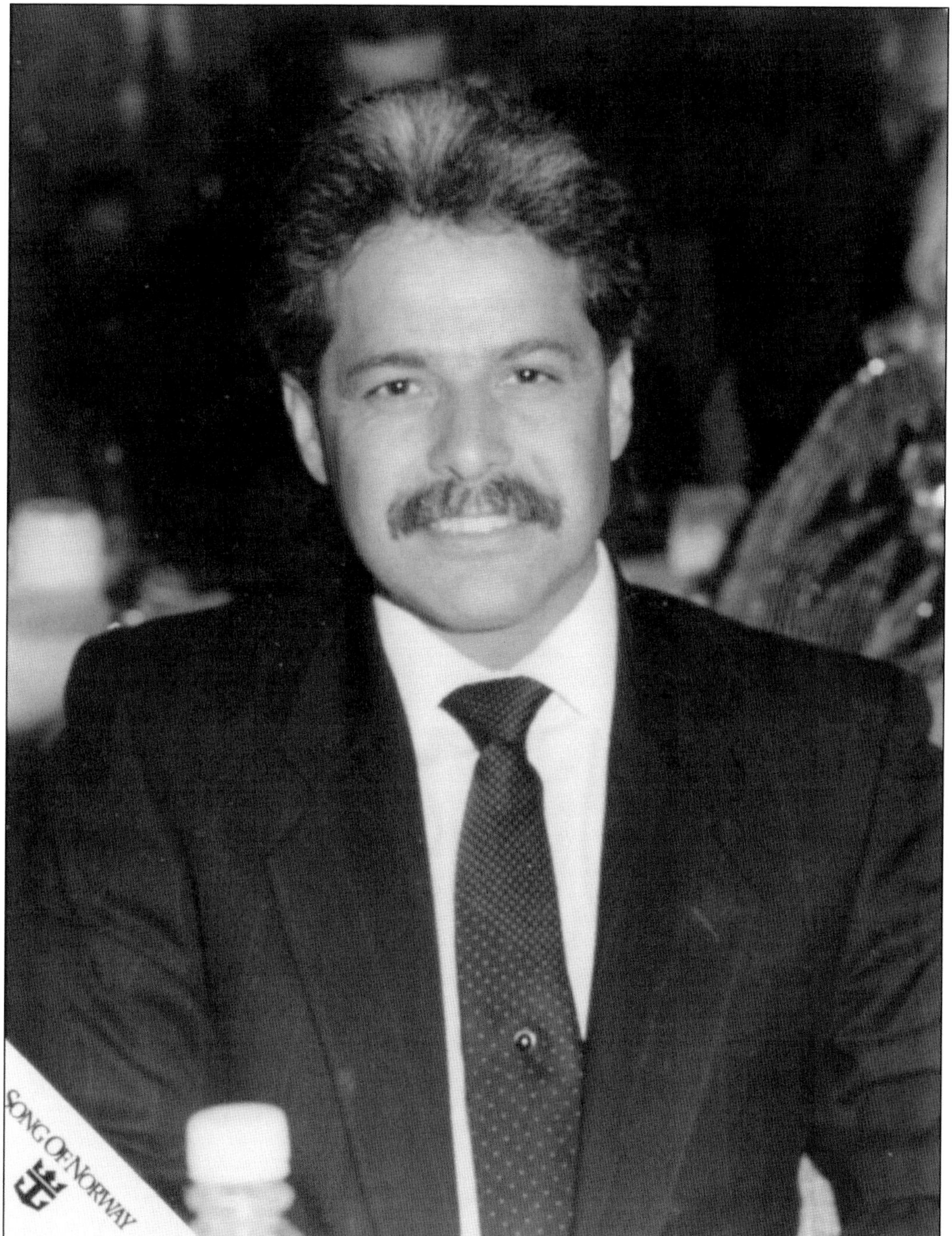

This picture of David White was taken in 1993. He is the son of Alfred and Bertha White. He attended Bishop Montgomery High School in Torrance and graduated from Cal-State University, Long Beach, with a bachelor's degree in 1973. He received his master's degree from Cal State University, Dominguez Hills, in 1993. White taught special education at West Torrance High School for 35 years. (David White.)

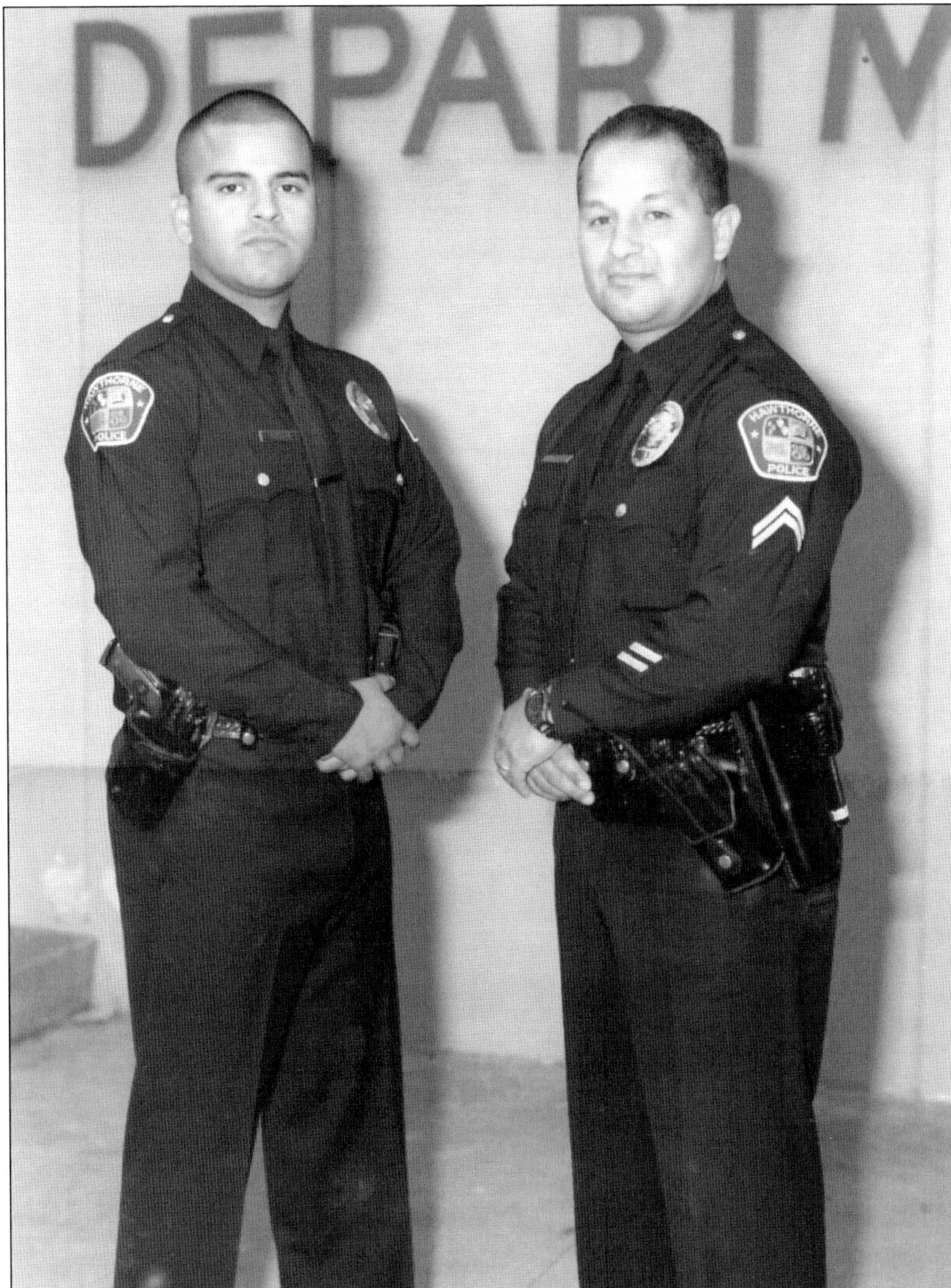

Brothers Michael Anthony (left) and Larry Grajeda are members of the Hawthorne Sheriff's Department. Michael Anthony graduated from Torrance High School in 1994, attended El Camino Junior College, and graduated from the Los Angeles Sheriff's Academy in 2000. Larry graduated from Torrance High School in 1981, also attended El Camino, and graduated from the Los Angeles Sheriff's Academy in 1990. (Armida Grajeda.)

James Yanes was born in Torrance in 1973. He is the great-grandson of Juanita and Rafael Solis and Artemio and Dolores Duarte. His parents are James and Jean Yanes. He graduated from Bishop Montgomery High School in 1991. He received a PhD in infectious diseases from the University of Arizona College of Medicine at Tucson in 2006. He is employed by Capital Medical Hospital in Olympia, Washington. (Jean Yanes.)

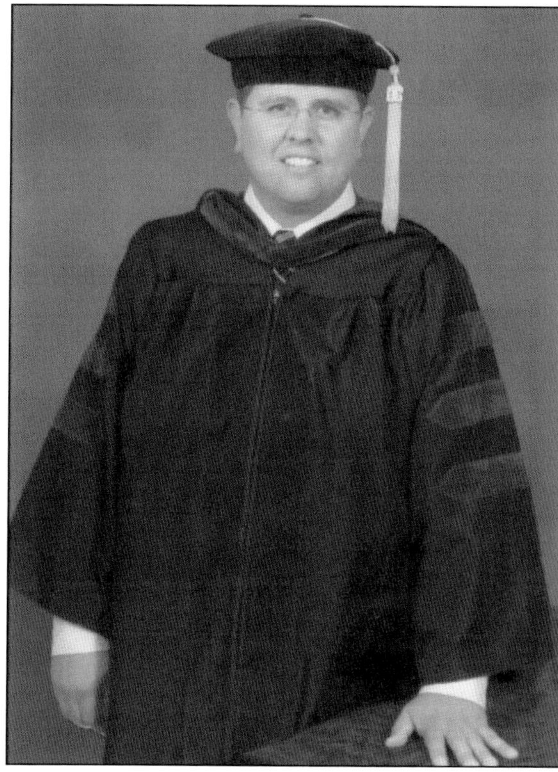

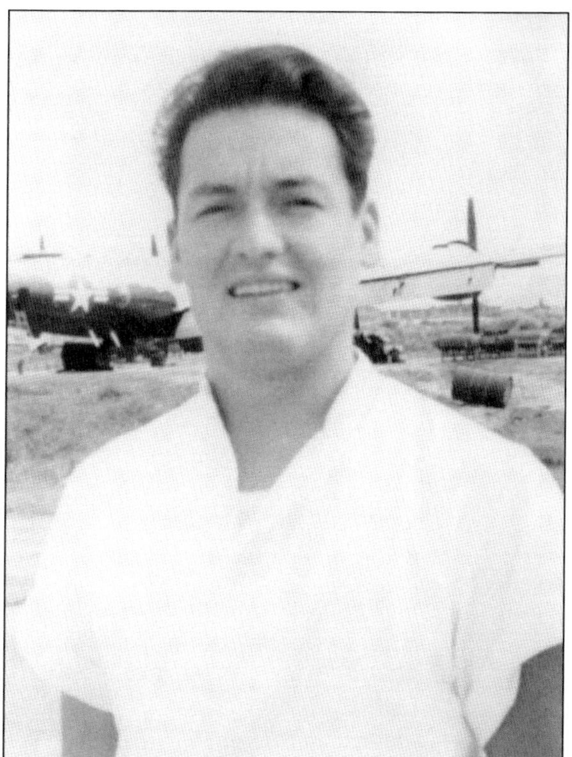

Alfonso (Ponchi) Ordaz is the son of immigrants Tula and Ruben Ordaz. He graduated from Torrance High School in 1948, attended El Camino College and the University of Santa Barbara (where he received his bachelor's degree) and California State University, Long Beach (where he received his master's degree). He taught English and Spanish at Santa Barbara High School for 40 years. (Stella Gassett.)

Consistent with our mission to preserve history on a local level, this book was printed in South Carolina on American-made paper and manufactured entirely in the United States. Products carrying the accredited Forest Stewardship Council (FSC) label are printed on 100 percent FSC-certified paper.

MADE IN THE USA